CAMBRIDGE STUDIES IN LINGUISTICS

General editors: B. COMRIE, C. J. FILLMORE, R. LASS,
D. LIGHTFOOT, J. LYONS, P. H. MATTHEWS, R. POSNER,
S. ROMAINE, N. V. SMITH, N. VINCENT, A. ZWICKY

English focus constructions and the theory of grammar

In this series

ENGLISH FOCUS CONSTRUCTIONS AND THE THEORY OF GRAMMAR

MICHAEL S. ROCHEMONT
University of British Columbia

PETER W. CULICOVER
The Ohio State University

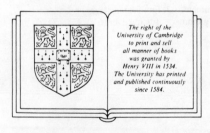

*The right of the
University of Cambridge
to print and sell
all manner of books
was granted by
Henry VIII in 1534.
The University has printed
and published continuously
since 1584.*

CAMBRIDGE UNIVERSITY PRESS

CAMBRIDGE

NEW YORK   PORT CHESTER

MELBOURNE   SYDNEY

Published by the Press Syndicate of the University of Cambridge
The Pitt Building, Trumpington Street, Cambridge CB2 1RP
40 West 20th Street, New York, NY 10011, USA
10 Stamford Road, Oakleigh, Melbourne 3166, Australia

First published 1990

Printed in Great Britain at The Bath Press, Avon

British Library cataloguing in publication data

Rochemont, Michael S. (Michael Shaun), *1950–*
English focus constructions and the theory of
grammar. – (Cambridge studies in linguistics: 52)
1. English language. Grammar.
I. Title   II. Culicover, Peter W. (Peter William)
482.2

Library of Congress cataloguing in publication data

Rochemont, Michael S.
English focus constructions and the theory of grammar
Michael S. Rochemont and Peter W. Culicover
p. cm. – (Cambridge studies in linguistics: 52)
Bibliography.
Includes index.
1. English language – Topic and comment.   2. English language –
Discourse analysis.   3. Generative grammar.   I. Culicover,
Peter W.   II. Title.   III. Series.
PE1385.C85   1989

ISBN 0 521 36412 4

PE
1385
.R63
1990

BS

Contents

Acknowledgments

The research reported on here is the product of a joint effort and the order of authors reflects an arbitrary anti-alphabetical ordering. We would like to express our gratitude to a variety of communities for their support and encouragement throughout the writing of this book and the development of the ideas contained herein.

To begin, we have individually benefited greatly from the opportunity to discuss this work at various stages of development with fellow linguists and friends who have offered advice and constructive criticism regarding both our analyses and our assumptions. We are grateful to Joan Bresnan, Noam Chomsky, David Dowty, Lyn Frazier, Jorge Hankamer, Kyle Johnson, Richard Kayne, Diane Massam, Shigeru Miyagawa, Fritz Newmeyer, Richard Oehrle, Geoff Pullum, Luigi Rizzi, Sue Schmerling, Randy Sharp, Marie-Thérèse Vinet, Tom Wasow, and Wendy Wilkins.

To the University community more generally, we express our gratitude to the linguistics departments at the following universities for allowing us to present our work and for providing stimulating discussion: The University of Arizona, the University of British Columbia, l'Université de Quebec à Montreal, McGill University, the University of Washington, the University of Texas at Austin, and the Ohio State University.

We acknowledge with gratitude the financial and other support of the Universities of Arizona and British Columbia and the Ohio State University which enabled us to maintain our collaboration over such great distances. We give special acknowledgment to the Social Sciences and Humanities Research Council of Canada (S.S.H.R.C.) for a leave fellowship for Michael Rochemont during 1986.

Introduction

In this study, we will be examining the properties of a set of English constructions first analyzed as a class, to our knowledge, in Rochement (1978) and exemplified below.

(1) a. A man came into the room with blond hair.
     b. Mary was talking to a man at the party that she went to school with.
(2) a. Into the room walked John.
     b. At the head of the table sat Bill.
(3) a. Standing in front of her was Mary.
     b. Happiest to see her was her mother.
     c. At the entrance to the park was an old statue.
(4) a. John invited to the party his closest friends.
     b. There walked into the room a tall man with blond hair.

The sentences of (1) illustrate PP and Relative Clause Extraposition from NP (henceforth EX), those in (2) Directional/Locative Inversion (D/L), those in (3) Preposing around *be* (PAB). Sentence (4a) exhibits Heavy NP Shift (HNPS) and sentence (4b) Presentational *there* Insertion (PTI). Rochemont (1978) argues that these constructions are defined as a class as a function of the grammatical model proposed in Chomsky and Lasnik (1977) and summarized below.

(5)

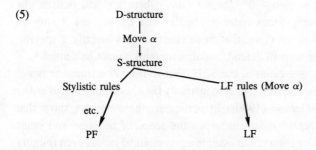

In particular, it is argued in Rochemont (1978) that the constructions of (1)–(4)

are derived by the category of stylistic rules in (5), and thus comprise a class of stylistic constructions in English. Following Horvath (1981, 1985), let us refer to this hypothesis concerning the sentence types of (1)–(4) as the Stylistic Rule Hypothesis (SRH).

Rochemont (1978) offers two main arguments in support of the SRH, and in particular for the claim that these constructions are stylistic in the sense of Chomsky and Lasnik (1977). The first argument that stylistic rules apply only to the output of rules of the syntactic component (i.e., applications of Move a prior to S-structure in (5)) accounts for the frozen character of the resulting constructions with respect to *wh*-extraction and similar syntactic operations. For example, consider the ungrammatical sentences below.[1]

(6)   a. *What color hair did a man walk into the room with?
     b. *Did into the room walk John?
     c. *Was standing in front of her Mary?
     d. *Nixon, John wrote for his mother a book about.
     e. *Who did there walk into the room?

As the sentences of (6) illustrate, *wh* movement, Subject AUX Inversion (SAI), and topicalization are barred from applying in general in stylistic constructions. This feature of these constructions is predicted as a function of the grammatical model in (5) if the rules deriving them are indeed stylistic, as Rochemont argues.

The second argument that Rochemont (1978) offers in support of the SRH is that the constructions of (1)–(4) appear to form a class in a further respect, in that they all of necessity identify a specific phrase as the focus of the sentence, and that they affect the interpretation of the sentence only in respect to the assignment of focus and not in general in respect to the truth-conditional interpretation.[2] We will discuss the focusing property of stylistic constructions in greater detail in section 4 of Chapter One, where we will outline our assumptions concerning focus more explicitly. For the present it suffices to observe simply that the claim that these constructions identify a specific phrase as focus is one we will defend, and that we think cannot be denied.[3]

However, the stronger claim of the SRH, that stylistic constructions never affect truth-conditional meaning, is demonstrably false, as argued in Culicover (1980) and also in Guéron (1980). In particular, these authors show that so-called stylistic operations can influence the scope of negation and other logical operators. If we continue to assume a grammatical model even roughly like that in (5), then the SRH can provide no account of this feature of stylistic constructions, since by assumption only S-structure representations provide information for the LF and semantic interpretation of English sentences. We conclude that the SRH provides too strong an account of the properties of stylistic constructions and must therefore be abandoned. For ease of discussion, we will continue to refer to the sentence types illustrated in (1)–(4) as "stylistic," but we do not mean to imply by this term either that they are stylistic in the sense required for (5) or that they are uniquely stylistic in some more literary sense.

While we have just seen reason to abandon the SRH, it must be acknowledged that to do so is to lose an account of the properties of stylistic constructions that the SRH otherwise correctly accommodates. With regard to the frozen character of these constructions, there are fortunately other conceivable accounts than that achieved by Rochemont (1978) through the ordering of components in a grammatical model. For instance, Wexler and Culicover (1980; Culicover and Wexler 1977) seek to describe the restrictions on these and other constructions in terms of a very general constraint on the operation of syntactic rules, the Freezing Principle. In this approach, the constructions of (1)–(4) are derived in the syntactic component, prior to S-structure, and are treated as a class only as a function of the configurational properties they exhibit after the application of the rules involved in their derivation. Since their S-structure representations are non-canonical in form, the constructions are frozen with respect to further transformational operation.

In this work, we will seek a different account of the frozen nature of stylistic constructions from that offered by the Freezing Principle, though we continue to assume the basic thrust of the approach forwarded by Wexler and Culicover (1980). Namely, we propose to attribute the restrictions in evidence in these constructions to the operation of independent principles of grammar in conjunction with specific features of the structural configurations associated with the constructions in question. In particular, we will present an analysis of stylistic constructions as derived by the general application of Move α and constrained by such principles of grammar as the ECP and Subjacency, under the specific formulations we present in Chapter One.[4] Analyzing stylistic constructions in terms of Move α allows us to characterize the thematic interpretations of these sentence types in terms of the assignment of thematic interpretation in their canonical counterparts, through the conventions of trace theory. To the extent that the structural restrictions in evidence in stylistic constructions can be made to follow from independently proposed principles of grammar, the analyses we advance and defend may in fact be seen as providing supporting evidence for these principles.

The other feature of stylistic constructions that is captured by the SRH is their ability to structurally focus a specific phrase in the sentence. We return to this focusing effect in Chapter Five, and we illustrate the effect and outline our assumptions concerning focus more precisely in section 4 of Chapter One. In the remaining sections of Chapter One, we reveal and to some extent defend our assumptions concerning the grammatical framework and principles used in this study. Chapter Two investigates the properties of EX, illustrated in (1). Chapter Three presents an analysis of D/L (2) and PAB (3), collectively termed Stylistic Inversion (SI). In Chapter Four, we analyze HNPS (4a). We follow Rochemont (1978) in grouping PTI in (4b) with HNPS, and we adopt the term NP Shift to refer more generally to the rightward displacement of NP in such examples.

1 _Theoretical assumptions_

1 The Autonomy Thesis

Our approach to linguistic theory is one that is characterized by a strong
notion of autonomy of grammatical components. Generalizations about syntactic structure are stateable independently of considerations about interpretation
or use. We take seriously a strong form of the Autonomous Systems view
(Hale _et al._ [1977], Culicover and Rochemont [1983]) as a methodological
principle of linguistic research. The Autonomous Systems view bears a close
relationship to the Autonomy Thesis of Chomsky (1975), which holds that
semantics plays a limited or no role in formal grammar (i.e. syntax).

The extension of the Autonomous Systems view that we entertain here
is most clearly articulated by Jackendoff (1983). According to this view,
a grammar consists of a set of components, each of which characterizes well-
formed representations at one or more levels. Each component of the grammar
has its own primitives, rules of combination and well-formedness conditions.
Moreover there are correspondence rules that map representations at one
level into representations at another. On this view the primitives of one component are not the primitives of any other and the well-formedness conditions
at one level do not make reference to aspects of representations at any other
level.

As can be seen, the Autonomous Systems view stands in direct contrast
to approaches such as generative semantics, in which there is no distinction
made between syntactic and semantic rules, and where syntactic well-formedness is expressed in part in terms of semantic primitives. (See Newmeyer
[1980] for discussion and criticism.) Much earlier work in generative grammar
outside of generative semantics shows occasional departures from a strict
observance of autonomy as well. For example, the rule of EQUI, a syntactic
rule, required coreference of NPs, which is plausibly a semantic condition.
But reference per se is a semantic or pragmatic phenomenon. Consequently,
we would not expect syntactic rules to refer to the referential properties of

5

noun phrases.[1] For example, while syntactic rules may take into account the syntactic category of a phrase (e.g. NP) we would not expect a syntactic rule to take into account the fact that the phrase refers to a human being ("Move α where referent of α is human") or to a member of the set of minerals occurring in nature, or that two NPs are in fact coreferential.[2]

There is no question, of course, that there can be strong correspondences, even partial isomorphisms, between two levels of representation. Montague grammar (and other versions of categorial grammar) assumes an isomorphism between the syntactic categories and the semantic categories. (See Montague [1973], and for an exposition, Dowty, Wall, and Peters [1981]. See also Gazdar, Klein, Pullum, and Sag [1985] for a related approach in Generalized Phrase Structure Grammar.) More generally, in any theory, a syntactic structure will determine in large part the formal representation of the meaning associated with it. Thus generalizations over one level often have their counterparts in the other.

2   The categorial component

We assume a context-free base component constrained along the lines of X-bar theory. More specifically, following Chomsky (class lectures 1986), we assume the following general X-bar schema for phrase structure.

(1) $X^j \longrightarrow \ldots X^i \ldots, i \leq j \leq 2.$

We follow Chomsky (1986b) in taking the structure of sentential and clausal phrases to conform to the general schema in (1), with C the head of CP (= S') and I the head of IP (= S), as diagrammed in (2).

(2)
```
            CP
          /    \
        α       C'
              /    \
            C       IP
                  /    \
                NP      I'
                      /    \
                    I       VP
```

We assume that the position of α in (1) is the ultimate landing site for *wh*-phrases in what has traditionally been termed "movement to COMP." We will refer variously to this position as SPEC, CP or as COMP.

We note that the schema in (1) is formulated to permit the base generation of adjoined configurations. We assume quite generally that internal arguments to a head are generated within the first maximal projection on the head, and that phrases generated in adjoined positions are either adjuncts or, in the case of small clauses, subjects. Consider in this connection the configuration below.

(3)
```
                    VP
                  /    \
               VP       β
             /    \
          VP       α
         /    \
       V'      XP
      /  \
     V    XP
```

From our assumptions it follows that V directly θ-marks either position of XP in (3), but does not θ-govern $α$ or $β$. We will assume that $α$ and $β$ are the typical positions for adjuncts at D-structure, and will sometimes refer to adjoined positions as "X, $γ$", where $γ$ is a maximal projection in general. Thus, $α$ and $β$ above are both in X,VP (adjoined to VP) position by this notation.

We make the very strict structure-preserving assumptions concerning Move $α$ proposed in Chomsky (1986b), in particular, that movement of X^{max} may be to SPEC or to adjoined positions only, and that movement of a head may be to the position of a properly governing head only.[3] We note that from these assumptions it follows that X-bar theory as outlined in (1) is satisfied at each level of syntactic representation.

3 Locality conditions on extraction

Our goal in this work is to investigate the structural properties of a class of English stylistic constructions, and to reduce the analysis of these constructions to independently motivated principles of grammar, including Move $α$. In this respect our line of investigation parallels that of Newmeyer (1987) and Coopmans (1987), though the specific analyses we propose and the general framework we assume are different than theirs. Restrictions on the application of Move $α$ are stated in the form of principles applying at or in the input to various levels of representation. We will make extensive use of two such principles that have been proposed: Subjacency and the Empty Category Principle (ECP). These principles are motivated on the basis of a broad range of empirical considerations in a variety of languages. See for example

Chomsky (1981), Huang (1982), Lasnik and Saito (1984), Rizzi (1982). The specific formulations we adopt are modeled on the proposals of Chomsky (1986b) and Lasnik and Saito (forthcoming), though our goal here is more modest than theirs. Our intention is to provide formulations of these conditions that will serve us consistently in the analyses and chapters to follow. We will not defend the specific formulations we propose by showing the full range of cross-linguistic applications they must inevitably encompass. Rather, where there is variation in the application of a specific principle that is relevant to its formulation with regard to English we will mention it. Otherwise, we restrict our attention to English specific cases, leaving the broader application of the principles for independent work.

As noted, we follow Chomsky (1986b), in taking the structure of clausal and sentential phrases to be consistent with the general X-bar schema for phrase structure, as in diagram (1) of section 3. This assumption has profound consequences for the specific formulations of Subjacency and the ECP we propose below.

3.1   Subjacency

It is a standard assumption that applications of Move α prior to S-structure are subject to a constraint of Subjacency, in particular, movement from one position to another is possible only if the latter is subjacent to the former. Our definition of "subjacent" is borrowed from Lasnik and Saito (forthcoming).

(1) α is *subjacent* to β iff for every $\gamma(\gamma = X^{max})$, if γ dominates δ, δ a barrier for β, then γ dominates α.

The definition for "barrier," also from Lasnik and Saito (forthcoming), is built on L-marking, following Chomsky (1986b).[4]

(2) α is a *barrier* for β iff   (i) $\alpha = X^{max}$
                                                     (ii) α dominates β
                                                     (iii) α is not L-marked.

(3) α *L-marks* β iff α is an $X°$ that directly θ-marks β.

Among the non-L-marked categories, then, are subjects and non-subcategorized complements (adjuncts).[5] Following Lasnik and Saito (forthcoming), we assume that in the typical case (i.e., in structure [2] of section 2), VP is L-marked and IP is not.

The formulation for Subjacency based on the definition in (1) correctly characterizes the full range of restrictions assumed to fall under that condition in English movement constructions.[6] In the configuration below, where δ is a barrier for t and β is a maximal projection, there can be no movement directly from t to a position outside β.

(4)　　$[_\beta \dots [_\delta \dots t \dots] \dots]$.

Consider then how the ungrammatical examples in (5) are characterized by this configuration.

(5)　　a.　*What do you wonder $[_\beta$ who $[_\delta$ saw $t]]$?
　　　　b.　*What did you $[_\beta$ leave $[_\delta$ after you saw $t]]$?
　　　　c.　*Who did $[_\beta$ that $[_\delta$ she talked to $t]]$ surprise you?
　　　　d.　*Who did $[_\beta [_\delta$ the articles about $t]]$ amuse you?
　　　　e.　*Who did you read $[_\beta$ the books $[_\delta$ that I sent to $t]]$?

Example (5a) illustrates the *wh* island condition. In this case, the barrier (δ) is IP. Example (5b) illustrates the Condition on Extraction Domain (CED) of Huang (1982). We will argue below that such adjuncts are adjoined to VP, but for the present purposes it is immaterial whether β = VP or IP; extraction from the adjunct (= δ) is excluded in either case, since the antecedent of the trace appears outside the maximal projection, whether VP or IP, most immediately dominating the barrier.[7] Example (5c) illustrates the Sentential Subject Condition, with δ = NP/CP and β = IP. In (5d), extraction from a subject is blocked, with virtually the same values for δ and β as for (5c). Example (5e) illustrates the Complex NP Constraint, with the assumption that the relative clause CP (= δ) is an adjunct and thus a barrier for t.[8]

As Lasnik and Saito (forthcoming) observe, this account of Subjacency effects also accommodates the island character of topic constructions, illustrated in (6), if it is assumed that topicalization derives by adjunction to IP.[9]

(6)　　a.　*I wonder what on the table John put.
　　　　b.　*Who did you say that this book, Mary gave to?
　　　　c.　*The man that a book Mary gave to left.
(7)　　　　I wonder [what$_i$ $[_\beta$ on the table$_j$ $[_\delta$ John put t_i $t_j]]]$.

Consider for instance (6a) with the structure in (7). Since δ (= IP) is a barrier for both t_i and t_j, the antecedent for both must be contained within β (= IP). Since the antecedent for t_i, however, is not, (6a) is ruled out by Subjacency.[10] A similar line of reasoning applies to the other examples in (6). The island character of IP adjoined configurations will play a central role in our discussion in later chapters.

Note that more generally when a phrase appears in an adjoined configuration it will constitute an island to extraction from it, under the definition of Subjacency provided above and with the further assumption that such phrases are not L-marked. Thus, any phrase in X, γ position will be a barrier to extraction. This consequence too will be of some significance in the coming discussion.

Lasnik and Saito (forthcoming) entertain and reject this consequence of their analysis for specific cases. In particular, they argue that extraction from constituents in A-bar position should not generally be excluded by Subjacency given the contrast in acceptability between extraction from a topic in (8a) and subject condition cases such as (8b).

(8)   a. ??John, I think that pictures of, Mary likes.
      b. *Who do you think that pictures of appeared in the newspaper?

They propose to exempt an A-bar binder from barrierhood, so that the derivation of (8a) does not violate Subjacency at all.

The problem with this account is that it licenses extraction from constituents in A-bar position very generally. As it turns out, however, extraction from a phrase in adjoined position is systematically barred, except for extraction from a topicalized *wh* moved NP. We will examine relevant cases with extraposed phrases, SI, and NP Shift configurations in later chapters. We note here simply that extraction from a topicalized PP or VP is barred, as is extraction from a *wh* moved PP.

(9)   a. *This car, I know that fix *t* well, John will.
      b. *John, I know that to *t*, Mary gave a book.
(10)   *This is the man who I wonder for which books about *t* Mary paid.

It seems to us, then, that a more profitable approach to the problem posed by (8a) is that such cases are a special effect of topicalized NP rather than the general case. We will not make any specific proposal here to accommodate (8a). Nevertheless, we do not adopt Lasnik and Saito's proposal to exempt A-bar binders from barrierhood. Note that extraction from a *wh*-phrase in COMP as in (8b) may be distinguished if necessary from extraction from an adjoined phrase by virtue of the former's appearing in SPEC position.

3.2   The Empty Category Principle

Following Chomsky (1981), we assume that traces must meet a recoverability requirement of sorts, in the form of the Empty Category Principle (ECP).

The standard view of the ECP, based on the analysis of Chomsky (1981), is that it is a disjunctive requirement on traces, that in order to be licensed they must be either lexically or antecedent governed. We return to the precise definitions for these notions below. For the present, it suffices to observe that lexical government refers to government/by a lexical category and antecedent government to government/binding in a local domain by an antecedent. Variations in the configurations that traces may appear in yield variations in whether given traces are lexically governed or antecedent governed.

The reason for the disjunction in the ECP of Chomsky (1981) stems from appeal to the ECP to explain the *that-t* effect illustrated below.

(11) a. Who do you think that John saw *t*?
 b. *Who do you think that *t* left?

As the contrast in grammaticality of these sentences illustrates, *wh* extraction of subjects is more restricted in English than that of objects. Suppose we attribute this difference to a difference in lexical government, since although it is $X°$ and governs the subject, I in English is not a lexical head. This account of (11b) presumes that traces must meet a requirement of lexical government, and since the trace in subject position in the S-structure of (11b) does not, the sentence is ruled out. But if the ECP were simply a requirement for lexical government, it is not obvious how we would be able to express the fact that (11b) is rendered grammatical when the complementizer *that* fails to be present.

(12) Who do you think *t* left?

We continue to assume for (12) that the trace in subject position is, like that in (11b), not lexically governed by I. Why then is (12) grammatical? The contrast between (11b) and (12) is accounted for if we assume that the ECP is also satisfied through antecedent government, and that the subject trace of (12) is antecedent governed whereas that in the S-structure of (11b) is not. Thus the subject/object asymmetry evident in the *that-t* effect is attributed to a difference in the potential for lexical government between the two positions. While objects are always lexically governed, English subjects can satisfy the ECP only through antecedent government.

An alternative approach would be to assume that C in the S-structure of (12) can act as a lexical governor, but not in (11b). We return to this possibility below.

This account of the paradigm in (11)/(12) hinges on a critical assumption concerning CP, that the presence of *that* in the head position of S'/CP blocks antecedent government from COMP/SPEC,CP. A common view in earlier elaborations of this account was that this assumption was taken to derive from the structure of COMP and the requirement for c-command in antecedent government. When the overt complementizer is present it occupies the base position, so preventing the intermediate trace in COMP from c-commanding the trace in subject position. (See Kayne [1980].) To allow for antecedent government from COMP when the overt complementizer is absent, we might assume that the *wh* phrase acts in some sense as the ''derived head'' of COMP, either through movement directly to the vacant head position (cf. Stowell [1981, 1985]), or through a mechanism of COMP Indexing, so that COMP no longer blocks c-command of the subject trace (cf. Aoun, Hornstein, and Sportiche [1981], Lasnik and Saito [1984]).

Nevertheless, however the foregoing account is realized in the S' system, it runs into difficulties when S' is subsumed under the X-bar schema, as in Chomsky (1986b) and outlined in section 3. In particular, in the structure below, it is not at all obvious how the presence of an overt complementizer can block antecedent government of t from the SPEC,CP position.

(13)

```
           CP
          /  \
        t'    C'
             /  \
           C     IP
                /  \
               t    I'
```

If antecedent government simply involves the binding of t by t', then the presence or absence of an overt head in CP in (13) is at least superficially irrelevant to whether a phrase in SPEC,CP c-commands something contained in IP. Further, Stowell's (1985) analysis that *wh* movement may involve substitution of t' for an empty head position in C runs counter to the restricted theory of movement proposed in Chomsky (1986b) and assumed here, which prevents (as a consequence of structure preservation) anything from moving to a head position apart from a head. Finally, the rule of COMP Indexing, while it presumably can make a distinction between empty and overt complementizers, again seems not to bear in any obvious fashion on the possibility for a phrase in SPEC,CP to bind a subject trace.

Chomsky (1986b) suggests a solution to this problem along the following lines. If antecedent government is a form of government rather than binding, then perhaps the closer possible governor C in (13) is what blocks antecedent government from the SPEC,CP position. Assuming the Minimality Condition,

Chomsky proposes that when C is lexically filled it is a minimal governor, and when C is empty it is not. A version of the Minimality Condition, based on the discussion in Chomsky (1986b, 42), is given in (14).

(14) α does not govern β in the configuration
$$\ldots a \ldots [\gamma \ldots \delta \ldots \beta \ldots] \ldots$$
if γ is an immediate projection of δ excluding α
α *excludes* β if no segment of α dominates β (Chomsky [1986b, 9]).

On this account, the overt complementizer acts as a closer possible governor for the subject trace, and thus blocks any government relation holding for the trace outside C'.

In Chomsky's proposal, Minimality is relevant because antecedent government is considered by him to be a form of government rather than a form of binding. In the account we will adopt below, however, we follow Lasnik and Saito (1984, forthcoming) in taking antecedent government to be a form of binding. The question then arises, as before, how does the presence of an overt complementizer in structure (13) block antecedent government from the SPEC,CP position? We suggest that a possibly appropriate response to this question is that it doesn't. In particular, antecedent government as a binding relation is satisfied in (13) whether there is an overt complementizer in C or not. If this is so, then the ungrammaticality of (11b) cannot be due to a lack of antecedent government, and antecedent government is evidently not sufficient to satisfy the ECP. Let us suppose then that the ungrammaticality of (11b) is due to a lack of lexical government for the trace in subject position. Consider once again the configurations for (11b) and (12), respectively, in (15).

(15)   a. *Who did John say $[_{CP} t' [_{C'} \text{ that } [_{IP} t \text{ left}]]]$?
        b. Who did John say $[_{CP} t' [_{C'} e [_{IP} t \text{ left}]]]$?

Clearly, the contrast in lexical government for t in (12) cannot be due to I. Since the variation in lexical government in (12) evidently coincides with the presence or absence of an overt C, suppose we attribute the well-formedness of (15b) to the possibility for the empty C to serve as a lexical governor for t. Adapting the COMP Indexing analysis noted above, let us suppose that C may be coindexed with a phrase in SPEC,CP position only if it is empty, perhaps as a form of SPEC-head agreement (cf. Chomsky [1986b]). Moreover, we assume that a coindexed C may serve as a lexical governor. Then if t' and e are coindexed in (15b), $[_C e]$ lexically governs t. Since the overt complementizer in (15a) may not undergo COMP Indexing, (15a) is out due to a lack of lexical government for purposes of the ECP.

Note that the definition of lexical government required for this analysis to go through must be stated in configurational terms, following Chomsky (1981), and not in terms of θ-government, contra Lasnik and Saito (1984) and Chomsky (1986b).[11] The specific definitions we adopt for government and lexical government that will be used throughout are given below.

(16) a *governs* β iff a c-commands β and for every γ ($\gamma = X^{max}$) that dominates β and excludes a, either

   (i) $\beta = \gamma°$, or
   (ii) $\beta = $ SPEC, γ, or
   (iii) there exists a segment of γ that does not dominate β.

(17) a *c-commands* β iff for every γ that dominates a, either

   (i) γ dominates β, or
   (ii) $\gamma = a^i$ and γ^n dominates β.

(18) a *lexically governs* β iff a governs β and a is a lexical $X°$.

It will be noted that the definition of government in (16) is purely configurational and makes no reference to barrierhood. Clauses (i) and (ii) of (16) allow government of the head and specifier positions of a governed X^{max}, following Chomsky (1986b). Clause (iii) of (16) allows government of all adjuncts of a governed X^{max}. This clause will play a role in our analysis of extraposition constructions in Chapter Two, where we will be concerned with government relations between maximal projections. It is useful also in allowing the verb to Case-mark the subject position of a small clause, in the configuration $[V [_a \text{ NP } a]]$, where a is a maximal projection . (See section 2.)

Turning now to the definition of lexical government in (18), as we have already seen there is categorial variation as to what is considered a "lexical" $X°$ in (18). In English, the lexical $X°$ heads are V,N,A,P but not I, and C only under COMP Indexing as outlined above. We assume that there is also parametric variation in what counts as a lexical $X°$ head. For instance, we follow Huang (1982) and Lasnik and Saito (1984) in assuming that I is a lexical $X°$ head in Chinese, so that lexical government for the trace of a subject is satisfied within IP, and without reference to the SPEC,CP position. We will see evidence of further variation regarding C as a lexical governor in our brief discussion of Vata in Chapter Four.

We note finally that "c-command" as defined in (17) incorporates a projection definition for heads in the fashion of Chomsky (1981). We will see evidence for this definition, beyond its application here, in the analysis of Stylistic Inversion in Chapter Three.

By the definitions in (16)–(18), C governs t in (13) and (15), and lexically governs t, we have assumed, only if it is empty (as in (15b)) and coindexed with SPEC,CP containing the antecedent of t. On this account, it would appear that the ECP requires lexical government.[12] In fact, it might appear that the ECP requires simply lexical government, since that is all that is needed to distinguish (15a, b). Nevertheless, antecedent government, taken to be a form of local binding relation, is still satisfied for t in (15b), so the account of the *that-t* effect just rendered would be equally consistent with a conjunctive version of the ECP, requiring both lexical and antecedent government, rather than simply lexical government.[13]

There is in fact evidence that the ECP should require antcedent as well as lexical government. Consider how the trace of the adjunct in (19) satisfies the ECP.

(19)   a. I wonder why John left.
       b. I wonder $[_{CP}$ why $[_{IP}$ John $[_{VP}$ $[_{VP}$ left] t]]].

As shown in (19b), we take it that adjuncts at least may be generated within VP, as the distributional evidence below suggests.

(20)   a. John said he would leave because it was too noisy,
          ... and he did.
          ... and leave because it was too noisy he did.
       b. What John did was leave because it was too noisy.

In (20), the adjunct clause patterns with the VP under ellipsis and in topic and pseudocleft positions. If t appears within VP in (19b), then it is lexically governed by V under our assumptions. If the ECP required only lexical government, then adjuncts would be permitted to undergo movement freely, without reference to antecedent government from SPEC,CP. But as Huang (1982) clearly established, adjunct traces must be antecedent governed from the local SPEC,CP position. This assumption allows the ECP to characterize the ungrammaticality of the English example (21a) below (compare (21b)), and parallel examples from Italian, Spanish, Chinese, and Japanese (cf. Huang [1982], Lasnik and Saito [1984]).

(21)   a. *Why do you wonder [who left t]?
       b. ?*What do you wonder [who bought t]?

To preserve this account of adjunct movement together with our new account of the *that-t* effect, we must evidently assume that the ECP requires both lexical and antecedent government.[14]

In this context, consider the following definition for antecedent government, modelled on that in Lasnik and Saito (forthcoming).

(22) α antecedent governs β iff α binds β and α is subjacent to β.

In light of the definitions for antecedent and lexical government above, let us consider how the ECP is satisfied for the subject trace in the configuration (15b), now modified to include the effects of COMP Indexing.

(23)   Who$_i$ did John say $[_{CP}\ t'_i\ [_{C'}\ e_i\ [_{IP}\ t_i\ \text{left}]]]$?

$[_C\ e_i]$ lexically governs t, as before. By (22), the antecedent governor for t must appear within CP to be subjacent to t, IP being a barrier for t. Thus, t_i in a configuration like (23) may be antecedent governed only if it has an antecedent in the most local SPEC,CP position. Similarly, the trace of an adjunct may be antecedent governed only if it has an antecedent in the most local SPEC,CP position. Under this analysis, subjects and adjuncts (at least in English) must behave alike under extraction by being sensitive to the presence of an antecedent in the most local SPEC,CP position.

What then of traces in object position? Clearly such traces are lexically governed. On the other hand, antecedent government in such cases is evidently not contingent on the presence of an antecedent in the most local SPEC,CP position, as evidenced by the contrast in (21), and parallel examples from Italian, Spanish, Chinese, and Japanese in the discussions of Huang (1982) and Lasnik and Saito (1984). Following Stowell (1981), let us assume that the subcategorization frame of a verb is given in terms of a θ-grid, and that θ-marking of an argument is achieved through coindexing between the phrase and a position in the θ-grid. Then V is coindexed with its subcategorized complements. Let us then suppose that if the head that lexically governs a trace is also coindexed with it, then the head may further serve as the antecedent governor of the trace. Now in the case of a trace in object position, the trace is both lexically and antecedent governed within VP, without reference to the SPEC,CP position.[15] On the other hand, an adjunct trace, not being the trace of a subcategorized argument, is lexically governed by V but not antecedent governed by it.

For completeness, we observe that both requirements of the ECP are satisfied for A-movement in cases such as (24).

(24)   John seems $[_{IP}\ t$ to like Mary$]$.

We assume that *seem* and similar verbs select and θ-mark IP complements. (See Chomsky [1986a, b], Massam [1985].) Then *seem* in (24) lexically governs t and since IP is not a barrier for t, t is antecedent governed by *John*.

This concludes our discussion of the grammatical principles we presuppose and will make appeal to in the analyses of the coming chapters. In the next section, we briefly elaborate our assumptions concerning focus.

4   The theory of focus

In the coming chapters we will be proposing syntactic analyses for a class of constructions in English. This class, termed "stylistic constructions," is unified in part through the property of always identifying a specific phrase in the sentence as a focus, as argued in Rochemont (1978, 1986).[16] Our purpose here is to illustrate this property, and to present our assumptions concerning focus. For defense of these assumptions, the reader is referred to Culicover and Rochemont (1983) and Rochemont (1986).[17]

4.1   Focus, accent, and information

In accord with a long-standing tradition in this regard, we assume that focus has a systematic phonological manifestation in the form of (sentence/pitch) accent. We will not enter into a precise characterization of the phonological/ phonetic nature of accent. On this issue there has been a great deal of discussion. See especially Pierrehumbert (1980), Selkirk (1984). We will assume simply that the accent is the intonational nucleus of the sentence, or the position(s) of greater phonological prominence in an intonational domain, which we take to correspond always to a syntactic constituent.

Whatever the exact nature of accent may be, we will proceed on the basis of an indisputable observation. This is that a sentence such as (1), even keeping the intonation contour to that of a simple declarative, allows various pronunciations, among them those indicated in (2), where upper case letters in a word signal the position(s) of greatest relative phonological prominence in the sentence.[18]

(1)   John likes Mary.
(2)   a. JOHN likes Mary.
       b. John LIKES Mary.
       c. John likes MARY.
       d. JOHN likes MARY.

Thus, in (2a) the lexical item *John* is more heavily stressed than the other two items, and in (2d) *John* and *Mary* carry relatively equal phonological emphasis, in contrast to *likes*. This variation in pronunciations for (1) we attribute to variation in the assignment of (sentence/pitch) accent to lexical items in a sentence.

The alternatives in (2) are phonologically and phonetically distinct. They are also in some sense interpretively distinct. That is, although they are truth-conditionally equivalent, each of these sentences implies something different concerning the point of information in the sentence that is deemed most valuable or relevant from the speaker's point of view. We will say that each position of an accent in (2) identifies a focus. Regarding the precise association of focus and accent, we assume for the present that if an item is focused then it must be accented. (This assumption is stated in revised form in (9) below.) It is the varying assignment of focus in (2) that is responsible for the variations in interpretation noted above. We claim here and have claimed in previous work that the assignment of focus is in part a function of well-formed discourse. In particular, we claim that the focus/foci of a sentence is/are predictable in terms of properties of the discourse and context that the sentence occurs in and of the sentence itself.

The relevance of focus and accent to the interpretation of the sentences of (2) is reflected in judgments of well-formedness for discourse sequences, such as question/answer pairs. For example, of the various pronunciations of (1) in (2), only (2a) qualifies as a well-formed response to the question in (3).

(3)   Who likes Mary?

Using the concept of focus, we characterize the observation that only one of the sentences of (2) qualifies as a well-formed response to (3) as (4).

(4)   In a well-formed *wh* question/answer sequence, all and only the information requested in the question is focused in the response.

Given (4), the requested information in a response must be focused, and therefore accented. (4) also requires that only the information requested is focused in the response, as evidenced by the oddity of (2d), for instance, as a response to (3).[19]

Our discussion thus far has made systematic use of a simplifying assumption that a focus is an accented lexical item. However, while we wish to preserve the claim, following Selkirk (1984), that accent is assigned to lexical items only, it is very clear that focus is not. In particular, a focus-related accent on a single lexical item can render a string of unaccented lexical items in focus. For instance, consider sentence (6) as a response to the question (5).

(5)   Who likes Mary?
(6)   The man in the blue hat likes Mary/does.

According to (4), the phrase *the man in the blue hat* in sentence (7) must be the focus of this sentence when it is used in response to the question in (5).

(7)   The man in the blue hat likes Mary.

Evidently, the single accent on *hat* in (6) is sufficient to allow the entire subject phrase to act as a focus for the purposes of (4).[20] More importantly, it is not the case that accent may be assigned anywhere within the subject phrase of (7) in order to identify the full phrase as focus. In particular, none of the various pronunciations of (7) given in (8) qualifies as a well-formed response to (5), in contrast to (6).[21]

(8)   a. The MAN in the blue hat likes Mary.
        b. The man in the BLUE hat likes Mary.
        c. The man IN the blue hat likes Mary.

These and similar examples show quite clearly that there is a systematic nature to the relation between assignment of a focus-related accent to a lexical category and the determination of focus status for phrasal categories containing the accented item. The precise nature of the rules involved in spreading the potential focus interpretation across a phrase is a matter of some dispute. (See Selkirk [1984], Rochemont [1986].) Revising our earlier assumption, we state the accent/phrasal focus relation as (9), which is based on the analysis proposed in Chomsky (1971), Halliday (1967), and subsequent other work.

(9)   If a is a focus, then a is an constituent dominating an accented lexical item on its right branch in S-structure.

While we actually think that (9) is mistaken, and that an empirically more adequate account requires much more careful elaboration, these issues will have little bearing on the discussion to follow. As a result, the much simpler view expressed in (9) will suffice for our purposes here.

Let us now reconsider (4). As a generalization, (4) provides a diagnostic for determining the focus of a sentence, as we have already seen. A similar diagnostic is based on the well-formedness of simple (*yes/no*) question/answer sequences, as below. (We will sometimes indicate odd or unnatural sequences by prefacing them with " % .")

(10)   A: Did Bill talk to his brother?
       B: (a) No, he talked to his SISTER.
          (b) %No, he TALKED to his sister.
          (c) %No, he TALKED to his SISTER.

The generalization that surfaces here is expressed in (11).[22]

(11)   In a well-formed simple question/answer sequence, all and only the information provided in the response that is not contained in the question is focused.

It is reasonable to ask why (4) and (11) should successfully yield diagnostics for focus. It is generally assumed that such generalizations follow from a principle that is presupposed, implicitly or explicitly, in virtually all work on focus, (12). The converse of (12) cannot of course be true, because of cases of Contrastive Focus, as will be seen below.

(12)   If a, a phrase in a sentence S, constitues new information in C, the utterance context to which S is being added, then a must be a focus in S.

Since the requested information in a *wh* question must constitute new information in the context of that question,[23] it must be focused, by (12). Similarly, any information provided in the response to a simple question that is not included in the question must constitute new and/or relevant information, if the sequence is to be judged well-formed. The published literature contains a multitude of views on (12) and the associated notion of "new information." Providing a satisfactory definition for the term "new information" is not a simple matter, and we will make no attempt to fully elaborate such a definition here. Instead, we will introduce some informal terminology that will prove useful in our subsequent discussion, overlooking a number of nontrivial issues. See Rochemont (1986), chapter 2 for discussion.

One very common approach to the concept of "new information" seeks to define "new" information as that which is not "old," or "given." Our own approach to this issue has been of this type. In prior work (Culicover and Rochemont [1983]), we have sought to characterize "old/given information" as that which is *c(ontext)-construable*, and we have employed this predicate in stating generalizations about the distribution and use of focus in discourse. (For elaboration, see Rochemont [1986].) Here, we will restrict attention to just one of the conditions that satisfy c-construal, namely "given" by virtue of being under discussion in the discourse at hand. In other words, we understand (12) to derive from (13). We emphasize that (13) is only partly true, even granted an understanding of the term "under discussion." (Rochemont [1986, chapter 2].)

(13)   If a is not c-construable (= under discussion), then a is a focus.

We recognize that this account is vague, in that the term "under discussion" is not defined. To provide a definition for it, however, would require the presentation of a complete and explicit theory of pragmatics. That is, to determine whether something has been "mentioned," and so is under discussion, would require not only a mechanism for providing semantic interpretations, but also an understanding of how ambiguity, reference, and the communicative intentions of speakers are resolved in communication. We think this is presumably as a function of relevance relative to context. (See Sperber and Wilson [1986].) Nevertheless, we take it for granted that whatever pragmatic theory one may ultimately develop that properly characterizes the use of focus, that theory must be capable of accommodating the principle stated in (12)/(13), and derivative generalizations such as (4) and (11).

It will be useful now to digress briefly to consider, and dispel, some common myths concerning the interpretation of focused phrases, even in terms of the oversimplified discussion we have presented thus far. First, (13) constitutes a sufficient but not a necessary condition for focus. In particular the converse of (13) in (14) is not true.

(14)   If a is a focus then a is not c-construable.

Consider for instance the question/answer pair in (15).

(15)   a. Who does John's mother like?
       b. John's mother likes JOHN/HIM.

Given the diagnostic in (4), *John* is a focus in (15b). But clearly, in the context of (15a) this lexical item is c-construable in the intended sense. But if this is so then (14) must be false.

The observation that (14) is false is sufficient to negate the often made claim that focus is uniformly interpreted as "new information." The use of focus in examples such as (15) is indicative not of a different syntactic notion of focus, but simply of a different use of a single syntactic notion of focus, what we in earlier work have termed the "Contrastive," in contrast to the "Presentational," use. In this connection, consider example (16).

(16)   John's mother likes MARY.

If we substitute (16) for (15b) in (15), then *Mary* in (16) is a focus in just the same way as *John* in (15b), though, assuming this to be the first mention of *Mary* in this discourse, one with a Presentational in addition to a Contrastive interpretation. In this modular view, focus is a uniform notion syntactically, but not interpretively.

A second misconception concerning the interpretation of focus concerns the attempt, popular in the generative literature, to fix a uniform interpretation for focus in terms of the concept "presupposition." This approach, initiated in Chomsky (1971) and further elaborated in Jackendoff (1972), identifies a focus as that information which when extracted from a propositional representation leaves a proposition (with lambda quantified variables) that is claimed to be presupposed. We in fact agree with this characterization, except that we think that the term "presupposed" in this usage is undefined, and in particular that it does not have the meaning it normally does in other contexts. For instance, the complements to factive verbs, generally assumed to be presupposed, are readily focused or not, purely as a function of context. In other words, that such complements are necessarily presupposed does not render them unfocusable. (For this and further arguments the reader is referred to Schmerling [1976] and Rochemont [1986].) Since the term "presupposed" has a different sense in the context of focus, we have abandoned it in our earlier work, and coined a different term ("c-construable"), seeking to provide a definition for it based on its intended range of empirical coverage. "Given" in the sense empirically relevant to the determination of focus shares nothing with the notion of logical presupposition, and use of this latter term in the former sense is potentially confusing, and even obscures the true nature of the problem.[24]

A third misconception we wish to discuss, again concerning the interpretation of focus, involves the use of the term "contrastive stress." We follow Bolinger (1961) in drawing a distinction between (lexical) stress and (sentence) accent. Stress is assigned within syntactically unanalyzed lexical items; accent is assigned to lexical items.[25] This distinction is one that is often overlooked, with damaging consequences, in applications of the term "contrastive stress." Let us then briefly consider some motivation for this distinction.

As we have already seen, the assignment of accent to lexical items is sensitive to the information content of the sentence relative to the discourse context in which it is embedded. It is, however, readily demonstrated that the assignment of stress is not sensitive to information in this manner. In point of fact, we think both stress and accent are assigned as a function of strictly grammatical, even phonological, processes. Nevertheless, accent has implications for the interpretation of a sentence relative to a context in a way that stress does not. For instance, the examples in (18) constitute possible responses to the question in (17), but (19) does not.

(17)   Did you see anything blue during your hike?
(18)   a. Yes, we saw several [$_N$ BLUEbirds].
        b. Yes, we saw several [$_{NP}$ blue BIRDS].
(19)   Yes, we saw several [$_N$ blueBIRDS].

That (19) is odd in the context of (17) provides a clear indication that stress within lexical items does not vary as an apparent function of information in context in the way that accent does.

This point is at first glance a trivial one, but it bears in a profound way on the use of the term "contrastive stress." Contrastive stress is usually motivated on the basis of examples such as (20), where lexical stress is assigned in violation of the grammatical rules of lexical stress assignment, seemingly as a function of the context.

(20) I didn't say blueBERRY, I said blueBIRD.

Such assignments of lexical stress are often said to be "contrastive," and are legitimately excluded from discussions of the systematic phonological nature of lexical stress assignment. The exclusion is legitimate because it can be shown that contrastive stress is associated with a very restricted class of discourse contexts, which we refer to as "contexts of repair." Examples (17)–(19) illustrate that acceptable use of contrastive stress requires that the context be one of repair, as in (20), and not just one where the flow of information in the discourse implies a contrast. This same point is illustrated by the examples in (21) and (22).

(21) a. We didn't find any BLUEberries, but we did see some BLUEbirds.
      b. *We didn't find any blueBERRIES, but we did see some blueBIRDS.
(22) We didn't find any blue BERRIES, but we did see some blue BIRDS.

As with our earlier examples, the oddity of (21b) shows that even when the flow of information implies a contrast, there is no shift of lexical stress to accommodate it. In (22), which provides a phrasal interpretation for the relevant NPs in (21b), the assignment of accent does reflect the flow of information.

Such cases underscore our claim that, except in contexts of repair, lexical stress is assigned as a function of grammatical rule, without influencing the structure of information in a discourse, in contrast to accent. We reserve the term *contrastive stress* to refer strictly to the assignment of stress in violation of principles of grammar, with the sole function of repair, as in (20). As we have seen, accent identified focus may have a contrastive interpretation (see also (22)), but this interpretation is a function of context more generally, and not simply or necessarily one of repair. In other words, following Bolinger, we claim that there is no such thing as "contrastive accent," contrary to widespread belief as reflected in conventional usage of the term contrastive stress.[26]

It is a consequence of the view just established that intuitions about the contrastive interpretation of a focus-related accent are irrelevant to the determination of grammaticality for a given example, contrary to common practice in the use of the term "contrastive stress." If a given sentence must have a specific intonation to count as grammatical, then the fact of the sentence's grammaticality is not in dispute. What must be explained is why it is acceptable only on that pronunciation in a given context. Where the pronunciation factor concerns the location of accent, it is likely that focus is involved. Since focus as we have already seen can constrain the discourse setting into which a given sentence may be embedded, it is not surprising that some sentences may be most easily judged grammatical if the focus-accented phrase is embedded in a context where that phrase receives a Contrastive Focus interpretation. But importantly, the notion of contrast of relevance here is more general than the "context of repair" variety that characterizes "contrastive stress."

4.2   Structural focus

We have seen in the preceding discussion that the assignment of accent to the extent that it determines the position of a focus can affect the ability of a sentence to be embedded naturally in a context. The syntactic form of a sentence can also affect the sentence in a similar fashion. For instance, it has long been recognized that the *it* cleft construction, exemplified below, functions to focus the phrase in postcopular position.[27]

(23)   It was a brand new fur coat that John purchased for his wife.

That the postcopular phrase in (23) must be a focus is shown by the fact that (23) is a possible well-formed response to the question in (24), but under no intonation is it a possible response to (25), and in particular, not with the pronunciation in (26).

(24)   What did John purchase for his wife?
(25)   Who purchased a brand new fur coat for his wife?
(26)   It was a brand new fur coat that JOHN purchased for his wife.

  Heavy NP Shift (HNPS) is also a construction in which there is an obligatory focus interpretation for a given phrase. Thus, sentence (27) below is a well-formed response to (28a), but not to (28b).

(27)   John purchased for his wife a brand new fur coat.
(28)   a. What did John purchase for his wife?
        b. For whom did John purchase a brand new fur coat?

It is a property of HNPS constructions that the postposed and focused phrase must be accented and, generally, preceded by an intonational pause, as in (29).

(29)   John purchased for his WIFE, a brand new fur COAT.

Since we assume that every intonational domain must contain an accent, then except in contexts of repair, sentences like (1) must always have at least two accents. Accordingly, the only acceptable accenting of (27) in the context of (28a) is that indicated in (29).

This observation underlies one of the arguments presented in Rochemont (1986) that accent is not sufficient to identify a focus, since *wife* in (29) need not be focused, in contrast to (30).

(30)   John purchased a brand new fur COAT for his WIFE.

In addition, notice that it is not possible to shift the focus of such sentences simply by altering the placement of accent. For example, (32a) is a well-formed reponse to (31), but (32b) is not.[28]

(31)   When did John buy that brand new fur coat for his wife?
(32)   a. John bought that brand new fur coat for his wife YESTERDAY.
         b. John bought for his wife YESTERDAY that brand new fur coat.

HNPS is then presumably functionally equivalent to the process of *it* cleft formation.[29] We will use the term *structural focus* to refer to the phrase in HNPS and *it* cleft constructions that must receive a focus interpretation.

It has been argued in various places that there are a number of English constructions which serve to identify a structural focus in much the same manner as HNPS and *it* clefts. See for example Guéron (1980), Rochemont (1978, 1986). The constructions that we will be concerned with, besides HNPS, are illustrated below.

(33)   a. A man came into the room who everybody recognized.
         b. Mary was talking to a man at the party who everyone knew.
(34)   a. A woman appeared at the door with blonde hair.
         b. John was talking to a woman at the party with blonde hair.
(35)   a. Into the room walked John.
         b. At the top of the stairs stood his mother.
(36)   a. Sitting in front of her was Bill.
         b. Under the table was a cat.
         c. Happiest to see him was his sister.
(37)   There ran into the room several overexcited fans.

The examples in (33) and (34) illustrate the Relative Clause and PP Extraposition from NP constructions (EX), (35) illustrates the Directional/Locative Adverbial Preposing constructions (D/L Inversion), (36) various instances of Preposing around *be* constructions (PAB), and (37) Presentational *there* Insertion (PTI), which we will analyze as a special case of HNPS.

Rochemont (1978, 1986) argues that, like HNPS, each of the constructions in (32)–(36) identifies a specific phrase as a structural focus. In the case of (33) and (34), the structural focus is the extraposed PP or CP, and in (35)–(37), it is the postverbal subject. Let us review briefly some of the evidence for this claim. What must be demonstrated is that each of these constructions is well-formed only if it is uttered in a context where the phrase in question may be interpreted as a focus. In terms of our *wh* question/answer diagnostic for focus, what this means is that these constructions may be used as responses to *wh* questions in which the constituent being questioned corresponds to the structural focus of the relevant construction, as we have already seen in the case of HNPS. This is illustrated for (33)–(37) in the examples below, drawn largely from Rochemont (1986, 111–113).[30]

(38)   a. Who just walked into the bathroom?
         That MAN just walked into the bathroom from INDIA.
      b. Which room did that man from India walk into?
         *That man walked into the BATHROOM from India.

(39)   a. What did you sell to Shirley?
         We sold that PAINTING to Shirley that was in the SHED.
      b. Who was that painting that was in the shed sold to?
         *We sold that painting to SHIRLEY that was in the shed.

(40)   a. Who ran into the forest?
         Into the forest ran ROBIN HOOD.
      b. Where did Robin Hood run?
         *Into the FOREST ran Robin Hood.

(41)   a. What was standing next to the fireplace?
         Next to the fireplace stood that old SOFA.
      b. Where did that old sofa stand?
         *Next to the FIREPLACE stood that old sofa.

(42)   a. What was at the edge of the lake?
         At the edge of the lake was a small BOATHOUSE.
      b. Where was the small boathouse?
         *At the edge of the LAKE was the small boathouse.

(43)   a. Who was sitting on the bed?
         Sitting on the bed was his long lost BROTHER.
      b. Where was his long lost brother sitting?
         *Sitting on the BED was his long lost brother.

(44)   a. Who do you think might be less fortunate?
         Less fortunate might be the people without JOBS.
      b. What about the people without jobs?
         *Less FORTUNATE might be the people without jobs.

(45)   a. Who stood beside him?
         There stood beside him his favorite BROTHER.
      b. Where did his favorite brother stand?
         *There stood BESIDE him his favorite brother.

The (a) examples above show that the structurally focused phrase may be a focus, and the (b) examples show that it must be. Thus HNPS and the constructions of (33)–(37) form a class in consistently identifying a structural focus. In part, this is the rationale for calling them "stylistic."

However, while the *it* cleft construction is also "stylistic" in the sense that it identifies a structural focus, it is not stylistic in the sense intended by Rochemont (1978), adapting the model of grammar elaborated in Chomsky and Lasnik (1977). As we have noted in the Introduction, Rochemont argues that the English constructions of (33)–(37) and HNPS form a class in a further sense, to the exclusion of *it* clefts. In particular, the former are more severely restricted than *it* clefts in a number of ways. For example, EX as in (33)–(34) exhibits varying restrictions concerning the specificity of the NP and the nature of the predicate involved, properties not typically associated with *it* clefts. (For discussion, see Guéron [1980], Rochemont [1978], and Chapter Two.) Moreover, constructions such as (35)–(37) are absolutely frozen with respect to further transformational operation. Consider for instance the application of SAI in (46) in contrast to (47).

(46) a. *Did into the room walk John?
      b. *Was sitting in front of her Bill?
      c. *Was under the table a cat?
      d. *Was happiest to see him his sister?
      e. *Did there run into the room several overexcited fans?
(47)   Was it John that walked into the room?

In order to characterize just the constructions in question as a class, Rochemont (1978) proposes to treat them as stylistic in the sense that they apply in the PF component of the grammar. In this way, their failure to interact with S-structure operations is accommodated. (However, it is accommodated too strongly, as we have noted in the Introduction.) Further, the failure of these syntactic manipulations in particular to affect truth-conditional interpretation is also accounted for. In order to express the structural-focus property, Rochemont suggests that some PF information must be allowed to feed a level of representation beyond LF, a level which is concerned with "pragmatic" aspects of grammatical information.

The bulk of our investigation here is devoted to showing that there is no need to assume these constructions to apply in the PF component in order to characterize their syntactic behavior. If this goal can be achieved, then the question of how to represent their effect on the systematic interpretation of a sentence reduces to the question of how to represent the effect of LF identified focus on the interpretation of a sentence, an issue that we will not be directly concerned with now. Our more immediate goal will be to reduce the syntactic properties of stylistic constructions to independently motivated principles of grammar. We return to the matter of their structural focusing ability in the concluding chapter of this book.

4.3   Focus and the Definiteness Effect

The Existential *there* construction in (48) is widely acknowledged to exhibit a restriction on the definiteness of the postcopular subject, as evidenced by the contrast between (48) and the unacceptable instances of this construction in (49).

(48)   There was a man walking into the room.
(49)   a. *There was the man walking into the room.
        b. *There was John walking into the room.
        c. *There was him walking into the room.

This restriction is referred to by Safir (1985) as the Definiteness Effect (DE).

Generative grammarians have long been concerned with predicting the association of the DE with existential constructions. For example, Milsark (1974, 1977) ties the DE to the presence of *there*. Safir (1985) argues explicitly against such a view, showing that the DE is not distributed across languages so as to cooccur always or only with a pleonastic item equivalent to *there*. Rather, in his approach, the DE is associated with the position of a lexically filled NP in chains that have the specific property that they are unbalanced (i.e., the lexical NP in the chain is not its head). In fact, Safir's claim is that the unbalanced chain is necessary for Case inheritance to the lexical NP. The reason the establishment of an unbalanced chain leads to the DE is that indefinite expressions may fail to satisfy binding Condition C at S-structure. Since these expressions presumably must satisfy Condition C at LF, however, the only way to avoid a binding violation is for the NP to be a quantified expression undergoing QR. Then *there* is re-interpreted as a variable at LF, being locally A-bar bound, and the trace of QR is in turn A-bound by *there*, so an anaphor (NP trace) at LF rather than a variable. In a much different approach, Belletti (1988) attempts to correlate the DE with assignment of partitive Case.

Our purpose in raising this issue here is not to decide among these and other alternative proposals nor is it to present an account of our own for the distribution of the DE. We wish simply to clarify a confusion in discussions of the DE. We think that this discussion had tended to confuse two differentiated effects, one of them related to the structural-focusing property. Our purpose in this brief section is to establish the distinction that we think important to any potentially fruitful investigation of the DE. We return to a more careful examination of the structural-focusing effect in Chapter Five: 3.

It has sometimes been claimed, as for example by Safir (1985), that the DE extends in some form to PTI constructions such as (50).

(50)   There walked into the room, a man that no one knew.

In particular, the sentences of (51) are not as fully acceptable as (50).

(51)   a. ??There walked into the room, the man.
       b. ??There walked into the room, John.
       c. ??There walked into the room, him.

It can be argued, however, that it is mistaken to attribute the oddity of (51) to the DE, on a par with (49). First, (51a) is much improved, even fully acceptable, if the NP is made heavier. For example, compare (52a) with a true instance of the DE in (52b).

(52)   a. There walked into the room, the one man she had no desire to see.
       b. *There was the one man she had no desire to see in the room.

Second, as observed by Bresnan (1976), examples such as (51b) are considerably improved when the postverbal subject is made heavier by the addition of a significant intonational pause preceding it, accompanied by a very heavy accent. Similar manipulation of example (49b), on the other hand, has no effect on the grammaticality of that sentence. Finally, as Rochemont (1978) demonstrates, (51c) is in fact fully acceptable when the pronoun is interpreted as deictic and not anaphoric, and with the same intonational properties just described for (51b). Once again, even this interpretation of the pronoun in (49c) is excluded for the Existential construction.

We have just seen that parallel manipulation of the examples of (49) fails to improve their acceptability in direct contrast to the corresponding examples in (51). It is therefore plausible to assume that the restrictions in evidence in PTI and exemplified above are not to be attributed to the DE. We conclude that of the two constructions in (48) and (50), only Existential but not Presentational *there* Insertion manifests the DE. If this is in fact correct, then accounts of how the Existential construction is associated with the DE that also include PTI must be mistaken. For example, the DE cannot be associated with a specific position in an unbalanced chain if it is assumed, as in Safir (1985) that PTI also requires the formation of an unbalanced chain. We will in fact argue in Chapter Four that PTI does not require the formation of an unbalanced chain, and that the postverbal subject in such cases is adjoined to IP and not VP. (Thus, *there* in (50) is in effect a bound variable at S-structure, but not in (48).) Accordingly, an account of the DE in terms of unbalanced chains can perhaps be upheld, but only with some qualification concerning PTI such as that just introduced.

If, as we have just seen, the oddity of examples (51) cannot be attributed to the DE, what can it be attributed to? Rochemont (1978) argues that the oddity of such examples is due to the requirement associated with this construction that the postverbal subject must be interpreted as a focus, as we have established earlier. The reasoning is that if a focus must be "new" information, then definite NPs and names require modification of some sort to be naturally interpreted as "new," and pronouns that must be interpreted as "new" cannot be interpreted as anaphoric. Adapting the terminology Safir (1985) develops to express the Definiteness Effect (DE), we might rephrase the claim of Rochemont (1978) as attributing the oddity of examples such as (51) to the Focus Effect (FE) induced in structural focus constructions.

However, while it is appealing, this account of (51) cannot be correct. The reason is that there are other instances of structural-focus constructions, also exhibiting the FE, which do not restrict the structural focus in the same manner as in (51).

(53)   a. Into the room walked the man.
        b. Standing in front of Mary was John.
        c. It was him that walked into the room.

In other words, of the constructions in (51) and (53), only PTI exhibits the effect illustrated in (51). The oddity of (51) can therefore not be attributed to the FE either, since this would falsely predict that (53) should be as odd as (51). Safir (1985) uses just such a contrast to develop a structural analysis of D/L and PAB as distinct from PTI. We argue against this analysis in Chapter Three.

We have just argued that the oddity of examples (51) must be due to something other than either the DE or the FE. We do not propose here to capture this effect apart from identifying it. In line with the terminology employed above, let us label this effect the Heaviness Effect (HE).[31] We believe that a profitable approach to predicting the distribution of the FE and the HE models the approach taken by Safir (1985) to the DE. In particular, we think it a promising line of analysis to attribute these varying effects to specific and identifiable structural relations.

It is important to recognize that just as with the DE, the HE cannot be associated directly with the presence of *there*. This is evident because of the very similar effect illustrated in the application of NP Shift to non-subjects, as in our earlier examples of HNPS and below.

(54)   a. ??Mary saw in the room the man.
      b. ??Mary saw in the room John.
      c. ??Mary saw in the room him.

Manipulation of the sentences of (54) in the manner suggested for (51) produces a similar effect on acceptability. So we cannot associate the HE with the presence of *there*, even if *there* is considered lexically ambiguous.[32] We suggest instead that the HE is associated with any postposing of NP to an adjoined position.[33] (We argue in Chapter Three that English Stylistic Inversion constructions involve no such operation.) We return to predicting the distribution of the FE in terms of structural configurations in Chapter Five, where we also provide a more careful elaboration of our proposal for capturing the HE.

2 *Extraposition from NP*[1]

This chapter considers the characteristics and analysis of sentences with extraposed adjunct and argument complements to NP, as in (1)–(4).

(1) a. A man that no one knew came into the room.
   b. A man came into the room that no one knew.
(2) a. A man with blond hair came into the room.
   b. A man came into the room with blond hair.
(3) a. John saw a picture of his brother in the paper.
   b. John saw a picture in the paper of his brother.
(4) a. A report that the ambassador was still in hiding was made public today.
   b. A report was made public today that the ambassador was still in hiding.

We term this construction Extraposition from NP (EX). We begin in section 1 by presenting an account of EX, adapting the main features of the analysis of Rochemont and Culicover (1988) and Culicover and Rochemont (to appear). In section 2 we extend this account of EX to the analysis of Result Clause Extraposition (RX) and Comparative Clause Extraposition (CX), illustrated below.

(5) Bill ate so much food at the party that he was sick.
(6) Bill ate more food at the party than anyone else.

We examine the interaction of EX, RX, and CX in sentences with multiple extraposition in section 3. Finally, section 4 addresses the several non-syntactic restrictions on EX, including the "definiteness" and focus effects.

1 Extraposition and the Complement Principle

As noted, our account presupposes the general validity of the arguments and conclusions of Culicover and Rochemont (to appear) (henceforth C&R). We briefly summarize here the main and relevant features of that analysis.

We argue in C&R that EX is base-generated, in that the extraposed phrase appears at D-structure in its S-structure position. The argument that EX is not derived by any application of Move α is built in part on the observation that EX does not share paradigmatic features of other movement configurations, being both less and more constrained. The examples below illustrate.

(1)　a. *Which actors would beautiful pictures of cost too much?
　　　b. *Of which actors would beautiful pictures cost too much
(2)　a. A man came into the room that no one knew.
　　　b. A man came into the room with blond hair.
(3)　a. *It was believed that John saw a picture in the newspaper by everyone of his brother.
　　　b. Who did Mary say that John saw a picture of in the newspaper?

The contrast between (1) and (2) shows that while *wh* movement may not normally extract a *wh* phrase from within a subject, EX can do so. On the other hand, EX is more strictly bounded than *wh* movement, as shown in (3). While a *wh* phrase may appear unboundedly far from its D-structure position, subject to Subjacency, an extraposed phrase may not.[2] The contrast in (3) has often been taken to signal the application of a movement constraint specific to rightward movement configurations.[3] The contrast in (1) and (2) has sometimes been taken to signal the non-applicability of standard restrictions on movement in cases of rightward movement.[4]

To us the contrast in (1) and (2) suggests that EX may not involve a movement operation at all, and that the more stringent bounding condition on EX seen in (3) is therefore due to the application of restrictions on the interpretive operation that relates the extraposed phrase to its interpreted position within NP.[5] Adapting the proposals of Guéron (1980) and Guéron and May (1984), we suggest that this interpretive relation is established at LF, and that it holds not between the extraposed phrase and a position within NP but rather between the extraposed phrase and the NP itself as antecedent. The interpretive relation is further subject to a locality restriction in the form of the Complement Principle (CP), whose specific formulation we consider below, but from which it follows that the extraposed phrase in (3a) may not be properly related to its antecedent, while that in each of the sentences of (2) may. Let us suppose that the CP regulates the interpretation of extraposed phrases in the following fashion. Suppose that β is a maximal projection that is governed by some $X°$ head at S-structure. Suppose further that β is not an argument to that head, and that it is also neither a predicate nor an operator. Then β can receive an interpretation only if it may be construed as a complement to some NP α that governs it.[6] If not, then the sentence fails to be fully interpreted, and the Principle of Full Interpretation (PFI) of Chomsky (1986a) is violated.[7] Seen in this light, the CP can in fact serve to satisfy the PFI for extraposed phrases without requiring the presence of a trace within the antecedent NP, and can also characterize the contrast between EX and *wh* movement in (3).[8]

In investigating the constituent structure of EX, C&R argues that phrases extraposed from object position (OX) are necessarily adjoined to VP, and that phrases extraposed from subjects (SX) may be adjoined to either IP or VP. Since this issue is of urgent relevance to the proper formulation of the CP, let us briefly review some of the evidence.

Following Baltin (1978, 1981, 1983) and Guéron (1980), among others, we observe that distributional evidence regarding OX favors the attachment of extraposed phrases in such cases to VP. Representative examples from the ellipsis, topicalization, and pseudoclefting of VP are provided in (4).

(4) a. John met a man last week (who was) from Philadelphia, and George met a man last week (who was) from Philadelphia/did too.
   b. John said he would meet a man at the party (who was) from Philadelphia, and meet a man at the party (who was) from Philadelphia he did.
   c. What John did was draw a picture on the wall of his brother.

The further claim that OX must attach to VP and may not be adjoined higher is supported by the observation that an extraposed phrase in OX may not contain a name that is bound by a phrase in subject position.

(5)   *She$_i$ invited many people to the party that Mary$_i$ didn't know.

Recall from our definition of c-command in Chapter One that if α is not a head, then α c-commands β if α does not dominate β and every node that contains α contains β. We also assume following Chomsky (1981, 1986b) that the binding conditions are stated in terms of this notion of c-command, and in particular that a pronoun may not c-command its antecedent. It must be then that the subject position in (5) c-commands the OX, which would not be the case were the latter possibly adjoined to IP.[9]

Given these arguments we assume that the constituent structure for OX can only be as in (6).[10]

(6)

```
            IP
          /    \
        NP      I'
              /    \
            I       VP
                  /    \
                VP      OX_i
              /    \
            V       NP_i
```

For convenience, we will sometimes represent the antecedent/complement relation as a function of coindexing (as in (6)), without meaning to imply that binding is required to represent this relation grammatically.

Consider next the position of attachment of extraposed phrases in SX. In C&R we argue contrary to prior work on SX that extraposed phrases in such cases at least may adjoin to VP. One argument we offer is based on the ellipsis of VP including SX, as illustrated in (7).[11]

(7)   a. A MAN came in with blond hair, and a WOMAN did [e] TOO.
       b. A MAN came in who had lived in Boston, and a WOMAN did [e], TOO.
       c. Although none of the MEN did [e], several of the WOMEN went to the concert who were visiting from Boston.

In each of the examples in (7), the conjunct with the missing VP allows a reading in which the extraposed phrase in the other conjunct is construed with its subject. We conclude that SX too may be adjoined to VP, but we find no evidence that it may not also adjoin to IP, as below.

(8)

```
                 IP
               /    \
            IP        SX
          /    \
       NP        I'
               /    \
            I         VP
                    /    \
                 VP        SX
```

The structures for OX and SX in (6) and (8) form the paradigm cases to be licensed by the Complement Principle.

Our specific formulation of the Complement Principle adapts the interpretive principle first proposed in connection with EX in Guéron (1980), and modified and refined by Guéron and May (1984). Our adaptation specifically accommodates the possible structural configurations for OX and SX in (6) and (8), so constituting an improvement over Guéron and May's account. The CP is given below in (9).

(9) β is a potential complement of α $(\alpha, \beta = X^{max})$ only if α and β are in a government relation.

The definition for government is that presented in Chapter One and reproduced below.[12]

(10) α *governs* β iff α c-commands β and for every γ $(\gamma = X^{max})$ that dominates β and excludes α, either

    (i) $\beta = \gamma^\circ$, or
    (ii) $\beta = $ SPEC, γ, or
    (iii) there exists a segment of γ that does not dominate β.

The CP as formulated in (9) correctly accommodates the possible antecedent/complement relations in (6) and (8).[13] In particular, in (6) the NP antecedent of OX is governed only if OX appears within VP, and in (8) a government relation holds between NP and SX is adjoined in either position, but not elsewhere.

    The CP also correctly predicts the distribution of judgments for sentences with SX and OX in interaction with the topicalization and pseudoclefting of VP. As our earlier examples (4b,c) illustrate, OX may pattern with VP for the purposes of both topicalization and pseudoclefting, but as the examples below show, SX may pattern with VP for neither of these processes.[14] (See also Baltin [1978, 1981], Reinhart [1980], Guéron [1980].)

(11) a. *They said that a man would come in with blue hair, and come in with blue hair a man did.
      b. *They said that a man would come in who had lived in Boston, and come in who had lived in Boston a man did.
      c. *What someone did was come into the room who had lived in Boston.
      d. *What a man did was come into the room with blue hair.

Given this contrast between OX and SX, the full range of possible EX configurations is diagrammed opposite in (12).

    In the configurations in (12), EX must be able to serve as a complement to either NP_1 or NP_2 in (a), but may only be construed as a complement of NP_2 in (b) and (c). Recall also that SX may serve as a complement to NP_1 in (a) but not to NP_2.

    The CP as formulated in (9) has the desired consequences outlined in (12). In particular, in structure (a) SX may appear adjoined to either VP or IP. In both cases, a government relation holds between NP_1 and the extraposed complement. In contrast, SX may not be construed with NP_2 in (a). When EX is construed with NP_2 in (a)–(c), a government relation is satisfied only if the extraposed complement appears no higher than the VP adjoined position, as required. Moreover, given the lack of a c-command relation between NP_1 and EX in (b) and (c), EX may not be construed as a complement to NP_1 in these configurations.

    The next point we consider concerns the point of application of the CP. In C&R we argue that for EX the CP must apply at S-structure. We adapt several arguments to this effect from other sources (see Ross [1967], Perlmutter and Ross [1970], Andrews [1975], Rochemont [1982], Baltin

(12) a.

```
              IP
           /      \
        IP          SX
      /    \
   NP₁      I'
          /    \
        I        VP
              /     \
            VP        EX
          /    \
        V        NP₂
```

b.

```
              IP
           /      \
        VP          IP
      /    \       /    \
   VP       EX   NP₁      I'
  /  \            \      /   \
 V    NP₂         I      t_VP
```

c.

```
              IP
           /      \
        CP          I'
      /    \       /    \
  ..NP₁..   I     VP
                /     \
              VP        EX
            /    \
          V        NP₂
```

[1987b]). We also present several additional arguments involving cases in which the extraposed phrases takes a *wh*-phrase as antecedent, as below.[15]

(13)   How many people did John say he visited last night that he has known for a long time?

We assume following Guéron (1980) that the CP requires that the antecedent of the extraposed complement must be a lexically filled phrase. Then if the CP applies at S-structure, it will be satisfied only if the extraposed phrase in (13) is in a government relation with its *wh*-phrase antecedent in SPEC, CP at S-structure.[16] This is possible only if the extraposed phrase is adjoined to CP or IP in the matrix clause, and no lower.[17]

That this is the correct constituent structure for such cases is shown by the following contrast, based on examples from Rochemont (1982, 152).

(14)   a. What secret documents did the British government announce they were about to reveal last week that would change our view of history?
       b. The British government announced that they were about to reveal several secret documents last week that would change our view of history.

In (14a), the temporal adverb may be construed with the higher verb, providing evidence that the extraposed phrase is adjoined outside the embedded clause. That this reading is unavailable in (14b) follows from the CP, which for this case requires the extraposed phrase to be adjoined no higher than the embedded VP, as we have already seen. This account of the contrast between (14a,b) is possible only if the CP is taken to hold for EX at S-structure.[18] We therefore adopt this conclusion here.[19]

We observe that Gazdar (1981), following Perlmutter and Ross (1970), notes that EX sometimes allows split antecedents, and cites this as an argument in favor of his analysis (cf. (15)).

(15) a. A man came in and a woman went out who were quite similar.
      b. A man came in and a woman went out who know each other very well.

The arguments we have levelled against a movement analysis similarly contradict the analysis of Gazdar (1981), as observed earlier. Moreover, our analysis correctly characterizes the possibility for split antecedents in EX in sentences such as (15), through the following structure.

(16)

$$
\begin{array}{c}
\text{IP} \\
\diagup \qquad \diagdown \\
\text{IP} \qquad\qquad \text{EX}_i \\
\diagup \ | \ \diagdown \\
\text{IP} \ \text{and} \ \text{IP} \\
\diagup \ \diagdown \quad \diagup \ \diagdown \\
\text{NP}_i \quad \text{I}' \ \text{NP}_i \quad \text{I}'
\end{array}
$$

Note that consistent with our analysis, though not with Gazdar's, is the prediction that split antecedents with EX in coordinate IP structures should be possible only when the antecedents are in subject and not object position, since in the latter case, the CP requires the extraposed complement to be adjoined to VP.

(17) a. ?*John talked to a man at the party and Mary met a woman on the subway who were quite similar.
      b. ?*John talked to a man at the party and Mary met a woman on the subway who know each other very well.
(18) a. A man just walked into the room and a woman just left who bumped into each other in the hallway yesterday.
      b. *A man just walked into the room and I saw a woman earlier who bumped into each other in the hallway yesterday.

The ungrammaticality of (18b) in particular might be attributed to a parallelism constraint on such cases, as observed by Andrews (1975), but not so (17). We note that some speakers seem not to share our judgment of ungrammaticality for cases such as (17). For instance, Andrews (1975, 78) claims the example below to allow only a OX reading on *woman* and *girl*, a reading precluded under our analysis.

(19)   A man saw a woman and a boy saw a girl who were similar.

On the other hand, another example discussed by Andrews (p. 79) is accommodated on our account here.

(20)   It is obvious that a man came in and (*that) a woman went out who were similar.

The failure of a complementizer to appear in (20) is accommodated by the CP since the extraposed phrase appearing outside the conjoined CPs would not be in the required government relation with its antecedent(s) in subject position.

Finally, we follow Baltin (1984) and Neymeyer (1987) in attributing the island effects induced by extraction from extraposed phrases to the CED, ultimately Subjacency, by treating these phrases as D-structure adjuncts, and so not L-marked. Extraction of any phrase from an adjunct, even by adjunction to the next higher maximal projection, results in a Subjacency violation as shown in Chapter One. Thus it will be possible in EX to extract from a non-extraposed phrase, or to perform an operation independent of the extraposed phrase, but not to extract from an extraposed phrase. These patterns are illustrated below.

(21)   a. Which party did John invite several people to that Mary doesn't know?
        b. Did John invite several people to the party that Mary doesn't know?
        c. *What did John invite several people to the party who gave to Mary?

The syntactic restrictions on EX are therefore fully characterized as a function of the CP and of Subjacency.[20] We discuss the non-syntactic restrictions on EX in section 4.

2   Further applications of the CP

2.1   Extraposed result clauses

In the preceding section, we gave an account of EX construction in terms of the CP, argued in these cases to apply at S-structure. We now consider, following Guéron and May (1984), LF applications of the CP, in particular characterizing the distribution of extraposed result clauses (RX) as in (1).

(1)   a. So many people came to the party that we left.
        b. Mary invited so many people to the party that we were upset.

Guéron and May extend their account to include *too* result clauses of the form in (2).

(2)   John got too drunk at the party to drive home.

We will specifically consider only *so* result clauses here, for the reason that *too* result clauses exhibit a number of properties not holding in the former construction. For instance, Baltin (1987a) observes that extraction from a *too* result clause is evidently possible.

(3)   Who was he too angry to visit?

Note that extraction is still possible even if the complement is obviously in extraposed position.

(4) Who was he too angry yesterday to talk to?

On the other hand, extraction from a *so* result clause is completely ungrammatical. Thus, compare (5).

(5)   a. *Who did Mary invite so many people to the party that John complained
            to?
       b. *How angry did Mary invite so many people to the party that John was?
       c. *Who was John so angry that Bill asked to leave?

In addition, *too* result clauses have a further complication in that they display control and extraction properties that indicate that they are sometimes complements to the A head and not just the Q. Thus, Chomsky (1986b) observes that sentence (6a) is ambiguous between a control and a noncontrol reading, but that the control reading correlates with the possibilities for extraction, given that (6b) has unambiguously the control reading only.

(6)   a. The demonstrators were too angry to hold the meeting.
       b. Which meeting were the demonstrators too angry to hold?

Consistent with these facts, we might assume that the noncontrol structure requires that the result clause be adjoined outside the c-command domain of the subject (cf. e.g. Baltin [1987a]). But this would be inconsistent with the observation that the result clause under both control readings may delete with the VP under ellipsis.

(7)   The demonstrators were too angry to hold the meeting, and the organizers
       were too.

Example (7) allows both the control and the noncontrol reading for the missing result clause in the second sentence. Note in addition that the example suggests that the control and noncontrol structures should nevertheless be distinguished structurally, to capture the observation that (7) is only two and not four ways ambiguous. That is, both result clauses have the same reading on a given interpretation of (7), either as control or as noncontrol complements.[21]

We therefore intend the term RX to refer only to *that* result clauses of the sort in (1). As Guéron and May illustrate, RX and EX exhibit certain systematic alternations. First, note that while an OX may not contain the antecedent of a pronoun in a subject position (as we have already seen), an extraposed result clause related to object position may, as seen in (8).

(8)   a. *She$_i$ met few people at the party who Mary$_i$ upset.
       b. She$_i$ met so few people at the party that Mary$_i$ was upset.

Second, whereas EX is strictly bounded at S-structure relative to its antecedent, RX is not.[22] Thus compare the examples below.

(9)   a. *Plots by many conspirators have been hatched that the government has jailed.
       b. Plots by so many conspirators have been hatched that the government has jailed them all.
(10)   a. *Autographed pictures of many famous people were for sale that have made donations to our organization.
       b. Autographed pictures of so many famous people were for sale that I ran out of money early.

Third, whereas an RX may take multiple antecedents simultaneously, an EX may not. (Chomsky [1981, 81ff.].)

(11)   a. A man approached a woman at the party who no one knew.
       b. So many people bought so much food that we sold out.

Thus, whereas (11a) may not be interpreted to mean that no one knew both the man and the woman, in (11b) the RX may be construed with both instances of *so*, so that neither *so* has a strictly exclamative interpretation, as in (12).

(12)   a. So many people bought food.
       b. Many people bought so much food.

Guéron and May argue that these contrasts between EX and RX may be characterized in terms of the positions of the respective antecedents coupled with the CP. They assume that the CP applies uniformly at LF and that in EX constructions the antecedent NP undergoes QR at LF. We reject both of these assumptions. Nevertheless, we think that the analysis Guéron and May provide for RX is roughly correct, apart from the issue of movement, and we adapt their account in what follows, consistent with our analysis of the CP as outlined in the previous section.

To begin, we assume that RX, like EX, is base generated and not derived by movement.[23] We further assume that the distribution of RX phrases is conditioned by the CP, that the antecedent of the RX phrase is the QP *so* contained within NP, and that the government requirement of the CP restricting the relation between *so* and the RX applies at LF in such cases and not at S-structure. It is this feature of RX that gives rise to the contrasts between RX and EX noted above. Note that also following Guéron and May, we assume that *so* undergoes movement at LF. We present evidence for this assumption below.

We have seen considerable evidence in the case of EX that the site of attachment of the extraposed phrase is conditioned by the S-structure position of its antecedent. By analogy, the site of attachment of a RX phrase must be conditioned by the position of *so* at LF.[24] Let us assume that *so* as a QP undergoes adjunction by QR to IP at LF. This assumption differs from that of Guéron and May (1984) but is consistent in general respects with the analysis of May (1985). Then consistent with the CP, the site of attachment of the RX must be either of the positions indicated below, both at S-structure and at LF.

(13)

```
                    CP
                  /    \
              CP        RX
            /   \
          C      IP
               /   \
          so_i      IP
                  /   \
               IP      RX
              /  \
         ...[_NP t_i ..]...
```

The contrast in pronominal binding properties noted in (8) between EX and RX follows directly from (13). In particular, given our assumptions concerning c-command, a name contained within the RX will not be bound by a pronoun in the subject position of IP.

That the RX may appear unboundedly far from its antecedent at S-structure, as in (9), is also accommodated in the analysis of Guéron and May, since LF applications of Move α are generally assumed not to be subject to Subjacency (cf. e.g. Chomsky [1981]), so that *so* may appear able to move unboundedly far at LF to satisfy the CP.[25] As Guéron and May (1984, 14) observe, this leads to further contrasts between RX and EX, given the interaction of the binding theory and the apparently less restricted bounding character of RX.

(14) a. *I told her; that the concert was attended by many people last year that made Mary; nervous.

  b. I told her; that the concert was attended by so many people last year that I made Mary; nervous.

In (14b) the RX phrase may be adjoined to the matrix CP or IP at S-structure, since *so* is free to take the widest scope possible under LF movement. Thus, (14b) allows an S-structure representation in which the pronoun may fail to c-command its antecedent contained within the RX. In (14a) on the other hand the CP requires the EX to be adjoined within the embedded sentence, so that the matrix pronoun may not fail to c-command its antecedent contained within the EX. Hence the contrast in grammaticality between (14a,b).

The assumption that *so* undergoes movement at LF is supported by three empirically-based observations. First, as Guéron and May note, this assumption allows us to adequately represent the ambiguity of an example such as (15) (cf. Liberman [1974]).

(15)   Mary believes that Harry is so crazy that he acted irrationally.

In particular, (15) may be construed to have either of the meanings below.

(16) a. Mary has the belief that Harry is so crazy that he acted irrationally.
  b. The extent to which Mary believes that Harry is crazy is such that he acted irrationally.

These two readings are characterized if we assume that *so* may be adjoined at LF either to the embedded or to the matrix IP, and that the respective readings in (16) correspond to differences in the scope of *so* seen as a function of its respective sites of attachment at LF.[26]

A related argument that *so* may take scope outside the clause most immediately containing it at S-structure is provided by the contrast in potential interpretations for the examples below.

(17) a. Bill said that John ate so many hamburgers and that Susan ate so many potatoes that we had to go shopping again.
  b. Bill said that John ate so many hamburgers and Susan ate so many potatoes that we had to go shopping again.

While both examples in (17) are grammatical, they differ in potential interpretations. In particular, (17a) can be interpreted to mean that the result clause is a consequence of Bill's having said such and such, whereas (17b) may not have this interpretation. Given the presence of a complementizer in each of the conjoined clauses of (a) and not (b), if *so* adjoins to IP then both instances of *so* can adjoin only to the matrix IP in (a) to take scope over the single result clause in sentence final position. In (b), the conjunction of IP rather than CP provides a possible LF attachment site for both *so*'s within the embedded clause.

Our final argument that *so* undergoes movement at LF is that it exhibits ECP effects characteristic of the LF and S-structure movement of adjuncts as analyzed in Huang (1982), Lasnik and Saito (1984) and Chomsky (1986b). This is illustrated in example (18).

(18) Mary wondered who was so crazy that he acted irrationally.

Under analogy with (15), it might be thought that (18) is ambiguous, with either of the readings in (19).

(19)   a. Mary has the belief that someone was so crazy that he acted irrationally, and she doesn't know who that person is.
       b. The extent to which Mary wondered whether someone was crazy was such that he acted irrationally, and Mary doesn't know who that person is.

In fact, (18) is unambiguous, and has only the reading in (19a). Evidently, *so* can take only a narrow scope reading in example (18). The wide scope reading, in which *so* is adjoined to the matrix IP at LF is excluded. If we assume that the relation between *so* and its trace at LF parallels that between a dislocated adjunct and its trace, then the lack of ambiguity in an example such as (18) may be attributed to the ECP. Note that this argument contradicts Guéron and May's claim that movement of *so* at LF is not subject to the ECP.

The scope interpretations for *so* interact with the possibilities for coreference, as expected. Specifically, where the complement to *so* within an embedded clause at S-structure contains the antecedent of a matrix subject pronoun, the *so* may only be interpreted with wide scope, as in (20).

(20)   She$_i$ believes that Harry was so crazy that Mary$_i$ left him.

Sentence (20) can only be interpreted to mean that the extent to which Mary believed that Harry was crazy was such that she left him. Notice that when (20) is interpreted with the *so* having narrow scope, coreference of the pronoun and *Mary* is excluded, as predicted.

If movement of *so* at LF patterns like that of an adjunct, as we have claimed on the basis of (18), we might expect to find other cases where RX is bounded. Specifically, it should not be possible to extract *so* from a non-subjacent domain to some higher position except successive cyclically in cases such as (15). This bounded character of RX is illustrated in the examples below.

(21) a. She$_i$ claimed that so many people left that Mary$_i$ must have been lying.

   b. *She$_i$ made the claim that so many people left that Mary$_i$ must have been lying.

(22) a. She$_i$ heard that so many people were coming that Mary$_i$ got nervous.

   b. *She$_i$ heard a rumor that so many people were coming that Mary$_i$ got nervous.

(23)   *She$_i$ invited several people who ate so much food to the party that Mary$_i$ was embarrassed.

(24) a. She$_i$ tried to do so many pushups that Mary$_i$ hurt herself.

   b. *She$_i$ bent to do so many pushups that Mary$_i$ hurt herself.

(25)   *She$_i$ hurried out after eating so much food that Mary$_i$ must have been sick.

(26) a. That so many people ate cheesecake that we had to order more surprised us.

   b. *That so many people ate cheesecake surprised us that we had to order more.

The impossibility of coreference in the relevant examples of (21)–(23) follows if *so* may not be extracted from a complex NP at LF and so govern the RX adjoined to the matrix clause. The examples in (24) and (25) show that *so* may not be extracted from an adjunct. Example (26b) shows that *so* may not be extracted from a sentential subject. If CP dominated by NP is always a barrier, and if *so* must antecedent govern its trace at LF as an adjunct, then it follows under our assumptions and the system of analysis of Lasnik and Saito (forthcoming) that LF movement of *so* must satisfy Subjacency, given the definition of antecedent government.

This conclusion contradicts a claim made earlier in this section on the basis of examples (9b) and (10b), repeated below.

(9b)   Plots by so many conspirators have been hatched that the government has jailed them all.

(10b)   Autographed pictures of so many famous people were for sale that I ran out of money early.

Guéron and May (1984) consider a further relevant example.

(27)   Critics who have reviewed so many books were at the party that I didn't have time to meet them all.

In these examples LF movement of *so* appears not to satisfy Subjacency, since *so* must evidently raise to the matrix IP to be in a government relation with the sentence final RX.

There is, however, an analysis of these cases that is consistent with our claim that LF movement of *so* must satisfy Subjacency. Note that the result clause in each of examples (9b), (10b) and (27) is interpreted as though *so* were construed with the head noun of the subject NP and not with the noun *so* is related to in its S-structure position. These interpretations are reflected in the content of the result clauses. When the result clause forces an interpretation for *so* as necessarily construed only with the lower noun, the examples become ungrammatical.

(28) a. *Plots by so many conspirators have been hatched that they've never even met each other.
      b. *Pictures of so many people were for sale that I couldn't talk to them all.
      c. *Critics who have reviewed so many books were at the party that I didn't have time to read them all.

Examples (28) illustrate the bounded character of RX that examples (20)–(26) lead us to expect.

We suggest that the contrast between (9b), (10b), (27) and the corresponding examples in (28) is due to the possibility that *so* may raise at LF to the SPEC position of the higher subject NP in the former, so yielding the appropriate interpretation. Thus, (27) for example is interpreted as (29).

(29)   So many critics who have reviewed books were at the party that I didn't have time to meet them all.

This hypothesis is reinforced by the observation that (9b), (10b) and (27) are all rendered ungrammatical when the SPEC position of the subject NP is filled. Thus, compare (27) and (30).

(30)   *Several critics who have reviewed so many books were at the party that I didn't have time to meet them all.

Example (30), in contrast to (27), may not be interpreted on a par with (29).

As may be readily verified, if (27) has an LF derivation in which *so (many)* raises to the higher SPEC,NP position, then the RX adjoined to the matrix IP in fact satisfies the CP by governing the raised *so* at LF. In (27) and related examples therefore, *so* has not escaped from NP at LF. Consider in this connection example (31).

(31)   *She$_i$ thought that pictures of so many famous people would be for sale that Mary$_i$ brought her credit card.

Although successive cyclic extraction of *so* is otherwise possible, as we have seen, our analysis predicts that in examples such as (31), *so* may raise only to the external position of the embedded subject where it is governed by the RX adjoined to the embedded IP. Since the CP is not satisfied for such cases when the RX is adjoined to the matrix clause, it is correctly predicted that the pronominal subject of the matrix clause must c-command its antecedent within the extraposed result clause in this example in contrast to example (32).

(32)   She$_i$ thought that the concert would be attended by so many people that Mary$_i$ decided not to go.

We conclude that examples (27) and related cases are not true counterexamples to our claim that LF movement of *so* must satisfy the ECP requirement for antecedent government, which we have assumed following Lasnik and Saito (forthcoming) requires that each trace have a subjacent antecedent.

This Subjacency-like LF effect with adjunct extraction may be used to account for an asymmetry in the behaviour of RX under ellipsis and dislocation of VP. First, we note that the formulation of the CP that we have provided also permits the RX to be adjoined at VP and properly related to its *so* antecedent adjoined at IP at LF.

(33)

```
              IP
            /   \
         so      IP
               /   \
            NP      I'
                  /   \
                 I     VP
               /   \
             VP     RX
```

In (33), *so* governs RX, given the definition of government we have assumed. Structure (33) predicts that the RX should be able to pattern with the VP for the purposes of ellipsis. As the examples below illustrate, this prediction is confirmed.[27]

(34)   a. John invited so many people to the party that Mary was upset, and Bill did too.
        b. So many men came to the party that Mary was upset, and so many women did too.

Examples (34) show that RX may appear in the adjoined to VP position in (33).

However, while the RX may pattern freely with the VP for the purposes of ellipsis in (34), it may not do so when the VP is dislocated rather than deleted. In particular, when the RX is construed with a *so* contained within an object NP at S-structure (ROX), the RX may appear with the VP in the topic position or in the focus position in a pseudocleft. But when the RX is construed with a *so* contained within a subject NP at S-structure (RSX), it may not appear with VP in those positions. Thus, we see a contrast between the examples in (35) and those in (36).

(35)   a. They said John would invite so many people to the party that Mary would get upset, and invite so many people to the party that she got upset he did.

        b. What John did was invite so many people to the party that Mary got upset.

(36)   a. *They said that so many people would come to the party that Mary would get upset, and come to the party that Mary got upset so many people did.

        b. *What so many people did was come to the party that Mary got upset.

Now note that if the RX is adjoined to the matrix VP in the examples of (36), then in order to satisfy the CP, *so* must undergo raising at LF by adjunction to the highest IP. Since we have assumed that VP Topicalization is derived by adjunction to IP, LF raising of *so* by adjunction to this derived IP node will yield a configuration in which *so* may not antecedent govern its trace in the LF corresponding to (36a). Similarly, in (36b) LF raising of *so* out of the sentential subject yields a configuration in which the intermediate trace of *so* fails to be antecedent governed. Thus, the ungrammaticality of examples (36) may be attributed to the Subjacency-like behavior of LF adjunct movement, assuming *so* patterns as an adjunct.[28]

Let us now consider the third distinction between RX and EX, that the former uniformly allows multiple antecedents for the extraposed phrase while the latter does not. As Guéron and May observe, if the relation between extraposed phrase and antecedent is represented as a function of coindexing, then the impossibility for a single extraposed complement to be related to multiple NP antecedents is readily characterized in terms of the binding theory. Since both NPs and the extraposed phrase would of necessity bear the same index, one of the NPs would (almost) inevitably be bound by the other, resulting in a violation of condition C.[29] On the other hand, no such binding theory violation results if multiple instances of *so* are coindexed with a single RX. Guéron and May assume that one of the QPs adjoins to the other at LF, in a process of apparent absorption, giving rise to a representation such as (37) (page 49). (Note that the CP is equally well satisfied if RX is adjoined to the CP most immediately dominating the higher IP.)

Adapting Guéron and May's analysis further, we note that it also follows from these assumptions that multiple instances of *so* with equal scope may not bind multiple RX phrases, as in (38).

(38)   *So many people ate so much food at the party that we had to order more that they were sick.

(37)

```
              IP
            /    \
          QP_i    IP
         /  \    /  \
       QP_i QP_i IP  RX
              \  /
        ..[_NP t_i ..]..[_NP t_i ..]..
```

In particular, consider the LF representation in (39) for (38).

(39)

```
                    CP
                  /    \
                CP      RX
              /    \
            CP      RX
          /    \
         C      IP
              /    \
            QP_i    IP
           /  \    /  \
         QP_i QP_i ..t_i..t_i..
```

In (39), RX in either position fails to govern the lower QP_i, its antecedent, because there is an intervening maximal projection (the higher QP_i) that excludes the RX.[30]

2.2   Extraposed comparative clauses

In this section, we consider the derivation of extraposed comparative clauses (CX), illustrated in (40), and the contrasts between these and both EX and RX.

(40)   a. More people came to the party than John invited.
       b. John invited more people to the party than he met there.

As Guéron and May (1984) observe, CX constructions of the type in (40) pattern with EX and not with RX in regard to the properties distinguishing these latter two considered in the previous section.

(41)   a. *She_i met more people at the party than Mary_i invited.
       b. *Pictures on more tables are for sale than I set up.
       c. More men met more women at the party than we invited.

The examples in (41) illustrate, respectively, that a CX with an object antecedent may not contain the antecedent of a subject pronoun, that the relation between CX and antecedent is strictly bounded,[31] and that a single CX may not simultaneously take multiple antecedents.[32]

Again, we continue to assume that CX is base generated, and not derived by any application of Move a, nor does the extraposed comparative bind a position within the NP with which it is construed.[33] Following Guéron and May, we also assume that in such cases both the *more* QP and the NP containing it are coindexed with the CX phrase. Note, though, that for purposes of the CP, it is the NP that satisfies the antecedent part of the antecedent/complement relation at S-structure. Evidently, as with EX, if the CP can be satisfied at S-structure it must be. In other words, if the antecedent of an extraposed phrase is NP, then the antecedent/complement relation must satisfy the CP at S-structure. We may assume in addition that *more* undergoes movement at LF in CX, adjoining to IP, and the CP is satisfied at LF for the QP/CX phrase relation.[34]

For completeness, we note that the government requirement of the CP is also satisfied in CX.

(42) a. John invited more people to the party than he met there, and Bill did too.
      b. More men came to the party than we invited, and more women did too.
(43) a. They said Mary would eat more oranges at dinner than pears, and eat more oranges at dinner than pears she did.
      b. What John did was invite more people to the party than he met there.
(44) a. *They said that more people would come to the party than we invited, and come to the party than we invited more people did.
      b. *What more people did was come to the party than we invited.

The examples of (42) show that the CX phrase may undergo ellipsis along with the VP, whether it is associated with subject or object position, as we expect. The contrasts between respective sentences in (43) and (44) show that only CX construed with an object may appear with the VP in topic and pseudocleft focus positions.

Guéron and May (1984, 26) observe, following Chomsky (1981, 81ff.), that not all CX are of the form (40). They provide the following minimal pair.

(45) a. More people arrived than I expected.
      b. More people arrived than I met yesterday.

The sentences in (45) differ in interpretation in that in (45a) the comparison may range over the entire clause, while in (45b) it is restricted to the phrase 'more people'. This difference of interpretation correlates with a difference in syntactic properties as well. In particular, CX of the form (45a) apparently patterns with RX, while CX of the form (45b), as we have just seen, patterns with EX. The following examples are drawn from Chomsky (1981, 81).

(46)   a. Pictures of more people are for sale than I expected.
        b. *Pictures of more people are for sale than I met yesterday.
(47)   a. More silly lectures have been given by more boring professors than I would have expected.
        b. *More silly lectures have been given by more boring professors than I met yesterday.

The contrast between (46a,b) shows that CX of the form (45a) appear not to exhibit the strict bounding that is characteristic of CX of the form (45b), and examples (47) show that only the former allow the extraposed comparative to take multiple antecedents.

Guéron and May propose to analyze the CX that pattern with RX (hereafter "sentence level CX") in the manner of RX. That is, the antecedent of the extraposed comparative in sentence level CX is the QP *more* only, and the CP is satisfied only after LF movement of the QP. We do not adopt this analysis here, however, for the reason that the parallels between sentence level CX and RX are not as extensive as such an analysis would predict. In particular, the site of attachment of the extraposed phrase in sentence level CX continues to be regulated to some extent by the S-structure position of the *more*. The examples in (48) illustrate.

(48)   a. She$_i$ talked to more people at the party than Mary$_i$ expected (to).
        b. *She$_i$ thought that more people came to the party than Mary$_i$ expected (to).

As (48a) shows, sentence level CX patterns with RX in that an extraposed comparative phrase related to an object may contain an antecedent for the subject pronoun, and therefore may be adjoined outside the c-command domain of the subject. However, (48b) shows that the CX may not appear unboundedly far from its antecedent at S-structure, in contrast to parallel examples with RX considered in the last section. Evidently, the scope of *more*, even in sentence level CX, is restricted to the embedded clause.

The clause bounded nature of *more* scope relations is further illustrated in (49).

(49)   a. Mary thought that more people came to the party than she expected.
        b. Mary thought that Bill invited more people to the party than she expected.

The examples of (49) may not be construed so that the *more* has wide scope. For instance, (49a) cannot mean that the extent to which Mary thought that people came to the party was more than she expected. These examples too, therefore, contrast with similar examples involving RX discussed earlier.

Yet further evidence for the clause bounded scope of *more* in sentence level CX is provided in (50).

(50)   a. More people thought that John invited more women to the party than I expected.
       b. *Autographed pictures of more famous people were for sale than I recognized.

Sentence (50b) contrasts with the minimally different sentence involving RX earlier in this section (cf. (10b)), and in this case even the sentence level CX patterns with EX. Example (50a), contrary to the prediction of Guéron and May's analysis, does not allow a multiple antecedent reading for the extraposed comparative.[35]

Thus, while sentence level CX pattern to a limited extent with RX, they also pattern to some extent with EX. We propose to capture the distribution of bounding properties just illustrated by assuming that sentence level CX differ from other CX in the following fashion. We have proposed that the S-structure antecedent for a CX is typically the NP that most immediately contains the *more*, and that the *more* undergoes movement at LF to serve as the LF antecedent of the CX. Let us suppose then that in sentence level CX the S-structure antecedent for the extraposed comparative is the IP that most immediately contains the *more*. This allows us to characterize the observation that in sentence level CX there is always a possible proposition-type gap in the extraposed phrase.

Thus, the differences in bounding properties for the two types of CX correlate with the type of the gap in the extraposed clause.

(51)   a. Pictures on more tables are for sale than I expected.
       b. *Pictures on more tables are for sale than I set up.
(52)   a. More people ate more food than I expected.
       b. More people ate more food than I expected to.
(53)   a. She talked to more people at the party than Mary expected.
       b. She talked to more people at the party than Mary expected she would.

Consequently, only in (51a) can the comparative phrase take an antecedent contained within a higher NP. In (52), only the (a) example allows a multiple antecedent reading for the comparative clause – the (b) example can only mean that more people ate more food than I expected to eat more food. Finally, while *she* and *Mary* may corefer in (53a), they may not in (53b).

If we assume in addition that LF movement of *more* by QR is clause bounded even where the Subjacency-like effect would otherwise be satisfied, then the distribution of judgments and the peculiar bounded character of sentence level CX are correctly accommodated.[36]

3   Relative order restrictions

3.1   Extraposition

It has long been observed in analyses of various types of extraposition that there are certain ordering restrictions on specific combinations of EX, RX, and CX.[37] These restrictions have often been used to argue that the site of attachment of whichever extraposed phrase is ordered first must be lower than that of the phrase which must follow.[38] However, we have seen evidence in the preceding sections that all extraposed phrases at least may adjoin to VP, whether they are instances of EX, RX, or CX. The issue of relative order restrictions, therefore, cannot be entirely reduced to considerations concerning the height of attachment of extraposed phrases of different types. Our purpose in this section is to present in a systematic fashion the relative order restrictions displayed by extraposition constructions in interaction with one another, and to provide an account of these restrictions.[39]

We begin with the observation that a given sentence may have two distinct and cooccurring instances of EX, one with a subject antecedent (SX) and the other an object antecedent (OX), as below.

(1)   A man came into the room last night that I had just finished painting who had blond hair.

In such cases, the SX must follow the OX.[40]

(2)   *A man came into the room last night who had blond hair that I had just finished painting.

This same pattern of judgments holds with CX. An extraposed comparative phrase with a subject antecedent (CSX) must follow a similar phrase with object antecedent (COX).

(3)   a.   ?More people ate more bananas at the party than cherries than I talked to.
          b.   *More people ate more bananas at the party than I talked to than cherries.

Since multiple antecedents in RX take a single extraposed complement, as we have seen, we cannot test the interaction of extraposed result clauses with *so* antecedents in subject (RSX) and object (ROX) positions. But as the examples in (1)–(3) illustrate, in EX and CX a subject antecedent extraposed complement must always follow one with an antecedent in object position.

What the foregoing generalization suggests is that in order to test the full range of relative order restrictions across extraposed complement types, we must test not only the interaction of differing types of extraposition, but also the interaction of differing complement types with antecedents in subject and in object positions. With this in mind, let us examine next the interaction of CX and EX. Consider the examples below.[41]

(4)   a. More people came to the party who were from Chicago than we invited.
       b. More people came to the party than we invited who were from Chicago.
(5)   a. John invited more people to the party who were from Chicago than we talked to.
       b. John invited more people to the party than we talked to who were from Chicago.
(6)   a. Someone went to more parties last year than we went to who was from Chicago.
       b. *Someone went to more parties last year who was from Chicago than we went to.
(7)   a. More people ate food at the party that was rotten than we talked to.
       b. *More people ate food at the party than we talked to that was rotten.

Examples (4)–(7), respectively, show the interaction of SX and CSX, OX and COX, SX and COX, and OX and CSX. The only restrictions arise in the latter two cases, where it is seen that a CX or EX with subject antecedent must follow a CX or EX with object antecedent.

Finally, let us consider the distribution of RX relative to the other two extraposed complement types. We begin with the observation, by now widely recognized, that RX phrases must always appear finally in interaction with other extraposed complement types. Consider first the interaction of RX and EX.[42]

(8)   a. Everybody is so strange whom I like that I can't go out in public with them.
       b. *Everybody is so strange that I can't go out in public with them whom I like.
(9)   a. So many people were at the party who were from Chicago that we had to serve pizza.
       b. *So many people were at the party that we had to serve pizza who were from Chicago.
(10)   a. We invited so many people to the party who were from Chicago that we had to serve pizza.

      b. *We invited so many people to the party that we had to serve pizza who were from Chicago.

(11) a. So many people invited several guests to the party who were from Chicago that we had to serve pizza.

      b. *So many people invited several guests to the party that we had to serve pizza who were from Chicago.

Examples (8)–(11) respectively show the interaction of RSX and SX, ROX and OX, ROX and SX, and RSX and OX. In every case where the EX phrase appears following the RX, the sentence is ungrammatical.

    Consider next the interaction of RX and CX.[43]

(12) a. So many more people came to the party than we had invited that we left.

      b. *So many more people came to the party that we left than we had invited.

(13) a. John invited so many more people to the party than we had invited that we were embarrassed.

      b. *John invited so many more people to the party that we were embarrassed than we had invited.

(14) a. ??More people came to so many parties last year than we invited that we stopped having them.

      b. *More people came to so many parties last year that we stopped having them than we invited.

(15) a. So many people ate more hush puppies at the fair than the vendor said they would eat that we ran out of them early.

      b. *So many people ate more hush puppies at the fair that we ran out of them early than the vendor said they would eat.

Examples (12)–(15) respectively illustrate the interaction of RSX and CSX, ROX and COX, ROX and CSX, and RSX and COX. The distribution of judgments in these examples exactly parallels that in (8)–(11). Wherever the RX phrase precedes the CX phrase the sentence is ungrammatical.

    To summarize, we have seen that CX and EX complement types pattern alike, in that a CX or EX complement with a subject antecedent must always follow a CX or EX complement with object antecedent, and that order is otherwise free. With RX, the generalization is that a RX complement must always follow a CX or EX complement, regardless of the argument status of the antecedent for either phrase.

    These generalizations suggest that antecedent/complement relations must satisfy an interpretive nesting requirement that parallels that motivated in previous work for A-bar movement constructions developed by Fodor (1978), Pesetsky (1982), and others.[44] If we assume that antecedent/complement relations satisfying the CP must also be nested, then in the configuration below, X_2 may be construed only with NP_2 if X_1 is construed with NP_2, X_2 may be construed with NP_1 only if X_1 is construed with NP_1 or with α, and X_2 may not be construed with α if X_1 is construed with either NP_1 or NP_2.

(16)

Since α is, we have assumed, the position occupied by the QP antecedent of a RX at LF, it follows that extraposed result clauses must always appear finally in any sequence of extraposed complements. Thus, if one choice of X in (16) is RX and the other is either EX or CX, then only X_1 can be RX, as required. Similarly, for any choice of X_2 in (16) as CX or EX, if X_2 is construed with the subject (NP_1) as antecedent, then X_1 may not be construed with the object (NP_2), also as required.[45]

That the interpretation of these interspersed phrases is subject to an intepretive nesting requirement is consistent with our account of extraposition constructions as not involving movement.[46] Moreover, the array of facts just reviewed may be seen as providing further support for this proposal. In particular, extraposition constructions do not pattern with movement constructions in regard to A-bar movement nesting requirements.[47]

(17)   a. *Which book did you wonder who John sent to?
        b. *?Who did you wonder which book John sent to?
(18)   Which of the rooms did a man walk into who you had never seen before?

Both of the examples in (17) violate Subjacency, but the much worse character of (17a) may be attributed to a nesting requirement on A-bar movement dependency relations under some formulation. However, in (18) the dependencies are non-nested, assuming that EX is derived by movement, yet no violation results. If we assume that nesting requirements characterize only like relations, then the required nesting of antecedent–complement relations on the one hand and A-bar movement dependencies on the other is consistent with the proposal that the former, and extraposition constructions in particular, do not involve any A–bar movement dependency.

3.2   Predication

The proposal that extraposition constructions are subject to an interpretive nesting requirement extends also to predication relations. Consider the examples below.

(19) a. John ate the meat nude.
      b. John ate the meat raw.
(20) a. John ate the meat raw nude.
      b. *John ate the meat nude raw.

As (19) shows, an adjunct predicate may be construed with either a subject antecedent (SP) as in (a) or with an object antecedent (OP) as in (b). Moreover, SP and OP may cooccur, as in (20a), but only with SP final. Compare (20b).

These facts might be thought indicative of differing heights of attachment for SP and OP, but as the examples below illustrate, both SP and OP may pattern with VP under ellipsis and dislocation.

(21) a. John ate the meat raw, and Mary did too.
      b. John ate the meat nude, and Mary did too.
(22) a. They said John would eat the meat raw, and eat the meat raw, he did.
      b. They said John would eat the meat nude, and eat the meat nude, he did.
(23) a. What John did was eat the meat raw.
      b. What John did was eat the meat nude.

Given that both SP and OP evidently may pattern with VP, the ungrammaticality of (20b) may not be taken as evidence that SP may not adjoin to VP. Rather, it appears that predication relations are subject to an interpretive nesting requirement of the same sort as antecedent–complement relations.

We note that predication relations apparently satisfy the requirements of the CP at LF without any modification of the latter. In particular, if we suppose that predicates undergo reconstruction at LF, then the relation between predicate and external argument meets the government requirement of the CP, if this is taken to hold for predicates only at LF. Thus, the paradigm cases of predication follow the same structural pattern as extraposition, as illustrated in (24) on page 58.

In (24), consistent with the evidence presented thus far, SP may appear in either IP or VP adjoined position. We have already seen that OP may be adjoined to VP. Example (25) shows that OP must be adjoined to VP.

(25)   *She$_i$ ate the meat last night cooked in Mary$_i$'s oil.

Since the OP may not contain an antecedent for the subject pronoun, the OP must be c-commanded by the subject position, as it is in (24).[48]

(24)

The observations that predication relations must be nested and that predication appears to satisfy the CP immediately raise the question whether predication and extraposition constructions interact for the purposes of nesting as if they were dependencies of the same type. There is in fact evidence that they do.[49]

(26) a. A man was painting the wall fully clothed (who was) from Philadelphia.
     b. A man was painting the wall (who was) from Philadelphia fully clothed.

(27) a. John ate some beans yesterday that should have been cooked raw.
     b. John ate some beans yesterday raw that should have been cooked.

(28) a. John ate some beans yesterday that should have been cooked in his bathrobe.
     b. *John ate some beans yesterday in the bathrobe that he got for Christmas that should have been cooked.

(29) a. Someone brought beans to the party cooked in oil imported from Italy who we didn't know.
     b. *Someone brought beans to the party who we didn't know cooked in oil imported from Italy.

The examples in (26) and (27) respectively show that the ordering of SX and SP is free (subject to relative heaviness considerations), and so is the ordering of OX and OP, as expected. As the examples in (28) and (29) show, OX may precede SP, but not vice versa, and OP may precede SX, but not vice versa, again as expected.

This same pattern of judgments arises when we examine the interaction of CX and predication.[50]

(30) a. More people came to the party nude than we invited.
     b. More people came to the party than we invited nude.

(31) a. John met more people at the party nude than he expected to meet.
     b. John met more people at the party than he expected to meet nude.

(32) a. *John came to more parties in the bathrobe that we gave him for Christmas than we invited him to.
     b. John came to more parties than we invited him to in the bathrobe that we gave him for Christmas.

(33) a. More people must have eaten beans at the party cooked in oil than we talked to.

b. *More people must have eaten beans at the party than we talked to cooked in oil.

Thus, CSX and SP are freely ordered in (30), and COX and OP are freely ordered in (31). The examples in (32) and (33) show the nested dependency restrictions parallel to (28)/(29) for CX and predication.

We note that in contrast to CX and EX, RX never exhibits freedom of ordering with respect to predication regardless of the relative positions of the antecedents of the extraposed result clause and the predicate. The predicate must always precede the extraposed result clause.

(34) a. So many people came to the party nude from the waist up that we had to close the curtains.

b. *So many people came to the party that we had to close the curtains nude from the waist up.

(35) a. John put so many letters in the garbage unopened and unread that we were shocked.

b. *John put so many letters in the garbage that we were shocked unopened and unread.

(36) a. So many people brought beans to the party cooked in oil that we left.

b. *So many people brought beans to the party that we left cooked in oil.

(37) a. John came to so many parties last year in the bathrobe that he got for Christmas that we stopped inviting him.

b. *John came to so many parties last year that we stopped inviting him in the bathrobe that he got for Christmas.

Recall that the relation between the extraposed result clause and its antecedent is established at LF and not at S-structure. Since we have assumed that the antecedent is a quantified expression adjoined to IP at LF, the nesting restriction will be satisfied just in case the extraposed result clause appears outside all other extraposed clauses and predicates. Thus the pattern of judgments in (34)–(37) is exactly as we expect if RX and predication are subject to the same nested dependency requirement.

To conclude, we have examined in this section an extensive range of relative order restrictions on the interaction of extraposition constructions with each other and with predication. These interactions provide empirical motivation for an interpretive nesting requirement on antecedent–complement relations, and provide further support for our claim that extraposition constructions are base generated in that the extraposed phrase does not bind a position within the antecedent phrase. We have also seen reason to extend the CP to constrain interpretive relations apart from complement relations between maximal projections at LF more generally, including specifically the predication relation.

4   Non-syntactic restrictions on EX

In this section we consider a range of non-syntactic restrictions specific to EX, so not displayed in CX, RX, or predication. Section 1 examines the well-known restriction on the definiteness and/or specificity of the antecedent phrase in EX, analyzed by Guéron (1980) in terms of the Name Constraint. Section 2 considers the specific realization of the Focus Effect in EX, and section 3 the predicate of appearance restriction specific to SX.

4.1   The Name Constraint

It is well-known that extraposition from certain definite NPs is impossible. The following examples illustrate this.

(1)   a. A man who is carrying a large package is here.
             The man who is carrying a large package is here.
         b. A man is here who is carrying a large package.
             *The man is here who is carrying a large package.

Guéron (1980) observes that the constraint on extraposition illustrated here cannot be expressed in syntactic terms, i.e. simply in terms of the feature [+DEFINITE] on the determiner. The reason is that the felicity of extraposition from an NP with a definite determiner depends on the discourse function of the NP. The difference can be seen most clearly when the definite determiner is *that*, as in (2).

(2)   That man came into the room that I was telling you about.

We note that if (2) is taken to be contrastive, that is, to be referring to *that* man versus *this* man, then extraposition is unacceptable. However, suppose that there is only one man. Then (2) is good. The difference in acceptability between these two readings is mirrored in their respective pronunciations. On the former reading, *that* carries sentence accent in (2), while on the latter, sentence accent is assigned to *man*. Under the latter pronunciation, (2) shows that the determiner constraint on EX is not stated in terms of definiteness.

The traditional approach in such cases is to assume that extraposition is Move α, and to seek an explanation for the constraint on extraposition in terms of well-formedness conditions on the distribution of the trace of the extraposed constituent. This is the approach taken by Guéron (1980). However, even in Guéron's analysis it is necessary to resort to semantic rather than structural notions. The question thus arises as to whether the correct characterization of the constraint on extraposition is to be given in terms of Move a and the trace of movement at all.

Guéron (1980) notes the distinction between NPs that allow extraposition and those that do not. She defines those that do not allow extraposition as "names," and stipulates in the form of the Name Constraint that a "name" cannot contain a trace under a movement analysis. While the Name Constraint may be an accurate statement of the facts, there is no reason other than convention why it needs to be formulated in terms of trace at all.[51]

Recall that at the heart of the analysis of extraposition is the question of how the interpretation is accounted for. On one view, the extraposed constituent is interpreted as though it is a constituent of NP, and on the other, it bears a somewhat looser relationship to the antecedent NP. In our formulation of the Complement Principle we have suggested that an interpretive rule for extraposition is sufficient to account for the standard cases. We claim that there is no need to posit a movement analysis, which may prove to be problematic.

Going beyond this, however, we can demonstrate that our approach to interpretation for extraposition is needed, in order to account for the full range of cases. Specifically, we find that the Name Constraint is a *consequence* of interpreting an extraposed clause in its S-structure position.[52]

An extraposed relative clause or non-argument, under the Complement Principle, will be interpreted as a modifier of its antecedent. A definite NP that is understood as a "name" cannot be modified, for reasons quite independent of extraposition. The government requirement of the Complement Principle, which we have already discussed, rules out the possibility that a constituent of a definite NP, or any NP for that matter, could be the antecedent of an extraposed constituent. Thus it follows that for the standard cases extraposition is ungrammatical.

But where the NP does not have the "name" interpretation, whether or not it is definite, it may serve as the antecedent for extraposition. Furthermore, where the extraposed constituent is not a modifier, the NP can serve as antecedent regardless of its interpretation.

Let us consider some examples that illustrate these generalizations. Note first that it is impossible to modify with a relative clause a proper noun NP, e.g. **John who I saw*. This NP denotes a unique individual or set of individuals. We presume that the problem here is with the precise formal interpretation of this structure. We assume that in contrast a relative clause or a common noun denotes a property. In the case of modification of an NP by a relative clause, the interpretation is usually a conjoined property, such that what is denoted is determined by a function whose arguments are not individuals, but the properties expressed by the relative clause and the common noun. The Name Constraint is a special case of this restriction on semantic structure, given that a proper name does not denote a property and hence cannot constitute a complex property in combination with a relative clause. Such a result follows from the formal approach to relativization of Montague (1973), for example.

The definite determiners may have the interpretation of picking out a unique set, in which case they form constituents that are similar to proper names. But alternatively, certain definite determiners may function pragmatically to indicate that the set of individuals otherwise denoted is not new to the discourse. (2) is an example of this sort. Here, the definite determiner crucially does not have the function of picking out a subset from a set on the basis of the description. That is, under the subset interpretation, a phrase such as *that man that I was telling you about* selects a particular man from the set of men that I was telling you about. On the "not new to the discourse" interpretation, such a phrase simply implicates that such a man has been mentioned before, but not that there are other men with the property that I was telling you about them.

The base generation analysis predicts precisely this distinction. The antecedent of an extraposed constituent must be a maximal NP, since only a maximal NP will locally c-command or be c-commanded by an extraposed constituent. Crucially, the extraposed constituent does not constitute part of the description that is within the scope of the definite determiner at S-structure. Thus, if the NP is interpreted as denoting a unique set, it is so interpreted independently of the extraposed constituent. The extraposed constituent can only be interpreted as a modifier of the definite NP, which thus yields ill-formedness.

The desirability of this approach becomes clear when we consider cases of extraposition from NP in which the extraposed constituent is not a modifier of the antecedent, but an argument. In these cases, the interpretation does not involve set-intersection, but rather argument satisfaction. Consider the following examples.

(3)   a. The mayor just called you of a large Eastern city.
     b. The destruction was ordered of a new bridge from Italy to Boston.
     c. The parents attended the meeting of many students.

    d. The idea has been around for some time that we should all band together
       on this problem.

Here, the restrictive definite determiner does not block the interpretation, precisely because set-intersection is not involved. In these cases the composit- ional semantics ignores the relative position of the definite determiner and the extraposed constituent. In fact there is no reason why they should interact, in contrast to those cases where what is extraposed is a modifier, since the rules of interpretation are entirely different.[53]

Along similar lines, consider the case of those adjectives that take scope within NP, such as *former*, *alleged*, and *big*. In each case we get an ambiguity with a relative clause, depending on whether or not the relative clause is understood as being in the scope of the adjective.

(4)   a. A former marine who was assigned to Paris during the last war just came
        in.
     b. An alleged physician who gave illegal prescriptions to his patients was at
        the party.
     c. A big mouse that was raised on beer is in this box.

In (a) the ambiguity consists of whether the marine was formerly assigned to Paris, or whether the assignment to Paris during the last war is independent of being a marine. In (b) the ambiguity consists of whether the person was alleged to be a physician only, or one who gave illegal prescriptions. In (c) the ambiguity is between *big for a mouse* and *big for a mouse that was raised on beer*.

When we extrapose the ambiguity is lost. This is shown in (5).

(5)   a. A former marine just came in who was assigned to Paris during the last
        war.
     b. An alleged physician was at the party who gave illegal prescriptions to
        his patients.
     c. A big mouse is in this box that was raised on beer.

As predicted by the Complement Principle, but not by a movement analysis, the relative clause modifies only the antecedent NP as a maximal projection. There is no possibility of the relative clause falling within the scope of the adjective, since no constituent of this maximal projection may serve as the antecedent of the extraposed relative clause.[54]

4.2   The Focus Effect

As we observed in Chapter One:4, EX constructions often exhibit a focusing effect on the extraposed phrase. This accounts for the oddity of the sequences below.

(6)   A: When did you buy a book about Chomsky?
       B: *I bought a book on TUESDAY about Chomsky.
(7)   A: Who did you sell that old bicycle to that you found in the garage?
       B: *I sold that bike to JOHN that I found in the garage.

There do exist well-formed sequences, however, in which the extraposed phrase appears not to be in focus.[55]

(8)   A: Is there anyone here that Mary likes?
       B: YEAH, a SOLDIER just came in that Mary likes.

In (8), it is the antecedent that is focused and not the extraposed phrase. This case, in fact, accords with the analysis of Guéron (1980) and of Rochemont (1978), who claim that NP must be focused to serve as antecedent to an extraposed phrase. In (6)–(7) as well, both antecedent and extraposed phrase are focused, consistent with the Guéron–Rochemont claim.

   But as the examples of (9) show, it is also possible for just the extraposed phrase to be focused, contradicting the claim that a proper antecedent must be focused.[56]

(9)   A: Did Mary meet any soldiers at the party?
       B: YEAH, she met a soldier at the party that she really LIKES.

In fact, in the context of (9A) the antecedent *a soldier* may not be focused at all. Hence, (10) is not a possible response to (9A).

(10)   YEAH, she met a SOLDIER at the party that she really LIKES.

The claim that a possible antecedent in EX must be focused therefore cannot be maintained, contra Guéron (1980) and Rochemont (1978). Rather it appears from examples (6)–(10) that in EX either the antecedent or the extraposed phrase is focused or both are. This same generalization is illustrated in the further exemplary paradigm below.

(11)   A: Did John get anything for his mother?
        B: YEAH, John bought a PICTURE for his mother that he saw in PARIS.
(12)   A: Did John get any pictures for his mother?
        a. B: YEAH, John bought a picture that he saw in PARIS for his mother.
        b. B: YEAH, John bought a picture for his mother that he saw in PARIS.
        c. B: YEAH, John bought a PICTURE for his mother that he saw in PARIS.

(13) A: Did John get anything that he saw in Paris for his mother?
      B: YEAH, John bought a PICTURE for his mother that he saw in Paris.

In (11) both the antecedent and the extraposed phrase are focused. In (12), (a) and (b) are possible responses to (A), but not (c); only the extraposed phrase is in focus in (b). In (13) the antecedent alone is focused.

The distribution of the Focus Effect then in EX is slightly different than in the other cases considered in Chapter One:4 in that the focus requirement is not restricted in EX to a single structural position. In Chapter Five, we will reconsider this difference, suggesting a possible account for it.

4.3   The predicate restriction on SX

As discussed at length in Guéron (1980) and Rochemont (1978), SX is subject to a restriction concerning the class of verbs/predicates that tolerate it.[57] Thus, (14a) is a felicitous instance of SX, while (14b) sounds distinctly odd.

(14) a. A man arrived who wasn't wearing any clothes.
      b. A man screamed who wasn't wearing any clothes.

If SX is subject to the restriction that the predicate in the sentence must be one of appearance, then the contrast between (14a,b) would appear to be accommodated. Both Guéron and Rochemont argue that the predicate of appearance restriction is contextually rather than lexically defined. Thus, it is possible to improve the acceptability of SX with a verb like *scream* by embedding the relevant example in an appropriate discourse context, as below.

(15)   Suddenly there was the sound of lions growling. Several women screamed. Then a man screamed who was standing at the very edge of the crowd.

Similarly, as Rochemont (1978, 12ff.) demonstrates, the idiomatic predicate of appearance reading is most natural in example (16) out of context, but the literal interpretation can be rendered natural in the appropriate context, as in (17).

(16)   A book hit the newsstand by Chomsky.
(17)   Many of the books which fell out of the tenth story window hit a small newsstand situated directly below at the base of the building. Most of them did little damage, but when a book hit the newsstand by Chomsky, everyone thought the structure would collapse.

In sum, in the terms of the framework of Rochemont (1986), SX is subject to the restriction that the predicate must be c-construable (roughly, "old information"), whether directly or indirectly.

It is important to recognize that the predicate restriction in SX is not equiva-lent to the superficially similar predicate restrictions in Stylistic Inversion (SI) and Presentational *there* Insertion (PTI) constructions as is commonly supposed. In SI and PTI the predicate restriction is more specifically grammati-cal, even lexical. Thus, for SI, compare the following.

(18)   a. Into the room walked John.
       b. *At the station arrived the train.

Example (18b) is not subject to the same sort of contextual manipulation as (14b). The same point holds for PTI, as shown in (19), corresponding to (14a).

(19)   There arrived a man who wasn't wearing any clothes.

Nevertheless, unlike (14b), (20) is unacceptable even in the context established in (15).

(20)   *There screamed a man who was standing at the very edge of the crowd.

By the same token, compare (21a,b) and (22a,b).

(21)   a. *There phoned her up a man who she didn't know.
       b. A man phoned her up she didn't know.
(22)   a. *There asked Mary to dance a man who she didn't know.
       b. A man asked Mary to dance who she didn't know.

We conclude that the predicate of appearance restriction in EX is contextually rather than lexically defined and not reducible to the superficially similar restriction in evidence in PTI and SI. In the remainder of the discussion in this section, we reserve the term "predicate restriction" to refer to the contextually defined predicate of appearance restriction in evidence in SX.

The claim that the predicate restriction is contextually rather than grammati-cally defined sets a requirement for any proposed account of this restriction. In particular, the contextually defined nature of the restriction implies, consis-tent with the Autonomous Systems view espoused by Guéron (1980) and Rochemont (1978), that the class of predicates that tolerate SX is not expressed in the grammatical description of this construction at all. On the Guéron–Rochemont view, the predicate restriction in SX is claimed to follow from the focusing requirement on the subject. We will criticize this account in detail below. Let us first consider an alternative analysis, proposed by Coop-mans and Roovers (1986). These authors propose to treat the class of predicates that tolerate SX as a grammatical class lexically identified as unaccusative. This view is appealing on a Move a account of EX, since it overcomes the difficulties for such an account posed by SX in particular, as we have discussed at length earlier in this chapter. If the predicates that tolerate SX are in fact unaccusative, then the S-structure subject in a SX construction is a derived subject that originated at D-structure in a VP internal position. Under this account, SX may be systematically excluded by Subjacency and/or the ECP, and apparent cases of SX derived as instances of OX with subsequent movement of the antecedent phrase to subject position.

In our view, there are two major difficulties for such an analysis. First, as we have already noted, an account that proposes to capture the predicate restriction on SX by lexically marking specific items in some fashion as predicates of appearance cannot accommodate the variable character of certain predicates in and out of context, as with (14b)/(15). In terms of the unaccusative analysis, status as an unaccusative predicate would be forced to vary as a function of discourse context and information structure, robbing the term ''unaccusative'' in this analysis of any independent motivation. The *ad hoc* nature of the term ''unaccusative'' in its use in such an analysis is further illustrated in cases where SX applies in the presence of a transitive predicate, as in (23).

(23) a. A man entered the room who wasn't wearing any clothes.
b. A man just bought that restaurant who everyone says is an entrepreneur.

To claim that the predicates in (23) are unaccusative in the required sense leads inevitably to circularity in the definition of ''unaccusative'' as it is intended to apply in deriving the predicate of appearance restriction.

A second difficulty with the unaccusative analysis concerns the claim that the appearance of a trace of extraposition within a subject NP is possible only due to the ''unaccusative'' character of the predicate. This account leads us to expect that subject condition violations are generally possible for subjects of ''unaccusative'' predicates. This prediction, however, is incorrect, as shown by the contrast in grammaticality between the examples below.

(24) a. A book *t* just appeared on the possibility of nuclear war.
b. *On what subject did a book *t* just appear?

Even with ''unaccusative'' predicates, there is a clear asymmetry between SX and *wh* movement. In short, the ''unaccusative'' analysis of the predicate restriction is at best *ad hoc*, and therefore unrevealing.

Consider now the alternative account, that the predicate restriction is due to the function of SX in focusing the subject.[58] Guéron (1980) and Rochemont (1978) claim that the discourse function of SX is solely to introduce the subject into the discourse. Since the subject is being presentationally focused, it would appear to follow that the predicate must be "given," or c-construable. The problem with this argument is that it requires that any sentence which presentationally focuses the subject must require a predicate of appearance, which is clearly false.

(25)   A MAN just ran into your HOUSE.

Example (25) may be used to initiate a discourse in which the predicate is not c-construable and the subject is nevertheless presentationally focused. Thus it is not generally true that presentationally focusing a subject requires that the predicate be c-construable. (See also Culicover and Rochemont [1983], Rochemont [1986].) What is special about SX is that the predicate *must* apparently be c-construable. As it stands, then, the predicate of appearance restriction on SX does not follow from the presentational focusing function of the construction either.

In this discussion we have considered and rejected two possible accounts of the predicate restriction on SX. Given the contextually defined nature of the restriction we think a functional account is more likely to be successful. At present, however, we can provide no such account. It would appear that SX occupies a special niche among constructions that function to (presentationally) focus a given phrase, in that in SX it is required that the predicate be c-construable.

3   *Stylistic inversion*

In this chapter we analyze a set of constructions in English that have typically been viewed as involving inversion of the subject to the right around the VP, often called Stylistic Inversion (SI). The constructions are exemplified below.

(1)   a. Into the room walked John.
       b. In front of her sat her mother.
(2)   a. Sitting in front of her was her mother.
       b. Happiest to see him was Bill.
       c. Under the table was a large box.
       d. Found at the scene of the crime was an axe.

(1a, b) exemplify Directional and Locative Inversion (D/L), respectively. The examples of (2) are all instances of what Emonds (1976) refers to as Preposing around *be* (PAB) constructions. As we argued in Chapter One, each of the constructions in (1) and (2) identifies the postverbal subject as a structural focus.

The question to be addressed in this chapter is what is the syntactic analysis of SI sentences, and in particular, what is the configurational position of the structurally defined focus? Although we will ultimately maintain that SI constructions form a unified class, our discussion focuses mainly on D/L, where the correct analysis is less obvious. Section 1 defends in general terms a particular view of the derivation of D/L, concluding with an account of PAB along similar lines. This account of D/L is defended more extensively in section 2. In section 3 we provide a more detailed syntactic analysis consistent with our theoretical assumptions as outlined in Chapter One. Section 4 considers some problematic aspects of one feature of the analysis of D/L resulting from our discussion in sections 1 and 2. In section 5, we discuss complications with our analysis of D/L arising from extraction facts. Finally, in section 6 we summarize and critically review some of the prior analyses of these constructions that have not figured in our prior discussion.

1   D/L Inversion

We begin our discussion with the D/L Inversion constructions reproduced below in (1). These sentences are truth-conditionally equivalent in meaning to the corresponding sentences in (2).

(1)   a. Into the room walked John.
         b. In front of her sat her mother.
(2)   a. John walked into the room.
         b. Her mother sat in front of her.

Taking the order of elements in sentences like (2) to be canonical, the question we face with the sentences in (1) is how the non-canonical order they exhibit gives rise to the same thematic interpretation as their counterparts in (2).

1.1   The Presentational *there* analysis

A superficially plausible, and in fact widely adopted, analysis would assign a thematic interpretation to (1) in a manner identical to (2), and treat the non-canonical order as derived by movement of the internal and external arguments of V to sentence peripheral positions. Thus the sentences of (1) would have S-structure representations in which the preposed PP and post-posed NP bind traces in their respective D-structure positions, as in (3):

(3)   [PP_i t_j V t_i NP_j]

Such an analysis accounts for the identity of thematic interpretation of the corresponding sentences in (1) and (2). It also entirely reduces the derivation of the non-canonical structures to independently attested movements. The preposing of PP parallels the topicalization of PP in such sentences as (4), and the rightward movement of the subject is also manifested in the Presentational *there* construction in (5).

(4)   Into the room John walked.
(5)   There walked into the room a man no one recognized.

The essentials of the analysis just outlined are realized in different ways by a number of authors. We will critically examine these analyses in sections 5 and 6 of this chapter. There are, however, a number of features of D/L that argue against any analysis of this general type. In particular, it can be demonstrated that neither PP Topicalization, i.e. the application of Move α that yields sentences such as (4), nor Presentational *there* Insertion, which yields (5), are involved in the derivation of sentences such as (1).

1.2   Predicates in D/L

The feature of D/L constructions which suggests that PP Topicalization is not involved is that it is not always simply a PP, or even obviously a constituent, that precedes the verb in sentences of this type. Consider for instance the examples in (6).

(6)   a. Into the room nude walked John.
       b. In front of her smiling stood Bill.

As always, it is important to recognize that sentences with contextual requirements of the sort that accompany the Focus Effect (FE) can only be reliably judged against an appropriate context. Since D/L requires that the sentence final phrase he focused, each of the examples in (6) is best judged in a specific discourse, as illustrated in the respective contexts below.

  (i) They said someone might walk into the room nude, and into the room nude
      walked John.
  (ii) She had the notion that someone might be standing in front of her smiling,
       and when she looked up, in front of her smiling stood Bill.

In such contexts the sentences of (6) are to our ears fully acceptable.[1]

   We assume that the sentences of (6) are derivationally related to the respective sentences in (7).

(7)   a. John walked into the room nude.
       b. Bill stood in front of her smiling.

It is generally agreed that in sentences like (7), the predicate phrase (*nude*, *smiling*) and the directional/locative PP do not make up a constituent apart from the verb. For instance, in *wh* questions, the predicate phrase may not "pied pipe" with the PP to the front of the sentence.

(8)   a. Into which room did John walk nude?
          *Into which room nude did John walk?
       b. In front of whom did Bill stand smiling?
          *In front of whom smiling did Bill stand?

Furthermore, it is not plausible that D/L sentences like (6) are derived in part by independent topicalization of the PP and the predicate phrase, for three reasons. First, while it is generally the case that topics are obligatorily separated from the rest of the sentences by an intonation break, sentences like (6) typically have no such pause following each of the fronted phrases.[2] Second, English, unlike some other languages (e.g. Chinese, Japanese, Hungarian), does not allow multiple topicalization in a single clause, as evidenced by the ungrammaticality of the sentences in (9).[3] (We revise this claim below.)

(9)   a. *Bill, John, I've never introduced to.
        b. *To John, a letter, Mary just sent.
        c. *That book, on the table, Bill just put.
        d. *With Bill, nude, Mary likes to play.
        e. *Nude, into the room, John walked.

And third, the order of PP and predicate phrase in cases like (6) is strictly fixed (compare (10)), an observation that is unexpected if such cases were derived by multiple topicalization.[4]

(10)   a. *Nude, into the room, walked John.
       b. *Smiling, in front of her, stood Bill.

The examples in (8) show that the PP + predicate phrase sequence in sentences like (7) is not exhaustively dominated by a single node. Let us now consider more carefully what the structure of such sentences is. We have already seen evidence in Chapter Two that the verb and the directional/ locative PP in these sentences make up a constituent that is contained within a broader constituent that includes the predicate phrase but not the subject, as in (11).

(11)

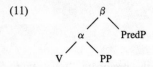

Recall that the operation of VP Ellipsis may apply to the V + PP sequence alone, as in (12), or to the entire post-subject sequence, as in (13).

(12)   a. Bill walked into the room smiling, and then John did nude.
       b. Bill sat in front of the house in his new car, and then Mary did on a motor-
          cycle.
(13)   a. Bill walked into the room nude, and then John did.
       b. Bill sat in front of the house on a motorcycle, and then Mary did.

Assuming that VP Ellipsis applies always to maximal projections of the same categorial type,[5] then such examples as (12) and (13) not only motivate the constituent structure in (11), but also suggest that the proper choice for α and β in (11) is VP.

The structure (11) is also motivated by examples with topicalization and pseudoclefting of VP. In such cases, just as with VP Ellipsis, the predicate phrase may either act as a constituent with the affected VP or not, as below.

(14) a. I was told that John would come into the room with a surprise, and come into the room he DID NUDE.
      b. I was told that John would come into the room nude, and come into the room nude he DID.

(15) a. ?What John did nude was walk into the room.
      b. What John did was walk into the room nude.

If we assume that only maximal projections can undergo topicalization, then the sentences of (14) and (15) provide evidence once again not only for the structure (11) but also that the proper choice for α and β in (11) is VP, as diagrammed immediately below.

(16)

```
              VP
            /    \
        VP        PREDP
      /    \
    V        PP
```

We will further assume that there is no non-maximal V^1 in such cases that dominates just V and PP, though nothing crucial hinges on this assumption in what follows. (See Culicover and Wilkins [1984] and Chomsky [1986b]).

VP Topicalization constructions generally sound best when they are embedded in a particular type of context, as below.

(17) They said John would come into the room nude, and come into the room nude he did.

In (17), the sentence final auxiliary is obligatorily prominent and focused. As is often the case with focused auxiliaries, it is the truth value of the proposition expressed in the sentence that is being focused.[6] VP Topicalization constructions such as (17) show two further restrictions, that nothing preceding the auxiliary may be focused, and that everything following it must be. Thus, whether the auxiliary is focused or not, example (18a) is odd because of the first restriction, and (18b) is odd because of the second.

(18) a. *They said someone would come into the room nude, and come into the room nude, JOHN did.
      b. *They said John would come into the room nude, and come into the room, he did/DID nude/NUDE.

We will not attempt here to formalize the focus and prominence properties of VP Topicalization constructions. But since these constructions form a focal point for our investigation below, these points must be borne in mind in assessing the relative well-formedness of relevant cases in our subsequent discussion.

1.3   An alternative analysis

1.3.1   VP Topicalization

Our conclusion that predicate phrases appear adjoined to VP, together with our prior assumptions, has immediate consequences for our analysis of D/L sentences such as those in (1) and (6). The relevant assumptions are that (i) the corresponding sentences in (1)/(2) and (6)/(7) are derivationally related, (ii) topicalization is restricted to constituents, and (iii) English marginally allows multiple topicalization in a single clause in a very restrictive fashion only. Given these assumptions, we are forced to conclude that the constituent that has undergone topicalization in sentences like (6) (and by analogy also [1]) is VP, since this is the only constituent containing both and only the subcategorized directional/locative PP and the predicate phrase. What is odd about this conclusion is that the VP seems to have been preposed without the verb.

However, despite the oddity of this conclusion, in section 2 we will consider a host of arguments to support the claim that the initial constituent in D/L is VP. We are consequently forced to conclude that V has escaped from VP in the derivation of D/L. For the present we will simply assume that V raises to I prior to the topicalization of VP, leaving a number of difficulties with this assumption for section 4. One piece of evidence favoring the assumption stems from our earlier observation that in typical VP Topicalization constructions such as (14), the auxiliary, and correspondingly the truth value, is obligatorily focused. Consider in this connection example (19).

(19)   They said John would walk into the room nude, and into the room nude
        he walked.

As (19) illustrates, and as we argue below in more detail, the reverse ordering of subject and verb in D/L is not a necessary feature of this construction. Now notice that in (19), as in (14), the obligatory focus in the sentence is on *walked*. Further, again as in (14), the interpretation of this focus is that of an auxiliary focus; that is, the focus is on the truth value of the sentence. In other words, for purposes of the interpretation of the focus in examples such as (19), the main verb *walked* functions as an auxiliary verb rather than as a main verb.

Focus on V in examples such as (19) can *only* be interpreted as auxiliary focus, and not as a simple V focus. This is shown by the oddity of an example such as (20).

(20)   *They said John would walk into the room nude, but into the room nude he RAN.

Similarly, focus on V itself cannot normally be interpreted as an auxiliary focus, apart from constructions such as (19), as evidenced by the oddity of examples such as (21d).

(21)   They said John would walk into the meeting late, and
  a. walk into the meeting late John DID.
  b. into the meeting late John WALKED.
  c. John DID walk into the meeting late.
  d. *John WALKED into the meeting late.

In other words, in constructions such as (19), the verb is behaving as though it were an auxiliary, a feature of these constructions that could be captured if the verb had been raised out of VP and into I, given a theory of the interpretation of focusing on I.

In section 3, we will elaborate an analysis of Stylistic Inversion constructions on the assumption that sentences such as (6a) and (19) (cf. (22a,b), respectively) are derived from the same D-structure as the corresponding sentence (7a) (repeated in (22c)) by raising of the verb to INFL (I), with subsequent topicalization of the remaining VP containing the trace of the raised verb. This derivation is schematically represented in (22d).

(22)   a. Into the room nude walked John.
  b. Into the room nude he walked.
  c. John walked into the room nude.

  d.

1.3.2   Inversion or subject postposing?

In the immediately preceding discussion, we have seen some evidence that D/L constructions generally involve topicalization of a different constituent than the self-evident topicalization of PP in (4). We have assumed that the constituent that has topicalized is VP. In section 2, we present further arguments to this effect. Let us now consider the second component of the analysis of D/L constructions outlined in (3), that the positioning of the subject in such sentences relative to the verb is a function of postposing of the subject to sentence final position. One specific realization of this account, that of Stowell (1981), considers this postposing to be identical to that in Presentational *there* constructions such as (5), repeated below.

(5)   There walked into the room a man no one recognized.

It is generally agreed that the postposed subject in sentences like (5) is in a VP adjoined position.[7] Safir (1985) also provides an account of D/L constructions as involving postposing of the subject, but he argues for a different realization of this analysis, in which the postposed subject in such cases is adjoined to IP rather than VP. These two accounts of the positioning of subjects in D/L are represented schematically below in (23).

(23)   a.   Stowell (1981)   b.   Safir (1985)

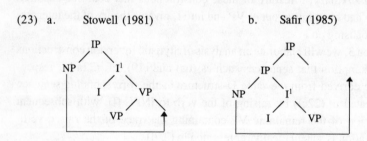

Both of the derivations in (23) predict that the postposed subject will follow all other elements in VP, including predicate phrases. This prediction is borne out for the postposed subject of the Presentational *there* construction in (5), as seen in (24).[8]

(24)   a.   There walked into the room nude a man no one knew.
       b.   *There walked into the room a man no one knew nude.

However, contrary to the predictions of either of the accounts of D/L represented in (23), the positioning of the subject in D/L relative to non-topicalized predicate phrases does not parallel that in evidence in the Presentational *there* construction in (24), but is in fact the reverse.

(25) a. *Into the room walked nude John.
      b. Into the room walked John nude.

Example (25b) is grammatical only under a specific intonation. For reasons that will become clear below, D/L constructions are similar to VP Topicalization constructions in imposing a restriction that all elements following the obligatorily focused phrase must also be focused and prominent. Thus, to be grammatical, (25b) must be pronounced as in (26).

(26)   Into the room walked JOHN NUDE.

But no pattern of prominence in (25a), and in particular neither of those in (27), can improve the judgment of ungrammaticality for this example.[9]

(27) a. *Into the room walked nude JOHN.
      b. *Into the room walked NUDE JOHN.

The contrasts of acceptability between the examples in (24) and (25) provide the basis for a convincing argument that D/L constructions do not involve any process of subject postposing of the type illustrated in (23). We assume that all other conceivable accounts of D/L in terms of a process of subject postposing are excluded as a matter of principle. In particular, Emonds' (1976) proposal to derive Locative Inversion constructions by postposing the subject NP to the position of an empty object in VP is ruled out by any principle that has the same effect as the Projection Principle of Chomsky (1981), that movement into an argument object position is blocked. Furthermore, if one assumes that adjunction can only be to a maximal projection, then any conceivable remaining alternatives are also excluded.

It has been suggested to us that (25b)/(26) might not be characterized structurally as we have proposed but rather with the postverbal subject and predicate phrase appearing as a small clause subject constituent of the sort analyzed in Safir (1983). Then, (25b) would presumably be derivationally related to (28).

(28)   ?John nude walked into the room.

There are several arguments against this view. We present here just two. Consider first the question of number agreement for a small clause subject such as *John nude*, or to pick a somewhat more felicitous example,

(29)   Mary bathing is a wonderful sight.

As (30) shows, number agreement in such cases is not with the NP itself, but with the small clause as a propositional subject.

(30)   Those men bathing is/*are a disgusting sight.

Now note that in D/L, number agreement is always with the postverbal NP and not with a small clause.

(31)   Behind her were/*was sitting three men nude.

A second argument is given on the basis of example (6b) of section 2, repeated below.

(32)   *Into the room walked Susan nude and out of the room Jack smiling.

Assuming that the gapped sequence can only be followed by a single constituent (see references in section 2.1), then it must be that *Jack smiling* is not a constituent. We conclude that the constituents following V in (25b) do not form a small clause unit.

There is a further argument that the reverse ordering of subject and verb in D/L is derived by preposing of the verb, rather than postposing of the subject as a function of PTI. This concerns the operation of quantifier float on a pronominal subject as in (33).

(33)   They all walked into the room.

As (34) shows, it is not possible to shift the subject NP in a sentence such as (33) to produce an instance of PTI.

(34)   *There walked into the room them all.

Nevertheless, such phrases can take part in D/L, as below.

(35)   ?Into the room walked them all.

Now note that (35) could not be derived through postposing of the subject, given the ungrammaticality of the intermediate stage in (34). Consider also the ungrammaticality of the related example (36).

(36)   *Into the room there walked them all.

These examples reinforce our conclusion that D/L is not derived through the dual operations of PP Topicalization and PTI.

Thus far, we have claimed that the sentences (6a) and (19a) are derived from the same D-structure as the corresponding sentence (7a) by the application of V-raising to I and VP Topicalization. In particular, we propose the following (partial) S-structure representations for these sentences.

(37)   a.   John [$_{VP}$ walked into the room nude].
        b.   [$_{VP}$ into the room nude] John [$_I$ walked].
        c.   [$_{VP}$ into the room nude] [$_I$ walked] John.

Of the two conceivable possibilities for deriving the reverse ordering of subject and verb in (37c) illustrated in (38), we have just argued that (i) is inconsistent with the available evidence.

(38)   (i)

                     | --------→

     [$_{VP}$ into the room nude] John [$_I$ walked]

             ←--------|

            (ii)

We conclude that the only plausible account of the ordering of subject and verb is that represented by (38ii).[10] In particular, we will assume that inversion of the I containing V around NP in (38) yields sentences such as (1) and (6), with the structure (37c). Failure to invert in (38) gives rise to such sentences as (19), with the structure (37b).

     Our analysis of the derivation of D/L constructions, then, contains three major components: VP Topicalization, V to I, and inversion of I containing V, each of which may be independently motivated for English. In the sections to follow, we will further defend and elaborate the details of analysis for these three components. Before turning to this task, though, let us return to the PAB construction mentioned at the beginning of this chapter and consider its relation to D/L.

1.4   Preposing around *be*

We have argued that D/L involves VP Topicalization and inversion of the verb around the subject. We must now consider whether PAB is susceptible to a similar analysis. The assimilation of PAB to the VP Topicalization construction is a straightforward matter, since the main verb of the sentence in a PAB construction does not escape prior to the topicalization of VP.

(39)   a.   Sitting in front of the camera smiling was Bill.
        b.   Rolling down the hill out of control was a carriage.
        c.   Standing at the edge of the park rusting was an iron statue.

Similarly, that it is the auxiliary verb that inverts and not the subject that postposes is shown by examples entirely parallel to (24)/(25).[11]

(40)   a. There was standing at the edge of the park rusting a large old iron statue.
      b. *There was standing at the edge of the park a large old iron statue rusting.
(41)   a. *Standing at the edge of the park was rusting a large old iron statue.
      b. Standing at the edge of the park was a large old iron statue rusting.

Examples (40) parallel (24) in that the postverbal subject in a Presentational *there* construction must follow a subject-oriented predicate in VP. As (40) show, however, PAB patterns with D/L in that the postverbal subject precedes rather than follows the subject predicate. It is thus plausible to assume that D/L and PAB are derived in essentially the same fashion, with the difference that in D/L the main verb has been reanalyzed in I.[12] This perspective justifies our initial assumption that D/L and PAB are instances of a more general construction in English, which we have referred to as Stylistic Inversion.[13]

2   Further arguments for VP Topicalization

Our argument has been that the constituent that preposes in D/L Inversion is a VP. This argument has relied exclusively on the behavior of predicate phrases in certain configurations. We will now consider additional evidence for this analysis.

2.1   Gapping

First, we draw on an observation in Culicover (1980) that manner adverbs may also prepose in D/L.

(1)   a. Quickly into the room went Bill.
      b. Gracefully down the staircase walked the Queen.
      c. Meekly under the table crouched the dog.

Culicover argues that the adverb is not simply topicalized in the examples of (1), but actually behaves as a constituent with the PP for purposes of Gapping. It is widely recognized that in Gapping, only a single constituent may precede the gapped verb. (This observation is made first, to our knowledge, in Sag [1976].) This, Culicover reasons, assuming that the initial adverb-PP sequence in the sentences of (1) is a constituent, allows us to characterize the contrast in grammaticality between the sentences in (2).

(2)   a. Quickly into the room went Bill, and slowly onto the roof, Mary.
      b. *Quickly Bill went into the room, and slowly Mary, onto the roof.

In contrast to Culicover (1980), who assumes the adverb is a constituent *of* the PP, we conclude that the adverb in each of the sentences in (1) is a constituent with the PP in VP.

Moreover, the line of argument that we applied in the case of predicate phrases applies here as well. The only constituent containing both the PP and the adverb is a VP, as seen by the operations of VP Ellipsis and VP Topicalization.

(3) a. Bill went into the room quickly, and Mary did slowly.
     b. Bill went into the room quickly, and Mary did too.
(4) a. Into the room Bill went quickly.
     b. Quickly into the room Bill went.

Thus, (1) gives further evidence that it is a VP that topicalizes in D/L and not simply a PP.

The argument we have just given on the basis of the behavior of adverbs in gapping constructions with D/L is valid also with predicate phrases. Consider for instance the example in (5).

(5)   Into the room nude walked Susan, and out of the room smiling, Jack.

If a gapped sequence must be preceded by a constituent, then the grammaticality of (5) is predicted on our analysis.

It has often been claimed that a gapped sequence may only be followed by a constituent as well.[14] Assuming this to be true,[15] we account not only for the grammaticality of (5), but also for the distribution of judgments in the sentences of (6).[16]

(6) a. *Susan walked into the room nude, and Jack out of the room smiling.
     b. *Into the room walked Susan nude, and out of the room Jack smiling.
     c. Susan walked into the room, and Jack out of the room.

Only in (6c) is the gapped material both preceded and followed by a constituent.[17] The contrast between (6a) and (5) is explained on our account by our analysis of D/L as involving topicalization of a constituent VP. As we will see in section 4, V-raising cannot apply in the derivation of (6a). In (6b), only the "small" VP has been topicalized, leaving two constituents to follow the gapped verb, hence the judgment of unacceptability.

In sum, our analysis of D/L as involving VP Topicalization allows us to explain an otherwise puzzling range of judgments in Gapping constructions involving D/L.

2.2   Multiple complements to V in VP

A second supporting argument for the conclusion that D/L involves VP Topicalization concerns the behavior of multiple complements to V. Consider first the examples in (7).

(7)   a. Beside her in the waiting room sat her husband.
      b. Down the stairs into the kitchen walked Mary.

As the corresponding sentences in (8) and (9) demonstrate, the PPs in (7) are all constituents of VP.

(8)   a. Sitting beside her in the waiting room was her husband.
      b. Walking down the stairs into the kitchen was Mary.
(9)   a. . . . and sit beside her in the waiting room he did.
      b. . . . and walk down the stairs into the kitchen she did.

That these PPs are separate constituents of VP is indicated by the examples below in (10). To be grammatical, in (10) the postverbal subject and the sentence final PP must be focused and accented.[18]

(10) a. Where did her husband sit beside her?
         Where did Mary walk into the kitchen?
      b. In the waiting room sat her husband beside her.
         Down the stairs walked Mary into the kitchen.

Again, our conclusion is that in (7) it is a VP constituent containing multiple complements to V that has been topicalized.

In this connection, consider also the following case.

(11)   Several guards ran into the room behind her.

This sentence is ambiguous. The two readings are paraphrased below.

(12) a. Several guards ran into the room that was behind her.
      b. Several guards ran into the room following her.

A plausible account of this ambiguity is that on the reading expressed in (12a), the PP *behind her* is a constituent of the preceding phrase *into the room*, as diagrammed in (13a), and on the other reading, (12b), it is a separate constituent under VP, as in (13b). It is irrelevant to our discussion whether a in (13b) is VP or V^1. (See Culicover and Wilkins [1984])

(13) a.   VP
            V   PP
               . . .   PP

      b.   VP
            a PP
          V   PP

This account is supported by the operations of VP Ellipsis and VP Topicalization on (11). Thus, (14a) and (15a) have only the reading (12b) with constituent structure (13b), and (14b) and (15b) remain ambiguous with either of the readings in (12) and constituent structures in (13).

(14)   a. Several ladies ran into the room before her, and several guards did behind her.
       b. Several ladies ran into the room behind her, and several guards did too.
(15)   a. ..., and run into the room, they did behind her.
       b. ..., and run into the room behind her, they did.

Now notice that the sentence (16) is ambiguous between the two readings in (12).

(16)   Into the room behind her ran several guards.

Given the structures in (13), (16) would be expected to have only the reading (12a) if the topicalized phrase in D/L constructions were necessarily a PP. That this sentence is in fact ambiguous provides further evidence that multiple constituents in VP act like a single constituent in D/L. Given the data in (14) and (15), it seems we are once again forced to conclude that this constituent is a VP.

2.3   Extraposed relatives

Let us now consider the behavior of extraposed relative clauses in D/L constructions. We have argued in Chapter Two that extraposed relative clauses are adjoined to VP. This suggests an additional test for the constituenthood of the sequence preceding the verb in D/L constructions. However, implementing this test is complicated by the following considerations. First, as we have seen in Chapter Two, a subject extraposed relative may not precede its antecedent. Furthermore, as we will see below, there can be no direct object in D/L constructions, thus ruling out extraposed relative clauses from object position as a test of constituenthood for D/L. However, in some cases extraposition is possible from the object of a preposition, as below.

(17)   An escaped convict ran into the storeroom this morning that Mary was working in.

In such cases it is predicted that there may be a D/L variant in which the extraposed relative precedes the verb. This variant is given in (18).

(18)   Into the storeroom this morning that Mary was working in ran an escaped convict.

Thus, extraposed relative clauses too support the proposal that the constituent preposed in D/L Inversion is a VP.

It is apparently also predicted, if our account of relative clause extraposition is justified, that there will be a D/L variant in which the extraposed relative follows the subject. The relevant example, however, is ungrammatical.

(19)   *Into the storeroom this morning ran an escaped convict that Mary was working in.

As shown in Chapter Two, the ungrammaticality of (19) is due to a violation of the CP. From this perspective, the ungrammaticality of (19) is related to that of (20), in which a subject extraposed relative has been topicalized along with the VP.

(20)   *Into the bank this morning that no one had talked to walked a man.

See Chapter Two for discussion.

2.4   Topicalized VPs and focus

We now wish to draw attention to further parallelisms between D/L and VP Topicalization constructions. Although we have not emphasized it, we have already witnessed parallels between these two constructions. We will now establish this point more generally.

As with D/L constructions, in VP Topicalization constructions, predicate phrases, adverbs, and multiple PPs and extraposed object relatives may topicalize with the rest of the VP. Below we present relevant examples of VP Topicalization constructions illustrating these points where they have not already appeared in our discussion.

(21)   a.   . . ., and walk gracefully down the stairs, she did.
             . . ., and walk down the stairs, she did gracefully.
        b.   . . ., and run into the room behind her, they did.
             . . ., and run into the room, they did behind her.
        c.   . . ., and run into the storeroom this morning that Mary was working in, an escaped convict did.

The reader is reminded that the second example in each pair of (21) must be read with prominence on both the auxiliary and the final constituent, as for instance . . ., *and run into the room they* DID BEHIND *her.*

The similarity of D/L and VP Preposing extends even beyond the parallels of constituenthood we have witnessed in the examples of (21) and throughout our earlier discussion. Our caution concerning the reading of VP Topicalization constructions holds also for D/L constructions. In 1:(16) and in (21), the auxiliary is necessarily focused and prominent, and everything following the auxiliary must be focused and prominent. If we replace the term "auxiliary" in the latter part of this statement regarding the distribution of prominence and interpretations as focus in VP Topicalization constructions with "verb," this statement holds equally of D/L constructions. Compare the examples of D/L Inversion in (22a,b), and (23) with the VP Topicalization examples in 1:(16), 1:(17b), and (21a), respectively.[19]

(22)   They said someone would walk into the room nude
     a. , and into the room nude walked JOHN.
     b.*, and into the room walked JOHN nude/NUDE.

(23)   They said someone would walk into the room with a surprise, and into the room walked JOHN NUDE.

What these examples show is that VP Topicalization and D/L constructions share restrictions on the distribution of focus and prominence. We will ultimately argue that these restrictions follow in virtue of specific structural similarities between the two constructions. For the present, we observe simply that such cases provide evidence that the parallels between D/L and VP Topicalization constructions extend beyond the constituenthood of the preposed phrase.

2.5   Purpose clauses

Purpose clauses are infinitival clauses of the sort given below.

(24)   a. The plumber came into the room to fix the sink.
     b. John went off to the store to buy the milk.

Evidence that purpose clauses are adjoined to VP includes the following.

(25)   a. John came into the room to fix the sink, and Mary did too.
     b. John went off to the store to buy a chocolate bar and Mary did too.
(26)   a. . . ., and come into the room to fix the sink he did.
     b. . . ., and go off to the store to buy the milk he did.

Of course, VP Ellipsis and VP Topicalization might also apply to the smaller VP to yield examples such as (27).

(27)   a. John came into the room to fix the sink and Mary did to clean up the mess.
     b. Into the room came the plumber to fix the sink.

Now note that in SI, a purpose clause can front with the directional PP, as below.

(28) a. Into the room to fix the sink came the plumber.
      b. Off to the store to buy the milk went John.

We conclude that sentences such as (28) support our claim that SI constructions are derived in part by topicalization of a VP constituent.

2.6   Pied piping

We present now one final argument in favor of the position that D/L involves fronting of VP. This argument concerns the ungrammaticality of the D/L sentence in (29).

(29) a. *Into which room walked John?
      b. *I asked into which room walked John.

In the analysis we are pursuing here, there is a natural account of the ungrammaticality of (29). In particular, if D/L involves fronting of a VP, and not a simple PP, constituent, then (29) is ungrammatical for the same reason as (30).

(30) a. *Walk into which room will John?
      b. *I asked walk into which room John will.

For whatever reason, VPs containing a *wh* phrase cannot appear in COMP to satisfy the requirement for a *wh* phrase in SPEC,CP position.[20] We return immediately below in section 3 to consider more explicitly the structural analysis we are proposing for topicalization of VP. For the present it suffices to note that we will argue that topicalization of VP is derived by adjunction to IP.

3   A structural analysis

Up to this point we have argued simply that the sentences of (1) are all derivationally related and derived from the same D-structure as (2).

(1) a. Into the room nude walked John.
     b. Into the room nude John walked.
     c. ... and walk into the room nude John did.
(2) John walked into the room nude.

In particular, we have determined that the derivation of (1a) is as in (3).

(3) $[_{VP} \ t_V$ into the room nude] $[_I$ walked] John $t_I \ t_{VP}$.

Let us now consider the structure given schematically in (3) in greater detail. As noted, we assume that t_V in (3) is the trace of V to I. We return to this feature of the derivation in the next section. We wish now to focus on the nature of the topicalization in (1a, b) and (3) and the positions of VP and the inverted V relative to the subject NP, which we have argued is in situ.

We adopt the Head Movement Constraint (HMC) of Travis (1984), Chomsky (1986b) and Baker (1985), which requires that a head may only move to the position of a head that properly governs it. It would be most natural to assume that the VP in (3) has moved to SPEC,CP and the verb to [C,CP], as in (4).[21]

(4)

On this view, the structure of (1a) would parallel that proposed by Chomsky (1986b) for *wh* constructions as in (5).[22]

(5) a. Who did John see?

     b.

Structures (4) and (5) are both in accord with the theoretical requirements of Subjacency and the ECP as outlined in Chaper One. Since Subjacency is trivially satisfied in these derivations, we restrict attention to the various applications of the ECP. In (5), t_j is lexically and antecedent governed by V, and t_I is antecedent governed by *did* in the amalgamated head of CP position. By our previous assumptions, since C and t_I are also coindexed, t_I is lexically governed by C. Given that the ECP is satisfied for t_I in (5), the HMC is also satisfied.

Consider now (4). Here, t_I and t_V are both lexically and antecedent governed by the amalgamated I/V in the head of CP position, so also satisfying the HMC. VP in SPEC,CP antecedent governs t_{VP}. But how does t_{VP} meet the requirement of lexical government? Note that while I can normally be a lexical governor for t_{VP} (cf. (6a)), t_I apparently may not be (compare (6b)).

(6)   a. ..., and walk into the room he will t_{VP}
       b. ..., *but walk into the room will he t_I t_{VP}?

The relevant feature of (4) that distinguishes it from (6b) is that t_I is coindexed with t_{VP} in (4) in virtue of the raising of V to I. In other words, VP has the index of V, and I acquires the same index once V is raised to I. Then like C, an empty I may serve as a lexical governor for a trace of VP only if it is coindexed with it.[23]

Despite its initial appeal, however, this analysis meets with three objections. First, this analysis requires that VP may appear in SPEC,CP position in English, but we argue against precisely this option for VP in section 2.6 of this chapter. Second, it is possible to embed SI constructions with the result that the preposed VP and the inverted verb appear to the right of the embedding complementizer, as in (7).

(7)   a. John was afraid that into the room next might walk his wife.
       b. Mary pointed out that under the awning could be seen an old piano.
       c. Bill insists that at the end of the table sat John.
       d. Sally failed to realize that into the room behind her had walked John.
       e. Mary was surprised to discover that sitting beside her would be Bill.

On the face of it, examples like (7) go directly counter to the predictions of (4) as an account of (3).[24] Note in addition that the simple cooccurrence of an overt complementizer and the inverted verb renders implausible the assumption that the V has moved to C, since it is a feature of I to C that inversion and overt complementizers are in complementary distribution (cf. Koopman [1983a]).

A further difficulty with the analysis arises when we consider that it is possible to have sentences that are parallel to D/L in all respects except they show no inversion of the verb, as with (1b)(=8b) and the examples below.

(8)   a. They said John would walk into the room that Mary was working in this morning, and into the room this morning that Mary was working in he walked.

        b. . . . and into the room nude he walked.

        c. . . . and into the room behind her they marched.

        d. . . . and slowly into the room he crawled.

If the structure of (1a) is as in (4), then the sentences of (8) must have the structure in (9).

(9)

In (9), t_{VP} is lexically governed by I/V under coindexing and antecedent governed by VP in CP. The problem with (9) is that t_V is neither lexically nor antecedent governed by V and so violates the ECP.[25]

One might attempt to resolve this difficulty with (9) by making appeal to a process of reconstruction of the VP to the position of t_{VP} prior to the application of the ECP in LF. There is, however, clear evidence that reconstruction does not feed the ECP. For if it did, one would expect the derivation of (10a) as characterized in (10b) to be good.[26]

(10)   a. *Pictures of, John wondered who Bill bought.

        b. [[pictures of t_i]$_j$ [John wondered who$_i$ Bill bought t_j]]

If the phrase *pictures of t* were to be reconstructed in the position of t_j in (10b), then the derivation of (a) would exactly parallel that of (11).

(11)   John wondered who Bill bought pictures of.

We conclude that the violation of the ECP evident in (10a, b) cannot be avoided through reconstruction. By the same token, it is not possible to circumvent the ECP violation in (9) by appeal to reconstruction. Reconstruction, then, apparently feeds only the binding theory. (See Barss [1986].)

We have now seen three reasons not to adopt the structural analysis in (4) for (1a)/(3). As an alternative to (4), we suggest that VP Topicalization is derived by adjunction to IP and that V, correspondingly, must also adjoin to IP. See (12).

(12)

```
                    IP
                  /    \
            VP          IP
          /   \       /    \
       t_v .... I/V        IP
                         /    \
                      NP        I'
                              /    \
                           t_I       t_VP
```

This analysis encounters an immediate difficulty, in the form of Subjacency. In particular, it would appear that VP is not subjacent to t_{VP}. Following Lasnik and Saito (1984), we have assumed that Subjacency is a condition on movement and not on representations. Structure (12), then, may be derived under this view by first topicalizing VP in accord with Subjacency to yield the structure in (13).

(13)

```
              IP_2
            /     \
        VP          IP_1
                  /     \
               NP         I'
                        /    \
                     I/V       t_VP
```

A further application of Move a in (13) adjoins I/V to IP_1, yielding structure (12). In this derivation, each of the applications of Move a satisfies Subjacency, seen solely as a condition on movement. Note that what is odd about the derivation just outlined is that the Strict Cycle Condition is apparently violated, since on the cycle defined on IP_2 in (13) an operation is performed completely within an apparently prior cycle defined on IP_1. We suggest therefore that the Strict Cycle Condition should be interpreted in accord with the following convention.

(14)   If Move a is cycling on γ, γ a maximal projection, then Move a may cycle on any segment of γ.

Given (14), the derivation of (12) just outlined is fully acceptable. Apart from the special case governed by (14), the Strict Cycle Condition maintains its traditional coverage.

Assuming then that (12) satisfies Subjacency, let us ask how the various applications of the ECP are realized. Note first that t_V is both lexically and antecedent governed by I/V under our definitions. Recall most importantly that since I/V is an X°, its government and binding domains extend to its highest maximal projection. I/V also lexically and antecedent governs t_I. Finally, consider t_{VP}. As we argued earlier, t_{VP} is lexically governed by the coindexed t_I. Since by the convention introduced in Chapter One a lexical governor of a trace that is coindexed with the trace may also serve as its antecedent governor, t_{VP} is antecedent governed by t_I. Thus, the ECP is fully satisfied for each of the empty categories in (12).

Furthermore, (12) overcomes the three difficulties with (4) that we noted above. First it is not required that VP appear in SPEC,CP position in English. Second, the cooccurrence and relative order of overt complementizer and topicalized VP/inverted V in embedded D/L is just as predicted under an adjunction to IP account as in (12). And third, there is no ECP violation in examples such as (8), since in the structure that corresponds to (9) on the adjunction to IP account (cf. (15)), there is no ECP violation for t_V.

(15)

In (15), t_V is both lexically and antecedent governed by I/V, under the definitions adopted in Chapter One.

However, although the structure (12) overcomes the difficulties noted with (9), there are a number of problems with (12) that must be addressed. First, (12) violates the HMC as formulated in Travis (1984) and Chomsky (1986b). As noted earlier, these formulations require that a head can only move to the position of a head that properly governs it. V_I in (12) has moved not to C, the properly governing head, but instead to a position adjoined to a maximal projection. Movement of heads by adjunction to X^{max} is specifically excluded in the framework of Chomsky (1986b), so as to block unbounded movement of V. Nevertheless, as Koopman (1983b) demonstrates, Vata and other languages do exhibit unbounded movement of V to A-bar positions in accord with established island constraints. Evidently, then, the HMC is too strong as formulated, as has already been observed by Koopman and Sportiche (1986).

In addition, as Chomsky (1986b) and Baker (1985, 1988) note, it is reasonable to assume that the HMC is not an independent principle, but follows instead from the ECP. In particular, the trace of the head is both lexically and antecedent governed within the minimal domain defined by the properly governing head. But then, adjunction of a head to the closest maximal projection is in fact to be anticipated under the HMC, since t_I is antecedent governed from the adjoined position occupied by V_I in (12). We conclude that (12) not only fails to encounter difficulty with the HMC, but in fact supports the attempt to derive its effects from the ECP.

A second problem with the adjunction to IP proposal is that it must be explained why the reverse order of I and VP in (12) is not possible, as in (16).

(16)   a.   *Walked into the room nude John.

b.

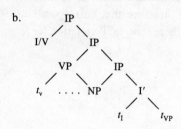

In fact, (16) is readily explained under our analysis. In particular, t_I, while lexically governed by its antecedent I/V, fails to be antecedent governed by I/V. The very lowest IP in (16b) is a barrier for t_I, and t_I fails to find an antecedent within the next higher maximal projection. On our account, the relative order of the topicalized VP and the inverted V is critical to the well-formedness of such examples in English. In fact, we claim that SI is possible in English only because in structure (12) the inverted verb can serve the dual function of antecedent government for both t_I and t_V, whereas it cannot in structure (16b).[27]

Finally, we can obtain support for (12) if we can show that adopting this structure for SI allows us to explain restrictions on the construction that are otherwise mysterious. We will show that SI exhibits two distinctive properties. First, it is strictly bounded, in that no unbounded movement of VP or V is possible, and second it is frozen with respect to extraction or movement of any constituent contained in it.

Let us look first at the boundedness of SI. We begin by observing that unbounded movement of the topicalized VP is not possible in D/L, as seen by the contrast below.[28]

(17) a. John didn't say that into the room had walked Bill.
          *Into the room John didn't say had walked Bill.
      b. Did John say that into the room would walk Bill?
          *Into the room did John say would walk Bill?

This is so despite the fact that unbounded movement of VP by topicalization is otherwise possible in constructions other than SI, as below (cf. Chomsky [1986b]).

(18)   Fix the car, I know (?that) he will.

The second examples of the pairs in (17) are in fact excluded on our account for the same reason that (9) is – the trace in the S-structure for (17b) that corresponds to t_V in (9) fails to meet the ECP since its antecedent is too far away, and reconstruction cannot apply to rectify the violation. In addition, it is not possible to overcome this difficulty with (17b) by moving the V unboundedly to a position where it would antecedent govern t_V, as in (19).

(19)   *Into the room had walked Mary didn't realize John.

Unbounded movement of V is excluded for several reasons. Most importantly, as Koopman and Sportiche (1986) demonstrate, movement of V displays the properties of movement of an adjunct, so that V may never be extracted from an island.[29] Further, V may not move unboundedly in English in any event, which is what distinguishes it from languages, such as Vata, which have predicate clefting constructions involving unbounded movement of V (cf. Koopman [1984], Koopman and Sportiche [1986]). Thus, (20) are also excluded.

(20)   a. *Had walked Mary didn't realize into the room John.
        b. *It was walked that Mary didn't realize that John (walked) into the room.

The boundedness restrictions on SI then follow in large part from the ECP and the failure of V to move unboundedly in English.

Let us now turn to the frozen character of SI. As observed in Rochemont (1978), the components that take part in SI are frozen with respect to any further grammatical operation. In particular, there can be no extraction of the subject (21a), formation of questions by SAI (21b), or extraction of any material contained in the preposed VP (21c,d,e).

(21)   a. *I wonder who into the room nude walked.
        b. *Did into the room nude walk John?
        c. *I wonder which room into nude walked John.
        d. *The room, into nude walked John.
        e. *I wonder how into the room walked John.

As we argued in Chapter One following Lasnik and Saito (forthcoming), structures of adjunction to IP create an island for further extraction of material dominated by the original node. Thus, in the structure below, nothing dominated by IP_1 may be extracted beyond IP_2.

(22) IP_2
      /   \
    α IP_1

Sentence (21a) is therefore excluded, since movement of the subject to SPEC,CP, the required landing position for *wh*-phrases, must be out of IP_1 in the analysis of SI that we have established. Furthermore, if we treat α in the adjoined position in (22) as an adjunct (as we argued in Chapter One), then it follows from the CED/Subjacency that there can be no extraction of material contained in α.[30] If so, then (21c,d) are also excluded, since the movement operations that have applied to derive these sentences have all extracted material from within α.[31] Finally, sentence (21b) is not derivable on our analysis since the tense features have been absorbed on our account by *walked* and so will not give rise to *do* support. (Further, extraction of a lexical modal/auxiliary verb from the verbal complex created by V to I must be restricted on independent grounds by the theory of restructuring.) We conclude that all aspects of the frozen character of SI follow from independent features of the grammar under the analysis we propose for these cases.

4   V-raising

In the previous sections we have argued that the sentences of (1) all involve an operation of VP Topicalization, and we have defended an analysis of this operation as adjunction to IP.

(1)   a. Walk into the room nude John did.
       b. Into the room nude John walked.
       c. Into the room nude walked John.

This result forces us to conclude that in (1b,c), the verb has escaped from the VP prior to the topicalization of VP, since the latter has evidently been topicalized without its verb. We have so far assumed, and will continue to assume, that the V escapes from VP by raising to I. However, it is worth pointing out that associated with this assumption are a number of difficulties that are perhaps serious enough to warrant considering alternative accounts of how V escapes from VP in the derivation of D/L. Let us briefly consider these difficulties, and some possible alternative accounts.

4.1   Problems with V movement in SI

There are two major problems that any account of how V escapes from VP in the derivation of SI must address. First, it is evidently the case that V raises to I in SI even when I is lexically filled, as below.

(2)   a. Into the room (will walk/has just walked) John.
       b. Across from him should sit Mary.
       c. Sitting in front of him will be Mary.

As Koopman (1983b) demonstrates, V to I is normally possible only when I is not lexically filled. But as the examples in (1) illustrate, this condition does not hold in SI, since in these cases the verbal sequence including the modal has inverted around the subject as a unit. Evidently, SI verbs can condition a restructuring of modal and other auxiliary verbs, perhaps on a par with the inversion of verb sequences in Spanish questions, as discussed in Torrego (1984). On the other hand, examples such as (1) provide a fairly solid indication that SI verbs must raise to I at some point in the derivation in order to condition the apparent restructuring of the auxiliary verbs in I in such cases.

A second problem for accounts of V movement in SI concerns the lexically highly restricted character of SI verbs. For instance, verbs that participate in SI must be intransitive. Thus, verbs that are optionally transitive can only function as intransitive when appearing in D/L constructions. Compare the examples below.

(3)   a. Mary walked into the park.
       b. Mary walked her dog into the park.
(4)   a. Into the park walked Mary.
       b. *Her dog into the park walked Mary.
(5)   a. John stood in front of the mirror.
       b. John stood the mirror in front of him.
(6)   a. In front of the mirror stood John.
       b. *The mirror in front of him stood John.

The obligatory intransitivity of SI verbs is in fact consistent with our V-raising analysis, given the proposal of Baker (1988) that traces may not assign Case.

There are additional restrictions on the preposed phrase in D/L even when it does not contain an object.[32] Consider the following.

(7)   a. *All night long lasted the party next door.
       b. *Into Bill ran John.
       c. *To his father talked Bill.
       d. *With his opponent briefly struggled Tom.

It is generally thought that verbs in D/L must cooccur with a directional or locative complement, which excludes the examples in (6).[33] It is natural to consider this coocurrence requirement to be tied to subcategorization or θ-marking, but this would require us to say that *stand*, for instance, subcategorizes/θ-marks a locative phrase and *arrive/appear/dug* do not, even though all four optionally cooccur with locative complements.[34]

(8)   a. John stood motionless (in the corner).
       b. Her mother finally arrived (at the train station).
       c. Mary suddenly appeared (in the doorway).
       d. John dug shirtless (in the garden).
(9)   a. Motionless in the corner stood John.
       b. *At the train station finally arrived her mother.
       c. *In the garden happily played Mary.
       d. *Shirtless in the garden dug John.

In addition, as Emonds (1976) observes, the locative/directional interpretation may be figurative rather than literal, as in the examples in (10).

(10)   a. To John fell the worst task.
       b. On that premise is built the entire argument.

Further restrictions include the requirement of a presentational interpretation on the verb, as noted in Rochemont (1978), and the cooccurrence of auxiliary verbs in specific cases. To illustrate the first point, (11b) does not allow the interpretation in (12), while (11a) does.[35]

(11)   a. His mother stood beside him.
       b. Beside him stood his mother.
(12)   Beside him, his mother stood up.

The second point is illustrated in the examples below.

(13)   a. Into the room came John.
       b. *Into the room was coming John.
(14)   a. At the head of the table sat the father.
       b. ?At the head of the table will sit the father.
       c. *At the head of the table will be sitting the father.
       d. ?At the head of the table should certainly sit the father.

As we observed in section 1.4, PAB is also lexically restricted, and it too gives evidence of restructuring of modals (cf. (2c)). But since the main verb preposes within VP in the derivation of PAB, it exhibits none of the other restrictions on D/L regarding cooccurrence of complements, auxiliary selection, or verbs of appearance.

(15) a. Walking her dog into the park was Mary.
      b. Standing the mirror in front of him was John.
      c. Talking to his father was Bill.
      d. Arriving at the train station is her mother.
      e. Digging in the garden shirtless was John.
      f. Standing up next to him is Mary.

4.2 A restructuring account

We have just witnessed two problems with our assumption that V escapes from VP in SI by V to I, on a par with V to I in other languages: this account fails to accommodate cases of SI involving restructuring of modal and other verbs, and also fails to accommodate the restrictions on SI verbs. We might seek to relate these two difficulties in the following way. It is widely acknowledged that restructuring is a lexically conditioned process. Since SI verbs evidently condition the restructuring of modals in I (cf. (2)), it is reasonable to suppose that the lexical restrictiveness of this class of verbs is tied to their restructuring function. In this section, we will briefly elaborate an account along these lines, and consider some of the problems it raises.

We begin with the observation that there is plausibly another lexically restricted process of V to I in English, that of the aspectual verbs *have* and *be*, as has been proposed in various forms in a number of places.[36] Let us refer to this process as V_{AUX} to I. We might seek to address the lexical restrictiveness of verbs in SI by assimilating this class to the class of V_{AUX}. However, to simply assume that SI verbs are lexically marked with the appropriate feature (say, [+AUX]) would be *ad hoc*. Further, such an account would not address the first difficulty we noted in section 4.1, involving the restructuring of modals in I, since V_{AUX} does not condition restructuring in V_{AUX} to I. Thus, compare the examples below with those in (2).

(16) a. *Will have John left?
      b. *Has left John?

Nevertheless, it may still be possible to characterize the SI verbs as V_{AUX} without lexically stipulating them to be such, by appealing to their role in the restructuring of auxiliary verbs, as noted earlier.

Let us suppose that SI verbs are lexically marked to optionally condition the restructuring of V_{AUX}. For instance, consider the derivation this assumption leads to for (17).

(17) a. In front of her was sitting her mother.

b. [$_{VP}$ *t* in front of her] [$_I$ was sitting] [$_{NP}$ her mother].

The restructuring account suggests that in (17), *sitting* has restructured the aspectual verb *was* to its left within VP, thereby acquiring the relevant feature that enables the restructured unit *was sitting* to raise to I under V_{AUX} to I. The lexical restrictiveness of SI is thus viewed as a function of the lexically governed process of restructuring of V_{AUX}. On this view, the derivation of a sentence such as (1c), *Into the room nude walked John*, would presumably involve the restructuring of an empty V_{AUX} in VP, to allow raising of what appears to be a simple verb.[37]

One potential problem we observe is that restructuring and V_{AUX} to I seem not to occur without topicalization of the remainder of VP in SI, as evidenced by the ungrammaticality of (18).[38]

(18)   a. *Was sitting her mother in front of her.(?)
       b. *Walked John into the room nude.(?)

A restructuring account might seek to exclude (18) by making appeal to directionality in the restructuring process. In particular, it appears that when the SI verb restructures V_{AUX} to its left and undergoes V_{AUX} to I, the trace it leaves behind in VP can only appear to its left in S-structure (by topicalization of the VP). This leads us to propose the following condition on restructuring.[39]

(19)   Given α, a lexical head conditioning restructuring, and β, the material α is restructuring, if α governs β to its left, then the restructured unit [$\alpha\beta$] governs only to the left, and if α governs β to its right, then [$\alpha\beta$] governs only to the right.

It follows from (19) that when a SI verb undergoes V_{AUX} to I, by restructuring of an (empty) aspectual verb within VP, it can only govern to its left thereafter. Since t_V must satisfy the ECP, as we have already seen in section 3, by (19) it must appear to the left of the restructured unit in I containing the SI verb, its lexical governor. In this way, we characterize the obligatoriness of VP Topicalization in SI related constructions.

Notice that (19) in fact forces V_{AUX} to I whenever a SI verb restructures V_{AUX}. Since the restructured unit no longer governs to the right, the complements to the SI verb will be ungoverned in S-structure in violation of the Projection Principle. We assume that direction of government by t_V is not restricted by (19), so it is only after V_{AUX} to I that the Projection Principle is satisfied.

There is some slight independent evidence in favor of (19), involving the behavior of adverbs in SI. Adverbs in simple declarative sentences may either precede or follow the verb, as in (20).

(20) a. The Queen walked slowly down the stairs into the ballroom.
b. The Queen slowly walked down the stairs into the ballroom.

And as we saw in section 3, sentences such as (20a) can give rise to VP Topicalization or D/L constructions such as (21). (As Rochemont (1978, 1986) argues, the subject of sentence (21c) cannot be a pronoun, except in a deictic reading, because of requirements it must meet as an obligatory focus in the D/L construction.)

(21) a. Walk slowly down the stairs into the ballroom she did.
b. Slowly down the stairs into the ballroom she walked.
c. Slowly down the stairs into the ballroom walked the Queen.

Notice, however, that there is an equally grammatical variant for each of sentences (21b,c) in which the adverb appears to have restructured with the verb.[40]

(22) a. Down the stairs into the ballroom the Queen slowly walked.
b. Down the stairs into the ballroom slowly walked the Queen.

The derivation of sentence (22b) is possible if we assume that the adverb may restructure with the raised verb. Interestingly enough, however, the very similar sentences in (23) are ungrammatical.[41]

(23) a. *Down the stairs into the ballroom, the Queen walked slowly.
b. *Down the stairs into the ballroom walked slowly the Queen.

The ungrammaticality of the sentences in (23) is explained under the assumption that the derivation of these sentences involves a restructuring process, and furthermore that this process is subject to condition (19). In particular, if the V must govern all the material it restructures in the derivation of such sentences in a single direction, then the adverb must appear to the same side of the verb as the empty auxiliary, as in (22), and not to its right, as in (23).[42]

There are, however, a number of difficulties with a restructuring account that makes appeal to a condition such as (19). First, while (19) receives some support from the behavior of adverbs, this evidence does not seem sufficiently strong to independently warrant its adoption. Moreover, while (19) is fully consistent with virtually all of the cases for which restructuring has been proposed, it finds no independent support in any of these uses.

(E.g. Akmajian, Steele, and Wasow [1979], Rizzi [1982], Zubizarreta [1985], Manzini [1983], Haegeman and van Riemsdijk [1986].) In short, (19) is relatively *ad hoc*.

A second difficulty with the restructuring analysis is the account it seems to force for examples such as (1c).

(1c)   Into the room nude walked John.

As we have already noted, in order for *walked* in (1c) to undergo V_{AUX} to I, it must presumably restructure an empty V_{AUX} in VP. The assumption of empty aspectual verbs, while certainly consistent with other features of our view of the grammar, is nevertheless surprising, being motivated solely for the purpose of generating examples such as (1b, c).

Finally, while the restructuring analysis provides us with a means for characterizing the lexical restrictiveness evidenced in SI, it suggests no explanation for the specific properties of the class of SI verbs, in particular regarding the restrictions on complement types discussed in 4.1. This feature of SI is one for which we have been able to provide only a stipulative account.[43]

These problems might lead us to abandon the restructuring account of V movement in SI. Nevertheless, any account of this raising must address the difficulties faced by the restructuring analysis. For instance, if we were to assume that all main verbs can undergo V to I freely, we could have no account of the lexical restrictions on SI. On the other hand, we might seek to revise our account by dropping the assumption that V escapes from VP in SI by raising to I. It presumably could not escape by adjoining to I, under a restrictive theory of adjunction (see e.g. Chomsky [1986b]). Furthermore, this would derive the wrong order of main and auxiliary verbs in SI examples such as (2).

The only remaining possibility is that V escapes from VP by adjoining to VP. This proposal encounters three difficulties. First, it does not suggest any way to solve the problem raised by (2). In fact, on this account the main and auxiliary verbs do not form a constituent. Second, an adjunction analysis would provide no account of the lack of inversion in SI without VP Topicalization (cf. [18]). And finally, such an analysis would still fail to characterize the lexical restrictiveness of SI.

In short, while there is little in the way of independent motivation for a restructuring account, the other accounts mentioned are not even possibly consistent with the desired coverage of data without considerably more stipulation than is required under the restructuring account. We suspect that the problems that remain can only be resolved through a more comprehensive study of V movement, in particular as exhibited in Spanish. For purposes of the present study we will assume the restructuring account, but it is important to recognize that the question of how V escapes from VP in SI is independent of our analysis of SI as involving topicalization of VP.

5   PP extraction from complex sentences

We turn now to an apparent difficulty for our analysis that arises on consideration of sentences such as (1), whose theoretical relevance was first noted by Bresnan (1977).

(1)   In which villages did Mary say could be found the best coffee in the world?

As Bresnan observes, extraction of PP in such cases shows the effect of her Complementizer Constraint on Variables, or the *that-t* filter of Chomsky and Lasnik (1977).

(2)   *In which villages did Mary say that could be found the best coffee in the world?

The contrast between (1) and (2) poses a difficulty for our analysis, if we assume, with Stowell (1981), that the ungrammaticality of (2) is due to the ECP. In particular, if we hope to relate the ungrammaticality of (2) to that of (3), we must claim that the presence of the complementizer in (2) blocks proper government of the trace of PP that is presumably in the position of the PP in (4).

(3)   *Who did John say that left?
(4)   Mary said that in those villages could be found the best coffee in the world.

We will proceed by first reviewing Stowell's account of such cases. We will then explain why Stowell's account cannot be adapted directly on our analysis of D/L to relate the oddity of (2) to that in (3). Finally, we consider some hitherto unnoticed data that suggest that sentences such as (1) and (2) are not instances of D/L.

5.1   Stowell's (1981) analysis

As we have already stated in section 1, Stowell provides an analysis of D/L which treats the postverbal subject in such cases as equivalent to the postverbal subject of a Presentational *there* construction such as (5).

(5)   There appeared before him a tall woman with blonde hair.

With this assumption, Stowell's analysis seeks to address two major questions:

(i)   Why is insertion of *there* mandatory in constructions such as (5), but not in D/L constructions?

(ii)   Why does extraction of the preposed PP in a D/L construction yield *that-t* violations, as in (2)?

Stowell's response to both questions is essentially the same: the preposed PP in D/L properly governs the empty category in the subject position vacated by the postposed subject, thus voiding the ECP violation that would normally result in insertion of *there*, as it does in (5). Since it is the preposed PP in COMP that properly governs the empty subject, the presence of a complementizer after extraction should block proper government from COMP in D/L in (2) in just the same fashion that it blocks proper government from COMP in (3). In order to allow the topicalized PP in (4) to properly govern the empty subject position, Stowell proposes that the PP moves through the vacated subject position on its way to COMP, thereby being coindexed with it. To summarize, on Stowell's analysis, the derived structure for D/L constructions is as in (6).

(6)

$$
\begin{array}{c}
S^1 \\
\diagup \quad \diagdown \\
\text{COMP} \qquad S \\
\mid \qquad \diagup \diagdown \\
\text{PP}_i \quad \text{NP}_i^j \qquad \text{VP} \\
\mid \qquad \diagup \diagdown \\
e_i \quad \text{VP} \qquad \text{NP}^j \\
\diagup \diagdown \\
\dots e_i \dots
\end{array}
$$

Since the empty category in subject position in (6) is properly governed by PP_i, extraction of PP_i will require the absence of *that* so that this empty category will remain properly governed by the trace of PP_i in COMP.

Following Chomsky (1981), Stowell also assumes that the postverbal subject is cosuperscripted with the empty category in subject position, from which it inherits Case. The postverbal subject is assigned its θ-role directly as sister to VP at S-structure. Stowell attributes the exceptional property of D/L constructions to the fact that the topicalized PP is associated with two A-positions at S-structure, the subject position and its original position within VP, and to the assumption that a PP in COMP must be reconstructed in a non-Case-marked A-position in LF.

We have already argued in section 2 that an account of D/L that treats the preverbal phrase as a topicalized PP and the postverbal subject as adjoined to VP faces serious difficulties when a fuller range of facts from D/L constructions are considered. For this reason, we reject Stowell's analysis of D/L constructions presented above. However, while our own analysis is designed to address precisely the difficulties encountered by an analysis of D/L like (6), it must be asked whether on our analysis there is any account of the contrast between (1) and (2), which Stowell's analysis adequately accommodates. Recall that on our account, D/L constructions are derived by topicalization of VP after restructuring and raising of the main verb. In order to derive a sentence such as (1), we might say that the PP has been extracted from the topicalized VP to COMP, and then undergoes further extraction to the matrix COMP, as outlined in (7).

(7)

However, if we accept this analysis of sentence (1), we can provide no account of the ungrammaticality of (2), since the trace of PP in VP should be properly governed by e_i independently of the presence of an overt complementizer in COMP. Moreover, there is generally no stranding of material in VP in configurations like (7), except for the empty verb under this analysis. Thus, consider the contrast between the sentences of (8).[44]

(8) a. In these villages rotting may be found the carcasses of dozens of farm animals.
     *In which villages did Mary say rotting may be found the carcasses of dozens of farm animals?
     b. On the wall ripped to shreds could be seen a large portrait of the order's founder.
     *On which wall did Mary say ripped to shreds could be seen a large portrait of the order's founder?

Given the contrast in the examples of (8), it seems incorrect to claim that the trace of V can be stranded in the topicalized VP in (7) by extraction of the PP to COMP. In fact, what seems to emerge from (8) is that there can be no stranding of material in A-bar position at all, so that in (7) either the entire VP moves to COMP, or nothing does. Since we assume that VP cannot move to COMP in structures such as (7), we predict that D/L constructions must be strictly bounded.[45] Indeed, this conclusion is reinforced by the observation that the sentences in (9) are ungrammatical.

(9)   a. *In those villages rotting Mary said might be found the carcasses of dozens of animals.
       b. *On the wall ripped to shreds Mary said could be seen a large portrait of the order's founder.

What then is the source of a sentence as (1) on this view?

5.2   A derivational ambiguity

Consider again the structure given in (6). Let us suppose with Stowell (1981) that Presentational *there* constructions such as (5) give rise to a representation in which the postverbal subject is adjoined to VP.[46] Suppose we further assume that a VP internal PP may topicalize in a Presentational *there* construction, as seems to be the case in (10).[47]

(10)   a. In front of her there sat knitting a woman she didn't know.
       b. Into her office there ran screaming a group of frantic young girls.

Observe that the presence of *there* in such sentences as (10) is apparently optional, as seen in (11).

(11)   a. In front of her sat knitting a woman she didn't know.
       b. Into her office ran screaming a group of frantic young girls.

The sentences of (11) cannot be derived as D/L constructions in the manner we have outlined in the preceding sections of this chapter. And while the verbs in (11) normally allow restructuring for D/L, these sentences could not have been derived through restructuring, since the relative order of subject and predicate phrase differs from that observed in true D/L sentences, as exemplified in section 1 for instance. Thus, compare (11a,b) with (12a,b), respectively.

(12)   a. *In front of her sat knitting Mary.
       b. *Into her office ran screaming Bill.

The grammatical counterparts of (12a,b) are (13) and (14), respectively.

(13)   a. In front of her knitting sat Mary.
       b. In front of her sat Mary knitting.
(14)   a. Into her office screaming ran Bill.
       b. Into her office ran Bill screaming.

Similar alternatives are possible also for (11a,b).

(15) a. In front of her knitting sat a woman she didn't know.
     b. In front of her sat a woman she didn't know knitting.
(16) a. Into her office screaming ran a group of frantic young girls.
     b. Into her office ran a group of frantic young girls screaming.

As we will see in detail in Chapter Five, there is a requirement in Presentational *there* constructions for the postverbal subject to be heavy. Since heaviness of the postverbal subject is all that distinguishes the sentences of (11) from those in (12), it seems reasonable to conclude that the sentences of (11) are derived by Presentational *there* Insertion. This conclusion is consistent with the observed order of predicate phrase and postverbal subject in these sentences, and relates the ungrammaticality of the sentences in (12) to that of the corresponding sentences in (17).

(17) a. *In front of her there sat knitting Mary.
     b. *Into her office there ran screaming Bill.

But if the sentences of (11) are derived in the same manner as those in (10), and not as D/L constructions as in (15) and (16), then it must be the case that the preposed PP in (11) serves to properly govern the empty subject position that arises by the application of Heavy NP Shift to the lexical subject, perhaps in the manner suggested by Stowell (1981) and represented schematically in (6).

It follows on this line of reasoning that sentences such as (18), in which the postverbal subject is heavy and the D-structure VP contains only a single complement to V, must be derivationally ambiguous.

(18)   Into the room walked a man no one recognized.

In other words, (18) may be derived either as a D/L construction, with restructuring, V-raising, and topicalization of VP, or as a Presentational *there* construction, with the presence of *there* made optional by the preposing of PP to COMP. We will assume that in this second derivation the PP properly governs an empty subject position in the manner Stowell (1981) suggests.

We will argue in Chapter Four that the postposed subject in a Presentational *there* Insertion construction (PTI) is adjoined at S-structure to IP. From this it follows, as we will show, that PTI is frozen with respect to all extraction to SPEC,CP. This would appear to create a problem for our analysis of sentence (1), which we are claiming is an instance of PTI but in which the embedded clause is evidently not an island to extraction. Note, however, that the basis for our claim that the shifted subject in PTI is adjoined to IP is that it is only in this configuration that the trace of the subject is antecedent governed for the ECP. Adapting Stowell's analysis of such cases as (1) obviates the need for the shifted subject to adjoin to IP, since the ECP is satisfied for the subject trace by the preposed PP. As we note in Chapter Four, the constituent structure evidence we consider is consistent with either an IP or a VP adjoined configuration for the shifted NP.

Let us return now to sentences (1) and (2), repeated below.

(1)   In which villages did Mary say could be found the best coffee in the world?
(2)   *In which villages did Mary say that could be found the best coffee in the world?

It might be thought that sentence (1), like (18), is derivationally ambiguous. Recall, however, our conclusion earlier in this section that true D/L sentences are strictly bounded, since there may be no stranding of elements in A-bar position (cf. (8b)). It follows that a sentence such as (1), then, is not derivationally ambiguous, but may only be derived by postposing of the subject, with the preposed PP (or more specifically its trace) properly governing the empty category in subject position, roughly as in (6). In other words, it is only on this derivation that unbounded extraction of the PP is possible, with the corresponding result that if the complementizer position is filled, the ECP will be violated for the empty subject position, as in (2).

If this account of (2) is correct, we predict that extraction of PP in examples such as (1) should correlate with two factors: (i) the position of predicate phrases in the embedded sentence, and (ii) the heaviness of the postverbal subject.[48] And indeed, these predictions appear to be confirmed.

(19) a. In front of whom did Mary say sat knitting a woman she didn't know?
      b. *In front of whom did Mary say sat a woman she didn't know knitting?
(20) a. Through which doorway did John refuse to say would walk nude the country's top military advisors?
      b. *Through which doorway did John refuse to say would walk the country's top military advisors nude?

The (b) examples of (19) and (20) violate Subjacency under the formulation adopted in Chapter One and as argued more carefully in section 3 of Chapter Four. The important point at present is that the contrast between the (a) and (b) examples of (19) and (20) shows that the predicate phrase must precede, not follow, the postverbal subject, when the PP has been extracted. In this respect, the sentences of (19)/(20) contrast with our earlier examples (15a, b). Prediction (ii) is confirmed by the contrast in grammaticality of the sentences in (21)–(23).

(21) a. *Into whose office did Mary say ran Bill?

   b. Into whose office did Mary say ran that group of frantic young girls?
(22) a. *Behind which desk does John think sits Mary?
   b. Behind which desk does John think sits the president of the company?
(23) a. *Through which window did Bill say could be seen his father?
   b. Through which window did Bill say could be seen a picture of the Queen?

The judgments relating to heaviness of the postverbal subject are admittedly not as firm as those relating to the position of predicate phases, though we think this is because in the former case the judgment is a relative and not an absolute one. As Bresnan (1976) and Rochemont (1978) observe, even proper names are marginally acceptable in cases of Heavy NP Shift, if the name is preceded by a sufficiently heavy pause and accompanied by a correspondingly strong accent. With this proviso, the ungrammatical examples of (21)–(23) may be improved, but only, we claim, by forcing a derivation of the type exactly parallel to the fully grammatical (a) examples. Granted this observation, examples (21)–(23) illustrate a correlation between unbounded extraction of the PP and heaviness of the postverbal subject in cases that otherwise closely resemble true D/L constructions. This is precisely what we expect if apparent D/L sentences are in fact derivationally ambiguous, and long extraction of PP is excluded in true D/L constructions.

We consider one final argument for this proposal. As we have already observed, for some reason it is not possible to negate the verb in D/L, as below.

(24)   *Into the room didn't walk John.

Negation of the verb is possible, however, in PTI. Compare (25).

(25)   There didn't walk into the room any of the most interesting people she had met at the party.

Since we claim that sentences such as (26) are derivationally ambiguous, we expect to find that the restriction against negation in an apparent instance of D/L is relaxed just in case the postverbal subject is sufficiently heavy. This prediction is confirmed in (27). (Compare (24).)

(26)   Into the room walked everyone she had met at the party.
(27)   Into the room didn't walk any of the most interesting people that she had met at the party.

We conclude that sentence (1) is not an instance of a true D/L sentence, and that the contrast in grammaticality between (1) and (2) provides only apparent difficulty for our analysis.

6   Alternative analyses

In the last section, we argued against Stowell's (1981) analysis of D/L. First, this analysis fails to account for much of the data that we have presented in prior sections of this chapter in connection with D/L. Second, this analysis fails to distinguish the derivational ambiguity underlying a sentence such as (1), and in so doing, also fails to characterize the correlations of heaviness and positioning of the postverbal subject and the nature of the extracted phrase on the one hand, and cases of unbounded extraction of the PP on the other, as for example in (2).

(1)   Into the room walked an old man with a cane.
(2)   Into which room (*nude) did Mary expect would walk (an old man with a cane/*John).

Our own account, motivated on the basis of the data in sections (1)–(4), can accommodate the derivational ambiguity of a sentence such as (1), in part through appeal to Stowell's (1981) analysis of what are only apparently instances of D/L sentences.

In this section, we will critically review two other proposals for the derivation of D/L and PAB sentences. The first of these, that of Emonds (1976), bears some similarity to our own proposal at least for a subset of the cases that we analyze. The second, that of Safir (1985), more superficially parallels the proposal of Stowell (1981), as we noted in section 1.

6.1   Emonds (1976)

Emonds (1976) argues that Directional Inversion constructions receive a derivation distinct from that of both Locative Inversion and PAB constructions. He proposes that the latter have a structure-preserving analysis whereby the subject postposes to a VP internal NP position, while the former are derived by preposing of PP with subsequent Subject Simple Verb Inversion (SSVI), a root transformation. Clearly this last derivation closely resembles our own account of Stylistic Inversion in English, though with important differences, to which we turn directly.

Emonds' reason for distinguishing these cases is part of the motivation for SSVI, namely that the Directional Inversion construction appears to exhibit an absolute restriction against auxiliary verbs that is not shared by the Locative Inversion or PAB constructions. He considers examples like the following in support of this claim.

(3) a. *In has come/was coming John.
    b. In each hallway has long stood a large poster of Lincoln.
    c. Waiting behind the door might be an unwelcome visitor.
    d. In front of the statue should be an ornate fountain.
    e. Just as shocking to witness would have been the manner of his death.

While we agree that (a) is certainly worse than (3b–e), we claim, following Rochemont (1978), that the auxiliary restriction on Directional Inversion is not absolute, as would be required by a rule of SSVI. This point is established by the examples in (4). (Examples (4) and (5b) are drawn from Rochemont [1978: 53, 27, 29, respectively].)

(4) a. Toward us was heading an ominous cloud with what looked like a tornado funnel leading down from it.
    b. When she finally got up to see what all the commotion was about, she discovered that into her house had walked a man she hadn't seen in years.

Moreover, the restriction on auxiliaries in some cases of Directional Inversion is shared also by Locative Inversion, but not by PAB. Consider in this connection the contrast between the respective examples in (5) and (6).

(5) a. *Into the room was coming John.
    b. *In the dining commons is being eaten the worst food on campus.
    c. *Among the guests would have been sitting an undercover agent.
(6) a. Coming in to the room was John.
    b. Being eaten in the dining commons is the worst food on campus.
    c. Sitting among the guests would have been an undercover agent.

We do not propose to explain the auxiliary restrictions on D/L. Nevertheless, such cases as (5)–(6) confirm our initial assumption that it is mistaken to treat Directional Inversion in a manner distinct from Location Inversion constructions. Rather, we hold that the differences between these two on the one hand and PAB on the other should be attributed to some property of auxiliary *be*, as distinct from main and other auxiliary verbs, that licenses the relatively greater freedom of derivation in PAB.[49] We emphasize that we have not, to our mind, provided any satisfactory account of this difference between *be* and other verbs, beyond the stipulations introduced in section 4.2. Nonetheless, we think it important to maintain a proper grouping of these constructions, even if they are all ultimately derived in essentially the same fashion, as we have claimed.

In addition to the criticism we have just raised against Emonds' (1976) account, it will be noted that Emonds, like Stowell, does not consider the range of data that has motivated our own analysis, in particular, the data we have used to support our claim that Stylistic Inversion is derived by VP, rather than PP, topicalization, and preposing of V_I around the subject, rather than postposing of the subject to a postverbal position.

6.2   Safir (1985)

We turn now to the analysis that Safir (1985) proposes for D/L and PAB constructions. Safir's interest in these constructions is motivated by his desire to predict the distribution of the Definiteness Effect (DE) in terms of syntactic properties of the structural configurations in which this effect is in evidence. In particular, as we have outlined in some detail in Chapter One, Safir seeks to associate the DE with constructions which require the formation of an unbalanced chain. This proposal forces Safir to claim that the Presentational *there* construction exhibits a Definiteness Effect, a claim which we have already shown to be factually incorrect. See Chapter One: 4.

Since Safir, like Stowell (1981), assumes without argument that D/L involves the postposing of the subject, these constructions raise a difficulty for his account of the DE. In particular, D/L does not exhibit the DE, and thus, under Safir's proposals, must not involve the formation of an unbalanced chain. Since Safir also assumes that Presentational *there* constructions do involve the formation of an unbalanced chain, he is forced to reject Stowell's (1981) analysis of D/L as structurally related to Presentational *there* constructions. As a result, Safir is obliged to provide an alternative account of D/L consistent with his proposal for predicting the distribution of the DE and with his Unity of Indexing Hypothesis. It is then not surprising that the analysis of D/L that Safir proposes treats the postverbal subject as adjoined to S (IP), as in (7).

(7)

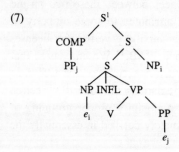

Since no unbalanced chain arises from (7), Safir correctly predicts the lack of DE in D/L.

However, the analysis in (7) faces a major difficulty, as Safir observes.

In particular, the empty category in subject position in (7) must not be properly governed in that configuration, at least not simply as a function of the coindexed NP in A'-position, for if it were, it would be falsely predicted that *Walked John* would be a grammatical English sentence.[50] In other words, the possibility for D/L to have a missing subject, in Safir's terms, must be made parasitic on the preposed PP in COMP. In fact, Safir assumes a version of the ECP that allows antecedent government only from COMP, so that e_i is not antecedent governed in (7). But Safir, unlike Stowell, may not assume that the PP passes through the subject position, given the Unity of Indexing Hypothesis. He is then forced to provide an alternative account of the relation between the preposed PP and the empty category in subject position.

To overcome this difficulty, Safir adopts Kayne's (1980) analysis of *wh* triggered Stylistic Inversion in French, exemplified in (8a), for which Kayne provides the representation (8b).

(8)   a. Quand a téléphoné Jean?

   b.
```
                    S¹
                  /    \
            COMP        S
              |       / |  \
          quandⱼ   NP INFL VP  eⱼ
                    |     /  \
                   eᵢ   VP   Jeanᵢ
                       /\
                   a téléphoné
```

Since the empty subject in (8b) is in violation of the ECP at S-structure, Kayne proposes to raise the postverbal subject to COMP in LF, where it undergoes absorption with the *wh* phrase in COMP, presumably in the manner suggested by Higginbotham and May (1981). Thus, at LF the empty category in subject position is properly governed by the NP that has been absorbed in COMP. Kayne further assumes that absorption in COMP must meet the uniform interpretation requirement (cf. Chomsky [1973]). This requirement is apparently not satisfied in simple non-*wh* questions or by *si* or *pourquoi*, hence the ungrammaticality of such sentences as (9).

(9)   a. *A téléphoné Jean?
      b. *Je ne sais pas si a téléphoné Jean.
      c. ??Pourquoi a téléphoné Jean?

Moreover, Kayne's account capitalizes on the parallel between Stylistic Inversion and multiple *wh* questions in French, which also involve absorption in COMP subject to a uniform interpretation requirement. Thus, (8a) and (9) are paralleled by the examples in (10).

(10)   a. Quand a-t-il tué qui?
      b. *A-t-il tué qui?
      c. *Je ne sais pas si il a tué qui.
      d. ??Pourquoi a-t-il tué qui?

For the interpretation in COMP in French Stylistic Inversion that satisfies the uniform interpretation requirement, Safir proposes the name "wh + focus." He further modifies Kayne's analysis, consistent with his own proposals, to provide (8a) with the S-structure (11) rather than (8b).

(11)

$$
\begin{array}{c}
S^1 \\
\diagup\ \diagdown \\
\text{COMP} \qquad S \\
| \qquad \diagup\ \diagdown \\
\text{quand}_j \qquad S \qquad \text{Jean}_i \\
\diagup\ | \diagdown \\
e_i\ \text{INFL VP}\ e_j \\
\text{a téléphoné}
\end{array}
$$

S-structure (11) then gives input at LF to raising of the postverbal subject to COMP and absorption in COMP, thus satisfying the ECP for the empty category in subject position.

Recall now that the difficulty Safir faces in proposing the structure (7) for D/L is that he must explain how the postposing of the subject in such cases is parasitic on the preposed PP. This problem is now easily remedied, he claims, if we assume that the English D/L construction as represented in (7) undergoes an LF derivation exactly parallel to the French Stylistic Inversion construction as represented in (11). In particular, the postposed subject raises to COMP in LF and undergoes absorption with the PP, thereby properly governing the empty category in subject position. Safir terms this interpretation of absorption in COMP "D/L + focus." He claims additional motivation for his analysis to stem from the observation that D/L constructions also occur in French, and he offers the following examples, taken from Atkinson (1973).

(12)   a. Dans le ciel flottait un nuage.
        "In the sky floated a cloud."
      b. Sur son front perlait en petits gouttes la sueur des voyous.

"On his forehead beaded in little drops the sweat of rascals."
c. De là partaient deux routes.
"From there left two roads."
d. De touts les côtés fumait un parfum de terre écrasée.
"From every side reeked the fragrance of crushed earth."
e. Devant lui, autour d'une allée, debout, le regardaient deux figures féminines.
"Before him around an alley, standing, regarded him two female faces."

Finally, Safir tentatively suggests extending this account to PAB, with the absorbed interpretation "X + focus."

There are a number of very serious difficulties with the analysis just outlined. To begin, it offers no account (as Safir acknowledges), of *that-t* violations in unbounded extraction of PP in examples such as (1) of section 5. In particular, since proper government of the vacated subject position is accomplished by absorption of the postposed subject in COMP at LF, extraction of the PP should be irrelevant to proper government of the subject position, just as it is in French *wh* triggered Stylistic Inversion (cf. Kayne and Pollock [1978]).

(13)   Quand penses-tu qu'est parti Jean?

In addition, the data we have presented in previous sections of this chapter motivating an analysis of D/L in terms of VP Topicalization and inversion of V_I cannot be accommodated under any conceivable version of the analysis Safir proposes.

Beyond this, the various interpretations which Safir suggests for the process of absorption in COMP are consistently of the form "α + focus." Clearly, some uniform interpretation is implied by this terminology, but we hold that the implied claim is without real empirical content. Instead, Safir is relying on an undefined and indefensible use of the term "focus" to imply that there is some consistency in the various uses of the uniform interpretation in COMP requirement on absorption to which his analysis appeals. Thus, it is simply not true, for instance, that in French *wh* triggered Stylistic Inversion constructions such as (8a) the subject is necessarily a focus. Thus, the question/answer sequence below is a well-formed one.

(14)   A: Jean a téléphoné.
        B: Quand a téléphoné Jean?

In addition, there is an implication in the specific interpretations that Safir provides that not only is the postverbal subject focused in D/L and PAB, but that the preposed phrase is also focused.[51] Again, while the preposed phrase may be focused, it need not be, in clear contrast to the postverbal subject in such cases. (See Rochemont [1986].)

Finally, Safir's claim that French exhibits instances of D/L on a par with English is very misleading, and probably false. Consider again the examples he gives, repeated in (12) above. Of these, only (a) and (c) are even marginally grammatical in English, suggesting at the very least that "directional/locative" or the class of verbs that participate in D/L, has a much broader specification in French than in English. Furthermore, Safir fails to mention the many examples in Atkinson (1973) which contradict his analysis and are not dependent on a preposed directional or locative phrase, as below.

(15)   a.   . . . en plein midi arrive un nuage rouge . . . (p. 73)
       b.   Avancaient vers nous l'expression, le regard . . . (p. 73)
       c.   Ainsi chante sous le front un cavillon allègre. (p. 75)
       d.   Et de nouveau le secouaient les sanglots . . . (p. 92)

Such cases are widely attested in literary French, both with and without preverbal phrases, and seem to parallel Presentational *there* constructions in English in imposing a heaviness restriction on the postverbal subject. We offer further examples below. (Example (16b) is taken from Rochemont [1979].)

(16)   a.   Sont représentées les universités suivantes, . . .
       b.   J'ai dit que lui seraient présentés tous les députés des villages du nord.

(17)   a.   ?Est arrivé ce matin une lettre de mon père.
       b.   ??Est arrivé ce matin une lettre.

The French constructions in (12) and (15)–(17) seem to pattern with English Presentational *there* constructions rather than with D/L in a further respect. The postverbal subject in the French examples is VP final, as may be seen by comparing the unaccusative construction in (18) with the Stylistic Inversion case in (17a).

(18)   *Est arrivé une lettre ce matin.

The expletive clitic *il* is apparently obligatory in unaccusative constructions such as (18), though not in the Presentational Stylistic Inversion construction.[52]

(19)   a.   Il est arrivé une lettre ce matin.
       b.   Il est arrivé ce matin une lettre de mon père.
       c.   J'ai dit qu'il lui serait présenté tous les députés des villages du nord.

There is another way in which French Presentational Stylistic Inversion bears a closer resemblance to English Presentational *there* constructions than to D/L. In particular, as the reader may have already noted, the classes of verbs participating in these constructions are more closely related in the Presentational constructions than with D/L. Moreover, all the relevant such verbs are either intransitive, or have the object expressed as a pronoun or as a clitic (cf. (20)/(21)), or may be reanalyzed as idiomatic intransitive predicates (cf. (22)).

(20)   a.   ?*There followed his sister into the park, a band of thugs on horseback.
       b.   There followed her into the park, a band of thugs on horseback.

(21)   a.   Les fenêtres donnent sur une dévolée de prés vides... Les couronne toute une chenille de mélancoliques petits bois. (Atkinson [1973: 76])
       b.   Tandis que la Princesse causait avec moi, faisaient précisément leur entrée le duc et la duchesse de Guermantes. (Atkinson [1973])

(22)   There will take place tomorrow evening the event of the century.

It is not our purpose here to enter into a detailed account of French Stylistic Inversion constructions or of the fascinating and presumably universal restrictions on verb classes participating in these and related constructions. However, it should be clear from what little we have said that French Presentational Stylistic Inversion differs from French *wh* triggered Stylistic Inversion and English SI radically enough that it appears inappropriate to attempt to provide a completely uniform account of these constructions in the manner Safir proposes.

4 *NP Shift*

In this chapter, we examine the properties of constructions such as (1).

(1) a. John bought for his mother a painting that he liked.
      b. There walked into the room a man with long blond hair.

Sentence (1a) exemplifies the construction known as Heavy NP Shift (HNPS) and (1b) Presentational *there* Insertion (PTI). We assume that both constructions are derived by the rightward application of Move a to the NP that appears sentence finally. (See Kayne [1979].) Thus (1a,b) are derivationally related to the corresponding sentences in (2).

(2) a. John bought a painting that he liked for his mother.
      b. A man with long blond hair walked into the room.

On this view, HNPS and PTI are in actuality instances of the same construction, which for convenience we will refer to simply as NP Shift. Rochemont (1978) expresses a similar viewpoint, referring to the generalized operation as Focus NP Shift. In light of the well-known heaviness requirement on the shifted NP in both constructions and the fact that in both cases the NP is an obligatory focus (see Chapter One:4), this seems to be a reasonable proposal.[1]

It also follows that whatever differences may be shown to exist between constructions of types (1a,b) must be attributable to either independent features of the target position for Move a or to properties of the configurations that result from the application of that rule in interaction with other principles of UG. For instance, *there* is obligatorily inserted in the position with respect to which the shifted NP is thematically interpreted in (1b) though not in (1a). This is an observation that requires an explanation on the view we espouse here. Moreover, while this is the most obvious difference between the two constructions it is by no means the only one, as we will see.

The assumption that (1a,b) are derivationally related by Move a to the respective sentences in (2) gives rise to the representations in (3).

116

(3) a. John bought *t* for his mother NP.
     b. *t* walked into the room NP.

The relation between each instance of NP and *t* in (2) must satisfy Subjacency, and in addition, *t* must be properly governed, for the ECP. These requirements impose rather severe restrictions on the range of possible constituent structure representations that may be associated with (3), and correspondingly with (1). First, to satisfy Subjacency, the NP in both cases of (3) may be adjoined no higher than the most local IP. In particular, since IP is a barrier for *t*, its antecedent under movement must be contained within the next higher projection dominating IP. If the NP adjoined to IP it would satisfy this restriction, but not if it adjoined to CP, for instance. Further, while NP in (3a) may be adjoined to either VP or IP and satisfy the ECP, in (3b) it may be adjoined only to IP if it is to bind *t* and so allow the antecedent government requirement imposed by the ECP to be satisfied. (Newmeyer [1987] makes an essentially parallel proposal which we discuss in Chapter Five:2.)

The discussion in this chapter proceeds in the following fashion. In section 1 we consider the constituent structure representations that our theoretical assumptions force us to adopt for (1a,b), and show that the structures we postulate are consistent with the results of constituent structure tests of the type employed in preceding chapters. Section 2 is concerned with predicting the distribution of *there* in the examples of (1), and in particular with the contrast between (1) and (4).

(4) a. *John bought there for his mother a picture that he liked.
     b. *Walked into the room a man with long blond hair.

In section 3, we examine a range of further contrasts and similarities between PTI and HNPS, showing how the properties in question may be seen to follow from the theoretical assumptions elaborated in Chapter One.

1   The constituent structure of HNPS and PTI

As noted in the Introduction to this chapter, the assumption that HNPS and PTI constructions are derived by Move a together with our theoretical assumptions elaborated in Chapter One force a restricted analysis of the derived constituent structures that must be associated with these constructions. Specifically, in structure (1) below, if the NP originates in object position (NP_2) it may be adjoined in the position of either a or β, but if it originates in subject position (NP_1) it can only be adjoined in the position of a.[2]

(1)

```
              IP
            /    \
          IP      α
        /   \
     NP₁     I'
           /   \
          I     VP
              /    \
            VP      β
          /   \
         V     NP₂
```

We will show that these specific predictions are consistent with the range of available evidence regarding constituent structure in such cases.

We begin with the prediction that an NP shifted from object position may pattern with VP under ellipsis, while one shifted from subject may not. Consider the operation of VP Ellipsis in the examples below.[3]

(2) a. John gave to Mary a picture of Lyndon Johnson, and Bill did too.
   b. John read in *The Times* a scathing review of his new book, and Sally did too.
   c. Sally noticed in the foyer a famous portrait by Rembrandt, and Bill did too.

(3) a. *There actually entered the room a veritable army of revelers, and for some reason I had thought that there might.
   b. *If Mary claims that there jumped out in front of her several friendly well-dressed Martians, then there did.
   c. *John said that there might walk into the room at any moment someone who would be perfect for the part, and there may.

The PPs and clauses following V and preceding the shifted object NP in sentences like (2) have sometimes been thought to appear optionally outside VP (Kuno [1975]). However, a consistent account can be given in which all of these constituents are attached to the maximal VP (see Culicover and Wilkins [1984]). The examples in (2) therefore support the claim that an NP shifted from object position may appear in the position of β in (1). (The same point is made in chapter 4 of Rochemont [1986].) The examples in (3) on the other hand show that an NP shifted from subject position may not undergo ellipsis with the VP, as would be expected were the NP adjoined to IP in the position of α in (1).[4] The evidence from VP Ellipsis therefore supports the claims that rightward movement of NP_1 is to α in (1) and that of NP_2 is to β.

We note that the data we consider here and below are consistent with a different hypothesis, that both NP_1 and NP_2 adjoin in the position of β

in (1). In this view, failure of NP$_1$ to pattern with the VP under ellipsis and so on might plausibly be attributed to restrictions on the relation between the position of NP$_1$ and β in (1). However, as we will see in section 3, such an analysis provides no account of the syntactic restrictions on PTI, and in particular of the frozen nature of PTI as distinct from HNPS.

Consider next the behavior of NP Shift with VP Topicalization.

(4)   a. Everyone said that John would give to Mary all of the money that he won at the track, and give to Mary all of the money that he won at the track he did.
      b. John was told to buy for Mary every book he could find, and buy for Mary every book he could find he did.
(5)   a. *They said that there would enter the room a herd of unruly elephants, and enter the room a herd of unruly elephants there did.
      b. *Mary was told that there might jump out in front of her several friendly well-dressed Martians, and jump out in front of her several friendly well-dressed Martians there did.

The examples in (4) show that an NP shifted from object position may topicalize with the VP, while those in (5) show that an NP shifted from subject position may not. Once again, these data are consistent with the proposal that the former appears in the position of β in (1), and the latter in the position of α.

Next, consider the interaction of NP Shift and pseudoclefting of VP.

(6)   a. What John did was buy for Mary every book he could find.
      b. What Mary did was put on the mantel an old soiled portrait of her husband.
(7)   a. *What there might do is walk into the room someone who would be perfect for the part.
      b. *What there did was jump out in front of her several friendly well-dressed Martians.

As (6) shows, an NP shifted from object may appear with VP in the pseudocleft focus position, but (7) shows that an NP shifted from subject may not.

Finally, we consider the evidence from the positioning of parentheticals.

(8)   a. John bought for Mary a picture of her father in a weird costume, I think.
      b. John, I think, bought for Mary a picture of her father in a weird costume.
      c. *John bought, I think, for Mary a picture of her father in a weird costume.
      d. John bought for Mary, I think, a picture of her father in a weird costume.
(9)   a. There entered the room behind her several uniformed officers, I think.
      b. *There, I think, entered the room behind her several uniformed officers.
      c. *There entered, I think, the room behind her several uniformed officers.
      d. There entered the room behind her, I think, several uniformed officers.

Assuming that what follows the parenthetical must be a constituent, the grammaticality of (8b) in particular is consistent with our proposal that the NP shifted from object position is adjoined to VP (Emonds [1976]). In contrast, the ungrammaticality of (9b) follows on our analysis of the NP in PTI as adjoined to IP rather than VP.

While the evidence in (2)–(9) is clearly consistent with the constituent structures for NP Shift that we have hypothesized in (1), there are a range of other related facts that should also be considered. First, note that if the NP shifted from object position appears in the position of β in (1), it might be expected not only that the NP may pattern with the VP in derived VP positions, as we have just seen, but also that it may fail to be included with the minimal VP in the same configurations. However, as the following examples illustrate, it is in general not possible to delete only the smaller VP in (1), excluding β, under VP Ellipsis (cf. (10a)), nor is it possible to place just the smaller VP in the focus position of a pseudocleft, as in (10b).

(10)   a.   *John bought for Mary a picture of her father, and Sally did every book she could find.
       b.   *What John did every book he could find was buy for Mary.

On the other hand, it apparently is possible to front just the smaller VP in a VP Topicalization construction, as in (11).

(11)   ?Everyone said that John would give to Mary something very valuable to him, and give to Mary he did [$_{VP}$ e] all of the money that he won at the TRACK.

That (11) is grammatical is to be expected, given our theoretical assumptions outlined in Chapter One. In particular, since V serves to both lexically and antecedent govern the trace of the object within the fronted VP, the ECP is satisfied. Moreover, after reconstruction has applied, the NP properly binds a variable within the VP. The alternative, that the NP is shifted from the topicalized VP and adjoined to IP, is excluded under our assumptions by Subjacency, since the topicalized VP is not L-marked in its derived position, and so behaves as an adjunct island to extraction.

What remains to be explained, then, is why the NP shifted from object position must be included with the VP under ellipsis or pseudoclefting as in (10). Consider first (10a). It has been noted that a phrase in A-bar position may not bind a variable trace within an elliptted VP, as in (12).[5]

(12)   *I know that Bill talked to someone, but I don't remember who he did.

Since (10a) is in relevant respects identical to (12), the restriction on (12) would provide an account of the ungrammaticality of (10a) as well. In (10b) on the other hand the problem would seem to be with the NP contained within the cleft clause. Evidently, this NP fails to find any interpretation whatsoever in the clause it is in, and so fails to satisfy the Principle of Full Interpretation of Chomsky (1986a).[6]

Let us now consider parallel cases where the NP must be in the position of a in (1), having been shifted from subject (NP^1) position. We have already seen that in these cases the NP fails to pattern with the VP under ellipsis or dislocation, as expected. Now note that ellipsis or dislocation of the VP is barred in PTI even when the NP is not included with the VP as a target of the operation. Consider the following examples.

(13) a. ?*You've been told that no one you know will walk into the room, but there will someone you haven't seen in years.
       b. ??You've been told that no one you know will walk into the room, but walk into the room there will someone you haven't seen in years.
       c. *What there did a man with long blond hair was walk into the room.

As these examples show, there can be no ellipsis, topicalization or pseudoclefting of VP in PTI. Example (13b), with topicalization of the VP, is somewhat better, we think, than either of the others. Consider also the examples below.

(14) a. ?We were warned that someone unusual might enter the room, and enter the room there did a tall man with blue spiked hair.
       b. ??Mary said that something unusual might jump out in front of us, and jump out in front of us there did several friendly well dressed Martians.

If these cases are in fact good, they would be consistent with our theoretical assumptions. In particular, assuming as we have that both VP Topicalization and PTI are derived by adjunction to IP, the relevant configuration would be as in (15).

(15) $[_{IP}$ VP $[_{IP}$ $[_{IP}$ there . . .] NP]]

Antecedent government for the ECP is satisfied for the trace of the NP in the position of *there* in (15) and, we assume, for the trace of VP by I, since VP is L-marked by I.[7] Moreover, since we take Subjacency to be a condition on movements rather than representations, there is a derivation of (15) consistent with the Strict Cycle Condition that does not violate Subjacency, as we have shown in Chapter Three:3.[8]

Example (13c), on the other hand, can be blocked under our assumptions by Subjacency. Note that the cleft clause in a pseudocleft construction plausibly involves movement of a *wh* phrase to the SPEC,CP position. Thus pseudoclefts show island constraints within the cleft clause for example. If the NP in PTI is in fact adjoined to IP, then extraction to SPEC,CP position must violate Subjacency in the configuration below.

(16) $[_{CP}$ wh$_i$ $[_{IP*}$ $[_{IP}$ . . . t_i . . .] NP]].

IP* in (16) is the node created by adjunction of the NP under PTI. Since IP is a barrier for t_i, extraction across IP*, the first maximal projection dominating IP, must violate Subjacency. Hence it follows that example (13c) should be ungrammatical.

Consider finally example (13a). We note that there is some variability of judgments for examples of this type. Thus, compare the examples below.[9]

(17)   a. ?There had actually entered the room a veritable army of revelers, but for some reason I thought that there hadn't.
       b. ??You may think that there will eventually fall on Bill a massive wall hanging, but I believe that there won't.
       c. ?There walked into the room many more people than there should have.
       d. ??Although there probably shouldn't have, there actually walked into the room at that time every one of the candidates.

Our theoretical framework, given the plausible assumption that the derivation of VP Ellipsis does not involve movement, provides no reason to consider any of the examples of the interaction of VP Ellipsis and PTI ungrammatical. We do not presently, therefore, have an account of why (13a) should be bad, nor of the contrast between (13a) and the examples in (17). Nevertheless, the existence of such cases does not disconfirm our hypothesis that the NP in PTI is adjoined to IP. The critical examples related to this hypothesis were presented in (3) and shown to be consistent with it. The ungrammaticality and/or oddity of the examples of (13), (14), and (17) is a problem on any account of the structure of PTI so far as we can determine irrespective of the site of attachment of the shifted NP.

2   On the distribution of Presentational *there*

As we stated at the outset of this chapter, one of the central claims in our analysis of PTI and HNPS is that these are really two surface realizations of a single construction. This point of view allows us to readily capture the properties they share, but requires that an explanatory account be provided of those properties which differentiate them. One such property is the obligatory appearance of *there* in PTI in the position with respect to which the shifted NP finds a thematic interpretation, and its obligatory absence in HNPS. Thus, we find the paradigm in (1) and (2).

(1)   a. John bought for his mother a painting that he liked.
       b. There walked into the room a man with long blond hair.
(2)   a. *John bought there for his mother a picture that he liked.
       b. *Walked into the room a man with long blond hair.

For the present, we will distinguish this use of *there* from its other uses in English by referring to the item that appears in a grammatical sentence such as (1b) as P-*there*. The problem we face now is to characterize the distribution of P-*there* in (1) and (2).

   Consider first the obligatory appearance of P-*there* in PTI. Our prior discussion has established that PTI as in (1b) is associated at some point in its derivation with the representation in (3).

(3) $[_{IP} [_{IP} t_i \text{ walked into the room}] \text{ NP}_i]$.

As we noted, adjunction of the NP to IP satisfies the antecedent requirement of the ECP: the NP binds and is subjacent to its trace from that position. Note, however, that t_i in (3) is not lexically governed, since by assumption I is not a lexical governor in English and C is a lexical governor only under COMP indexing. It is this feature of (3) that presumably gives rise to the ungrammaticality of (2b). By this line of reasoning, the contrast in grammaticality between (1b) and (2b) must be due to the insertion of P-*there* somehow voiding the requirement for lexical government. We propose therefore that P-*there* is inserted to "save" a trace from the requirement for lexical government. Assuming that the lack of lexical government is a necessary condition for the insertion of P-*there*, it follows that P-*there* may not be inserted in the position of the trace of an NP shifted from object position, since such a trace is in fact lexically governed. In this way, we correctly characterize the paradigm in (1) and (2).

   This view of the presence of P-*there* in PTI is extremely natural, even required, if we are to maintain the claim that HNPS and PTI are in fact instances of the same more general construction, derived by the rightward application of Move a. In particular, if it can be shown that the distribution of P-*there* is fully constrained by grammatical principles that systematically distinguish the cases where it may not and must appear in (1) and (2), then the analysis we suggest for sentence (1b) receives strong support. Let us therefore consider more carefully how the distribution of P-*there* may be predicted. We begin with a discussion of *there* Insertion in general, narrowing our attention to P-*there* as we proceed and returning in the subsequent discussion to the distribution of *there* in existential and unaccusative constructions as well.

As Chomsky (1981) observes, the optimal rule to account for the distribution of *there* quite generally is (4), with the specific details of distribution following from the interaction of independently established properties of *there* and principles of grammar. This is presumably a subcase of the more general rule Affect a of Lasnik and Saito (1984).

(4)   Insert *there* anywhere.

Since *there* has phonological content, it can only be inserted in a position to which Case is assigned. Note that it is not sufficient for *there* to simply appear in a chain to which Case is assigned. In fact, it can only appear at the head of a Case chain, assuming the head position to be the position in which Case is assigned. In addition, since *there* is pleonastic and so not a referring (or R-) expression, it cannot be inserted in a θ-position at D-structure. Finally, for reasons of recoverability, *there* can only be inserted in the position of an empty category.

There are, however, two properties of *there* that do not appear to follow from general principles. First, as Chomsky (1981) points out, (4) must be qualified with the stipulation, to distinguish *there* from *it*, that *there* is inserted in the position of an empty category that is coindexed with NP. This result may be guaranteed in a number of ways. Chomsky (1981, 87ff.) appeals to a number sharing account.[10] Safir (1985, 140) proposes the condition in (5).

(5)   Insert *there* if [*e*] is in a θ-chain, otherwise insert *it*.

Since not all languages that have impersonal formatives distinguish more than one of these, this extra stipulation is not unexpected. Whether all languages with multiple lexical impersonal formatives distinguish among them along the lines of (5) is a matter open to empirical investigation. Nevertheless, it appears that any account of the distribution of *there* must minimally assume some such statement as (5) in addition to (4).

The second stipulation that is apparently required is that *there* can only be inserted in the position of an empty category that is in subject position. At first glance, this might appear to follow from the θ-Criterion. In particular, if *there* is not an R-expression, then it cannot be inserted in a θ-position, and by the Projection Principle object position cannot be a non-θ-position.

However, it is by no means clear that this part of the distribution of *there* actually follows from the θ-Criterion. Rather, what seems to follow from the θ-Criterion is that *there* cannot be the sole lexical member of an A-chain that gets a θ-role. That is, *there* cannot be inserted in a θ-position at D-structure. It does not follow that *there* cannot be inserted in the position of an empty category that is a trace, as a phonologically realized trace of sorts for instance. As Safir (1985) observes, a general restriction against non-referential phrases appearing in θ-positions would block the appearance of NP-*t* in passive and raising constructions in the θ-position of the chain of which the NP-*t* is a member.[11] Thus, the requirement that *there* appears only in subject position does not in fact follow from the θ-Criterion. In Safir's analysis, this requirement is stipulated directly in the rule for insertion of impersonal formatives.[12]

(6)   Insert an impersonal formative for $[_{NP} e]$ if $[_{NP} e]$ is not a complete θ-set.

Under the definition for a ''complete θ-set,'' the only position which may not be a complete θ-set is the subject position. Thus, impersonal formatives may only be inserted in subject position by (6), but solely as a matter of stipulation. A preferable account would reduce (6) to (4), abstracting away from the language specific requirement in (5).

Let us now reconsider the structural analysis of PTI offered at the outset of our discussion. Our suggestion was that, assuming that the NP in PTI is adjoined to IP, the trace in subject position is antecedent but not lexically governed. Evidently, then, the presence of P-*there* is conditioned by the lack of lexical government for the trace of the NP. Since the requirement that P-*there* appear in subject position only is reminiscent of the typical subject/object asymmetries characterized by the ECP, such an account obviates the need for a stipulation such as (6) and permits the optimal description in (4), given (5), at least as concerns the distribution of P-*there*. Note that we are now assuming that P-*there* ''lexicalizes'' a trace, thereby voiding a potential violation of the requirement for lexical government. As we have further noted, since we must assume that P-*there* can be freely inserted in the position of an empty category, given (4), we must also assume the validity of the Principle of Last Resort, a principle which requires (4) to apply only in case it must.[13]

To claim that P-*there* may only be inserted in positions that are not lexically governed in the sense required for the ECP predicts that P-*there* is not in fact restricted to subject positions, but more specifically to lexically ungoverned subject positions.[14] In the cases we have witnessed so far, this turns out to be true, since we have considered only examples in which P-*there* appears in place of a lexically ungoverned trace in the subject position of a tensed clause. Consider, however, the behavior of the trace of a shifted NP in a subject position that is lexically governed, in particular in contexts of Exceptional Case Marking, as below.

(7)   a. I consider (*there) stupid anyone who would support a Socialist bid for power.
      b. I expect ?(*there) to win the race the horse that is ridden by the best jockey.
      c. I saw (*there) leaving the room someone I could not fail to recognize.
      d. I'd prefer *(?there) to walk into the room early someone who no one there will recognize.

In (7a–c) V governs, hence lexically governs, the position occupied by *there*, and P-*there* is evidently excluded. In (7d), on the other hand, V does not govern the embedded subject position (witness the inability of the embedded subject to undergo passivization in this case in contrast to the others), and P-*there* evidently must be inserted.[15]

   Note that Existential *there* (E-*there*), which appears in existential and unaccusative constructions as in (8), shows only partly the distribution of P-*there*. For instance, compare the examples in (9).

(8)   a. There was someone waiting to see me.
      b. There arose several objections during the meeting.
(9)   a. They showed *(there) to be a problem with the analysis.
      b. They showed (*there) to be false all of the claims he had made.

In particular, E-*there* is obligatorily present in any existential or unaccusative construction, we assume, for the purposes of Case assignment. Following Safir (1985), let us suppose the appearance of E-*there* to be intimately related to the requirement for the postverbal NP to receive Case even though it fails to bind the subject position on which it is dependent for Case.[16] Thus, on our account, P-*there* supplants an A-bar bound trace, while E-*there* does not supplant a trace at all, but rather a pleonastic pronominal empty category which heads an unbalanced chain at S-structure,[17] adapting the analysis of Safir (1985).[18] Since we take the ECP to be a condition on traces in particular (nonpronominal empty categories), the distribution of E-*there* cannot be determined as a function of the ECP. In what follows, then, we consider only the distribution of overt trace, which in English we claim is P-*there*.[19]

   While appealing, there is a difficulty with this attempt to limit the distribution of P-*there* in terms of the ECP. Recall from our discussion in Chapter One that we attributed the *that-t* effect to the failure of the trace in subject position to be lexically governed when *that* is present. Thus in the representations below, *t* is antecedent governed by *t'* in both cases, but lexically governed only in case *that* is not present and COMP Indexing has applied, as it may in (a) but not (b).

(10)   a.   who did you say [$_{CP}$ t' [$_{C'}$ e [$_{IP}$ t left]]].
       b.   *who did you say [$_{CP}$ t' [$_{C'}$ that [$_{IP}$ t left]]].

If P-*there* is in fact a "lexicalized" or overt trace of sorts satisfying the requirement for lexical government, we might expect the ungrammaticality of (10b) to disappear once *t* is replaced by P-*there*, as below.

(11)   *Who did you say that there left?

As indicated, P-*there* evidently cannot save *t* from the requirement for lexical government in cases such as (10b), although we have claimed that it can in PTI. Example (11), therefore, poses a serious problem for our approach.

Rather than abandon the attempt to characterize the distribution of P-*there* even partly in terms of the ECP, let us consider whether there is not some other account of the ungrammaticality of (10b) that also accommodates (11), while preserving the assumption that P-*there* can act as an overt trace and so void the requirement for lexical government. If P-*there* can in fact lexicalize trace to satisfy the ECP, then since it evidently cannot rescue *t* in (10b) from the ECP, it must be that *t* fails not only to be lexically governed in the presence of *that* but also antecedent governed, contrary to our assumption in Chapter One. Under this account, the appearance of *there* in place of *t* in (10b) as in (11) does not suffice to rescue *t* from the ECP, since *t* continues to fail the requirement of antecedent government.

Pursuing this line of reasoning further, we must ask how on this account the overt complementizer in cases such as (10b) blocks both lexical and antecedent government, since under our current assumptions it blocks only the former. Recall that we have followed Lasnik and Saito (forthcoming) in taking antecedent government to require that the antecedent be subjacent to the trace that it binds. Let us suppose instead that antecedent government requires a tighter notion than subjacent, which we will label *c-subjacent*, and define as below in (12).[20]

(12) α is *c-subjacent* to β iff for every δ, δ a barrier for β, if γ dominates δ then γ dominates α.

C-subjacent differs from *subjacent* only in that it lacks the restriction of γ to X^{max}. We now understand antecedent government to be as in (13).

(13)   *a antecedent governs β iff a binds β and a is c-subjacent to β.*

Given (13), *t* in (10) can only meet the requirement of antecedent government if it finds an antecedent within C'. Consider first (10a). In this case, we have assumed that the empty complementizer may serve as a lexical governor if it is coindexed with the phrase in SPEC,CP and correspondingly with *t*. Therefore *t* in (10a) may be lexically governed, if it is it is coindexed with the empty complementizer. Now recall from our discussion in Chapter One our assumption that when a is an $X°$ that lexically governs *t*, if a is coindexed with *t* it may also antecedent govern *t*. We required this assumption to accommodate the behavior of VP internal traces (of internal arguments in particular) under long extraction. Given (13), we must take this assumption to apply here in (10a) as well. Specifically, once the empty complementizer undergoes COMP Indexing, it serves to both lexically and antecedent govern *t*. Thus, *t* in (10) may satisfy the dual requirements of the ECP only if the complementizer is empty. In (10a), then, *t* is both lexically and antecedent governed within C'.[21] Since insertion of P-*there*, we assume, may satisfy only the requirement for lexical government, the contrast between (11) and (1b) now follows.[22]

Consider next (10b). We continue to assume that the overt complementizer is not a possible lexical governor in English. And since it is also not coindexed with *t*, neither is it an antecedent governor. Thus, *t* in (10b) fails the requirements of both lexical and antecedent government, as required.[23]

It is appropriate at this point to consider why P-*there* obviates the need for lexical and not antecedent government. It is natural to view the antecedent government requirement for trace as part of the definition of the very notion "trace." A trace is an empty category that has an antecedent as a consequence of movement. A trace without an antecedent would not be a trace. What the antecedent government requirement of the ECP amounts to is a condition that the antecedent of a trace be in a specific local relation to that trace.

It is a natural consequence of this view that no lexical item should be able to save a trace from having to be antecedent governed, since failure to be antecedent governed means failure to be a trace. We therefore predict that the lexicalization of traces should be restricted universally to contexts where only lexical government is lacking.

This view, that empty categories may be lexicalized only to void the lexical government requirement for non-pronominal empty categories, forces a very specific analysis of *wh* movement in Vata. The relevant properties of this construction are reported and analyzed in Koopman (1983b) and Koopman and Sportiche (1986), on which the following discussion is based. Briefly, the facts are these. Vata exhibits a by now clearly recognizable subject/object asymmetry under *wh* extraction.

(14) a. àlÓ   Ò/*[e]   nÙ   mí   là
         who   he-R   did   it   WH
         Who did it?
      b. àlÓ   n̄   gùgù   ná   Ò/*[e]   nÙ   mí   là
         who   you   thought   NA   he-R   did   it   WH
         Who did you think did it?
(15) a. yÍ   KòfínÙ   [e]   là
         what   did   WH
         What did Kofi do?
      b. àlÓ   n̄   gūgū   nā   Kófì   yÊ   [e]   yé   lá
         who   you   think   NA   see   PART   WH
         Who do you think Kofi saw?

The apparent resumptive pronoun (labeled R in (14)) is not a true resumptive pronoun, as Koopman and Sportiche argue, because as shown in Koopman (1983b), its distribution is subject to standard island constraints, from which true resumptive pronouns are typically exempt. Following Koopman and Sportiche, let us take R to be a lexically realized (overt) trace, thus the Vata equivalent of English P-*there* on our analysis. Significantly, R may not appear in the position of [e] in the examples of (15).

Koopman and Sportiche argue that the appearance of R is conditioned by the ECP. They assume that COMP Indexing is necessary for antecedent government from COMP. But they claim that *wh* movement in Vata cannot be movement to COMP, since preposed *wh* phrases appear at the left periphery of the clause in Vata, and COMP appears at the right periphery. Since COMP Indexing can only occur if the *wh* phrase is contained in COMP, Vata by their argument cannot have COMP Indexing. Preposed *wh* phrases therefore cannot be antecedent governed in Vata. Since lexical government is also lacking for the position of the subject trace, they propose that R is a "spell-out" of the trace, designed to satisfy the ECP.

Now notice that the discontinuity of *wh* phrase and COMP in Vata is readily accommodated in an analysis of S′ as CP.

(16)
```
              CP
            /    \
    wh-phrase     C'
               /    \
             IP       C
```

In Vata, in other words, the order of C and IP is reversed within C', in contrast to English. But then, the failure of COMP Indexing to apply in Vata is by no means transparent in (16) as it is in the S' analysis assumed by Koopman and Sportiche. In particular, it is not at all clear that C in (16) could not be an antecedent governor under COMP Indexing for a trace of the *wh* phrase in subject position, exactly as it is in our analysis of English.

We claim that there are two parameters that distinguish Vata and English. First, we have seen that in English, COMP Indexing applies only to the empty complementizer. But given the cooccurrence of *wh* phrase and complementizer in the Vata examples (14) and (15), we see that COMP Indexing is possible in Vata even for a lexically filled complementizer.[24] Vata differs from English in the further respect that a complementizer may never serve as a lexical governor even under COMP Indexing. Hence, the trace of the *wh* moved subject in (14) is antecedent governed by C under COMP Indexing, but not lexically governed. It is the lack of this latter property that forces insertion of R, the overt trace. It is the appearance of R in cases such as (14) that allows this parameter to be readily fixed by the learner.

There is in fact some support for our claim that a trace in subject position may be antecedent governed solely in virtue of the presence of an antecedent in SPEC,CP position, though on our analysis subject to the application of COMP Indexing. This concerns a subject/complement asymmetry that arises in Vata in extraction from a *wh* island. Compare the examples below.

(17)
*àlÓ n̄ nĺ   [, zĒ   mĒmÉ gbÚ Ò   dĺ ' -6Ót mÉ] yì   là
who you NEG-A reason it-it   for he-R cut REL it   know WH
    Who don't you know why cut it?

(18)   àlÓ n̄ nĺ   [, zĒ   n̄   kà   -6Ó [e]   nyÉ] yì   là
        who you NEG-A thing   you FUT-A REL   give know WH
        Who don't you know what you will give to?

If the ungrammaticality of (17) is to be attributed to the ECP, then it cannot be that the ECP is satisfied simply by insertion of R, since R appears in (17). In our view, lexical government is satisfied in (17) by the insertion of R. The example remains ungrammatical nevertheless, because antecedent government is lacking. But if antecedent government is a requirement for the ECP, then antecedent government must be satisfied for the subject trace in the examples of (14). There must therefore be antecedent government of a subject trace from C in Vata, just in case the trace has an antecedent in SPEC,CP to appropriately condition the COMP Indexing operation.

Like P-*there*, R is inserted to satisfy only the lexical government requirement of the ECP.[25] Moreover, as already noted, it is clear that the insertion of R in (17) is not sufficient to save the structure from the ECP, since the antecedent government requirement remains unsatisfied independent of the appearance of the overt trace. Thus, (17) is the theoretical equivalent in Vata of the English example (11).[26] While the distribution of R might be predictable under a weaker version of the ECP,[27] one requiring either lexical or antecedent government, such a version does not succeed in constraining the distribution of P-*there*, as we have already seen. Thus, the distribution of both Vata R and English P-*there* cannot be reduced on this view, as it is on ours, to the ECP.[28]

To conclude, we have attributed the obligatory presence of P-*there* in PTI and its obligatory absence in HNPS to the lack of lexical government for the trace that arises in the former but not in the latter. This analysis led us to reformulate slightly the definition of antecedent government. We then showed how the analysis might be extended to account for the distribution of the overt NP trace in Vata, with very minimal crosslinguistic parameterization of relevant aspects of the proposal.

3   Restrictions on NP Shift

In this section, we consider a range of restrictions on NP Shift, arguing that these restrictions follow from the specific configurational properties of the constructions in question in interaction with principles of UG. Consider first our proposal that in PTI the sentence final NP appears at S-structure in adjoined to IP position. Elaborating more fully, the structure we propose is given in (1).

(1)

$$
\begin{array}{c}
\text{CP} \\
\diagup \quad \diagdown \\
\quad \text{C}' \\
\diagup \quad \diagdown \\
\text{C} \quad \text{IP*} \\
\diagup \quad \diagdown \\
\text{IP} \quad \text{NP} \\
\diagup \quad \diagdown \\
t_{\text{NP}} \quad \text{I}' \\
\diagup \quad \diagdown \\
\text{I} \quad \text{VP}
\end{array}
$$

In the last section our concern was with the status of t_{NP} with respect to the ECP. Here, we wish to concentrate on a separate feature of (1). Note that the version of Subjacency that we have adopted predicts that IP in (1) is frozen with respect to further extraction. In particular, movement to any position outside IP* in (1) can only be in violation of Subjacency, since

IP is a barrier for everything it dominates.[29] Consider in this connection the examples in (2).

(2)   a. *Which room did there enter a man with long blond hair?
      b. *I don't remember which room there walked into a man with long blond hair.
      c. *Did there walk into the room a man with long blond hair?
      d. *This is the room that there walked into a man with long blond hair.

All of the examples in (2) are derived by movement of a phrase to C or SPEC,CP position in constructions with the form (1). As predicted, they are all ungrammatical.

Note that with E-*there*, in cases where the shifted NP may have originated within VP, it is predicted that the resulting configuration will not be frozen in the same fashion as a true instance of PTI. This prediction is correct, as the examples below illustrate.

(3)   a. Will there be sitting at the head table any of the victim's closest relatives?
      b. Did there arise during the meeting any unresolved issues?
(4)   a. ?At which table will there be sitting a large number of the victim's closest relatives?
      b. During which meeting did there arise a number of unresolved issues?

This state of affairs in PTI contrasts sharply with HNPS. Thus, compare the examples in (2) with the corresponding examples in (5).

(5)   a. For whom did Bill purchase last week an all expense paid ticket to Europe?
      a'. Which of these people purchased from you last week an all expense paid ticket to Europe?
      b. I don't remember for which of his sisters Bill bought in Europe a fourteenth-century gold ring.
      c. Did Bill buy for his mother anything she really liked?
      d. This is the woman from whom Bill purchased last week a brand new convertible with red trim.

The contrast in grammaticality between (2) and (5) is in fact as expected when we consider the constituent structure we have proposed for HNPS in (6).

Given that the postposed NP in HNPS is adjoined to VP* in (6), extraction to C or SPEC,CP position from within IP is consistent with Subjacency. This is because the only relevant barrier to extraction in (6) is IP, and movement to any position within CP in (6) will therefore satisfy the Subjacency requirement on movement.

The contrast between (2) and (5) is complicated by the interference of an effect independent of Subjacency. As Chomsky (1986b, 39) observes,

(6)

```
              CP
            /    \
                  C'
                /    \
              C        IP
                     /    \
                   NP       I'
                          /    \
                        I        VP*
                              /      \
                            VP        NP
                          /    \
                        V       t_NP
```

this effect arises in cases of multiple extraction from VP, where the phrases in question are of the same categorial type. Thus, Chomsky contrasts examples such as (7a), with a simple Subjacency violation, with the much worse (7b), where Subjacency is also violated and where the difference in acceptability must be attributed to this further effect.

(7)   a. *?To whom do you wonder what John gave?
       b. *Who do you wonder what John gave to?

With HNPS the effect is illustrated in the contrast between the relevant examples of (5) and the parallel examples in (8).[30]

(8)   a. *Who did Bill purchase for last week an all expense paid ticket to Europe?
       b. *I don't remember which of his sisters Bill bought for in Europe a fourteenth-century gold ring.
       c. *This is the woman who Bill purchased from last week a brand new convertible with red trim.

Given the grammaticality of the examples in (5), the ungrammaticality of (8) cannot be due to a general freezing of HNPS constructions, contra Culicover and Wexler (1977).

The effect in evidence in the contrast between (8) and (5) surfaces also in a range of cases with PTI. As we noted in connection with (1), extraction from the higher IP to a position within CP can only be in violation of Subjacency. There is a subset of extractions, however, that we predict should be possible. Recall from our discussion in section 3 of Chapter Three that on a specific interpretation of the Strict Cycle Condition, and with the assumption that Subjacency is a condition on movement and not on representations, it is possible to adjoin multiple phrases to IP without violating Subjacency, just so long as all other relevant conditions are satisfied (in particular, the ECP and the Strict Cycle Condition, under the interpretation that we have provided). As we saw in Chapter Three, this account makes possible the multiply adjoined configuration required for the analysis of Stylistic Inversion.

Now note that multiple adjunction to IP is possible also with PTI, as seen by the grammaticality of topicalization of PP in PTI as in (9).[31]

(9)   Into this room, there walked twelve jurors and a sheriff.

However, despite the possibility for multiple adjunction to IP exemplified in (9), topicalization of a constituent categorially equivalent to the postposed subject in PTI is nevertheless excluded. Thus, compare (9) with the minimally contrasting (10).

(10)   *This room, there walked into twelve jurors and a sheriff.

The contrast between (9) and (10) may be attributed once again to the condition motivated on the basis of examples (7)–(8) above.

We note that this same condition is also seen in cases of multiple topicalization in English, which as we observed in Chapter Three:1 are highly restricted. We considered there such examples as (11) and (12).

(11)   a. ?For John, a book, I would never buy.
       b. ?A book, for John, I would never buy.
(12)   a. *John, a book, I would never buy for.
       b. *A book, John, I would never buy for.

Note that the condition barring multiple extraction of categorially equivalent phrases from a given domain will account for the contrast between (11) and (12) as well.[32] Given the rather extensive support for this condition, we conclude that our claim that PTI is frozen in cases where HNPS is not stands, despite the ungrammaticality of the examples in (8).

Let us now consider a further prediction that arises from the configurations we propose for PTI and HNPS in (1) and (6) above. In both of these structures, the sentence final NP is in the position of an adjunct, and should therefore serve as a barrier to extraction from it. This prediction too is confirmed. Consider first that in HNPS extraction from the shifted NP gives rise to ungrammaticality, even though in at least some instances extraction from the non-shifted NP is possible.

(13)   a. Who did you buy a beautiful picture of *t* yesterday?
       b. Of whom did you buy a beautiful picture *t* yesterday?
       c. *Who did you buy yesterday a beautiful picture of *t*?
       d. *Of whom did you buy yesterday a beautiful picture *t*?
       e. I bought yesterday a beautiful picture of Sam.

While extraction from NP is possible in (13a,b), it is blocked in (13c,d) derived from the structure related to (13e). Since the shifted NP is an adjunct in its derived position, the relation between the *wh*-phrase and *t* in (13c,d) is in violation of Subjacency.[33]

Example (14a) shows that extraction from an NP shifted subject is also ungrammatical.

(14)   a. *Which famous actor did there appear in the newspaper a picture of?
       b. *Which famous actor did a picture of appear in the newspaper?

Recall that extraction from a subject NP in general, as in (14b), is excluded by Subjacency since the subject position is not L-marked. Not surprisingly, the postposing operation in PTI does not change the non-L-marked status of the shifted NP, so that (14a) is also excluded by Subjacency.

We turn now to the well-known restriction against NP Shift of the object of a preposition illustrated below.[34]

(15)   a. *Mary put the money on yesterday a table that was sitting at the entrance to the hall.
       b. *John threw a look at as he was walking by a man who was standing outside his office.
       c. *I mailed a letter to on my way to work an old friend from high school.

As the reader may easily verify, the ungrammaticality of the examples in (15) may be attributed to neither the ECP nor Subjacency. In fact, parallel cases under *wh* movement and other leftward movement operations are fully grammatical. It appears then that the ungrammaticality of such cases can only be due to some restriction on specifically rightward movements. Evidently, there is a very strict bounding constraint on rightward movement. Note that the required constraint is much stronger than either the Right Roof Constraint of Ross (1967) or the Generalized Subjacency Condition of Baltin (1981, 1983).[35] We propose that rightward movement in English obeys a condition that is roughly equivalent to the Uniformity Condition on inherent Case assignment of Chomsky (1986a, 194).[36] The condition we propose is given in (16).

(16)   *Local government condition on rightward movement:* In a configuration C where t is the trace of rightward movement and t is governed by $\beta = X°$, β must govern the head of the chain containing t.

Condition (16) requires that if a phrase moves rightward from a position governed by $X°$ then its ultimate landing site must also be a position governed by $X°$.[37] It follows from (16) that there can be no rightward extraction of NP from PP to VP adjoined position. Hence the ungrammaticality of the examples (15).

Condition (16) has a number of other advantageous consequences. First, (16) excludes long distance extraction of an NP through SPEC,CP with subsequent adjunction to the right VP adjoined position in a higher clause. That this must be excluded for both HNPS and PTI is shown by the ungrammaticality of the examples below.

(17) a. *It was believed that Mary bought for her mother by everyone an ornate fourteenth-century gold ring.
      b. *It was believed that there walked into the room by everyone a man with long blond hair.

In the relevant derivation for either example of (17), the matrix VP has the structure in (18).

(18)

```
                VP
              /    \
           VP       NP_i
          /   \
         V     CP
              /   \
            t_i    C'
```

The relation between NP_i and t_i in (18) satisfies Subjacency, and in addition, t_i satisfies the ECP (if it is relevant). However, condition (16) is not satisfied in (18) since there is an $X°$ (namely the C head of CP) that governs t_i and not NP_i. This consequence of (16) is a welcome result, since there is no independent way to exclude derivations of the sort just outlined.

There is perhaps some reason to strengthen (16) to require that the entire chain containing a trace of rightward movement be governed by a single head, to block the derivation of (19) indicated in (20).

(19)   *Walked into the room a man with long blond hair.
(20) $[_{CP} [_{CP} t'' [_{C'} e [_{IP} [_{IP} t \ldots] t']]] NP]$.

In (20) the shifted NP has adjoined first to IP in the position of t', then moved to SPEC,CP (t'') and subsequently adjoined to the right of CP. If we assume that COMP Indexing allows lexical government of t in the configuration indicated, then t and t' are both lexically governed by C and antecedent governed, the former by t' and the latter by C. If t'' is also lexically governed by C, then nothing apart from condition (16), revised in the manner indicated, would block this derivation.

It also correctly follows from (16), and from no other condition, that there can be no rightward extraction of the NP subject of a small clause, even though this is a position that is otherwise available for leftward extraction. Thus, compare the examples below.[38]

(21) a. Who does John want in New York on Monday?
        b. ?*John wants in New York on Monday every actor who has ever worked for him.
(22) a. Who did you see leave the room last night?
        b. ?*I saw leave the room last night a man with long blond hair.
(23) a. ?Who did you make angry while you were a student?
        b. ?*I made angry while I was a student every woman I ever dated.

Further, condition (16) provides an account of the ungrammaticality of (24), with the derivation indicated in (25).

(24)   *I wonder who there left.

(25)

```
                CP
             /     \
         whoᵢ        C'
                   /    \
                        IP
                      /    \
                  IP          tᵢ
                /    \
            there     I'
```

The relation between t_i and *who* in (25) satisfies Subjacency, and t_i moreover satisfies the ECP (as does the original trace of movement in the position of *there*.) However, since I governs *there*, under our analysis an overt trace, it must also govern the head of the chain containing *there*, which it does not in (25). Example (24) and similar examples are therefore excluded by condition (16).

We observe finally that it follows from condition (16) that NP Shift of an object may adjoin the shifted NP no higher than the VP adjoined position, despite the fact that Subjacency and the ECP are otherwise satisfied if the NP moves by adjunction to IP in such cases. Thus, (16) restricts the range of possible derivations associated with NP Shift of an object in a rather natural fashion.

Condition (16), together with the formulations for Subjacency adopted in Chapter One and the ECP as reformulated in this chapter, provide a complete account of the full range of syntactic restrictions on NP Shift, and of the differences and similarities between HNPS and PTI as regards these restrictions.

4   Conclusion

We have argued that PTI and HNPS are both derived by the rightward application of Move a, here referred to as NP Shift. While this analysis allows us to express similarities between the two constructions, it forces us to seek explanatory accounts of their differences. Our theoretical assumptions lead to differing constituent structures for both types, as a function of the site of origin of the shifted NP. This consequence, in interaction with the principles of UG that we have adopted, has allowed us to capture the differing behaviors of PTI and HNPS, in particular as regards the distribution of P-*there* and the more rigidly frozen character of PTI in contrast to HNPS. We have been led in the course of the discussion to propose a more narrow definition of antecedent government for the ECP than that adopted in Chapter One, and to suggest a very tight locality restriction on rightward movement in general, which bears some resemblance to the Uniformity Condition of Chomsky (1986a).

We argued in section 1 that the available evidence is consistent with the differing constituent structures we have been led to propose for HNPS and PTI. We observed briefly there that this evidence is also conceivably consistent with an account of NP Shift that uniformly shifts the NP to VP adjoined position regardless of its origin.[39] In this latter view, failure of the shifted NP in PTI to pattern with the VP under ellipsis and dislocation, in contrast to HNPS, might very well be attributed to restrictions on the relation between the shifted NP and P-*there* in the vacated subject position. A plausible candidate is the *there* replacement analysis of Chomsky (1986a), which it seems to us may be adapted to capture this failure of the shifted NP to pattern with VP. Nevertheless, while the hypothesis that NP Shift uniformly moves an NP to a VP adjoined position is potentially consistent with the constituent structure evidence, it provides no evident account of the more rigidly frozen behavior of PTI. In our analysis, on the other hand, the explanation for this behavior hinges critically on the contrast in adjunction sites between PTI and HNPS.

Note that the feature of our account that motivates the attachment of NP shifted from subject position to IP is the requirement for antecedent government in the ECP. As we observed in Chapter Three:6, the shifted NP may adjoin to VP just so long as the antecedent government requirement for the trace in subject position is independently satisfied. In this very restricted circumstance, the frozen character of the construction is also relaxed, as expected.

(1)   Behind which door (did you say) stood the woman that looked like your mother?

(2)   Into which room walked the man that you said had been following you?

See Chapter Three:5 for more extensive discussion and examples.

Finally, note that it follows on our account that the possibility for extraction in examples such as (1) and (2) is tied to the absence of P-*there* with the shifted subject. This prediction is correct, as the examples below illustrate.

(3)   a. In which park did you say could be seen last week a portrait of Chairman Mao?

        b. *In which park did you say (that) there could be seen last week a portrait of Chairman Mao?

Thus our proposal that the site of attachment of the shifted NP differs as a function of its site of origin is consistent with a broader range of evidence than the alternative proposal that NP Shift uniformly moves an NP to a VP adjoined position, all other things being equal. We conclude that our proposal is to be preferred over the alternative.

5   *English focus constructions*

As indicated in the Introduction, our major goal in this work has been to eliminate from syntactic theory the class of stylistic rules of Rochemont (1978), and to provide an account of their distributional properties in terms of their specific structural configurations in interaction with principles of Universal Grammar. We have grouped the relevant constructions into three classes, EX, SI, and NP Shift, and argued that with the theoretical perspective outlined in Chapter One and a detailed systematic investigation of their constituent structures the respective properties of these three construction types are indeed properly characterized.

We have two major objectives in this chapter. One is to review the major consequences of our analysis for the theoretical assumptions elaborated in Chapter One, and for the particular view of Universal Grammar that we have endorsed. This we do in section 1. In section 2 we contrast our specific reduction of the stylistic rule component to independent principles of UG with several other proposals with a similar goal.

Our second major objective is to reconsider the Focus Effect (FE) and the problems that arise in associating this effect with the constructions that have been the object of our primary analysis. In section 3 we suggest a particular solution to the problem that this property poses for the language learner, adapting a proposal of Rochemont (1986). In section 4 we propose to accommodate the Heaviness Effect (HE) in a similar fashion.

1   Theoretical consequences

1.1   The ECP

The ECP has been instrumental throughout our study in characterizing various properties of the constructions we have analyzed in terms of movement. We have assumed this principle to require both lexical and antecedent government of traces at LF, and possibly also at S-structure. We refer to this version of the ECP as the "conjunctive ECP." Following Lasnik and Saito (forthcoming), the version of antecedent government that we adopted in Chapter One required that the antecedent of a trace be subjacent to it. In order to capture the distribution of P-*there*, we saw reason in Chapter Four to amend the definition of antecedent government to require instead that the antecedent of a trace be c-subjacent to it, with c-subjacency defined as a special case of subjacency.

This revision of the definition of antecedent government is consistent with our other uses of the ECP, and with our original defense of this principle given in Chapter One. It is a consequence of this revised approach that in all cases of A-bar movement, apart from adjunction with no intervening barriers to a maximal projection that may be a barrier, the antecedent of a trace must be a lexical head. This consequence is consistent with our assumption in Chapter One that a lexical head may serve as antecedent governor for the trace of a maximal projection only if they are coindexed, either under θ-government or under COMP Indexing.

Our analysis of P-*there* in Chapter Four: 2, and of overt traces more generally, also provides support for the conjunctive ECP as outlined in Chapter One. In particular, the assumption that the ECP requires both lexical and antecedent government for traces makes it possible to characterize the distribution of Vata R and English P-*there* in terms of the ECP. As Koopman and Sportiche (1986) argue, the distribution of overt traces (at least Vata R) may not be fully characterized in terms of a disjunctive version of the ECP without some further principle. In our view, the distribution of overt traces may be attributed specifically to the requirement for lexical government.[1]

The assumption that lexical government is a requirement for traces forces a definition of lexical government in configurational terms rather than in terms of θ-government, contra Lasnik and Saito (1984) and Chomsky (1986b). Consider for instance the trace of NP Movement in a raising configuration as in (1).

(1)   John seems [$_{IP}$ *t* to like Mary]

t in (1) is antecedent governed by *John*, under either of the definitions of antecedent government we have considered. It is lexically governed by *seems*, however, only if lexical government is not θ-government. Similarly, the intermediate trace of *wh* Movement in SPEC,CP must be lexically governed by the higher verb without being θ-governed by it. The arguments provided by Lasnik and Saito (1984) that lexical government is not sufficient to guarantee well-formedness are consistent with the view presented here, because lexical government by itself is never sufficient to guarantee well-formedness with respect to the ECP, since antecedent government must be satisfied as well.

In defining lexical and antecedent government in Chapter One, we adopted the version of c-command proposed in Chomsky (1981) rather than that of Chomsky (1986b). The former but not the latter extends the c-command domain of a head beyond the first maximal projection that dominates it to the highest projection of the head. This definition of c-command is supported by our analysis of SI in particular. As we noted in Chapter Three: 3, the raised V in I in the configurations below serves to both lexically and antecedent govern its trace in the preposed VP.

(2)   a.

```
              IP
            /    \
          VP      IP
         /\\      /  \
      t_v...    NP    I'
                    /    \
                  I/V    t_VP
```

b.

```
              IP
            /    \
          VP      IP
         /\\      /  \
      t_v...    I/V    IP
                     /    \
                   NP      I'
                         /    \
                       t_I    t_VP
```

Without a projection definition of c-command for heads of the sort we have adopted, t_v in (2) could not satisfy the ECP under any definition of this principle. We conclude that the version of c-command proposed in Chomsky (1981) is to be preferred.[2]

1.2   Subjacency

The definition of Subjacency borrowed from Lasnik and Saito (forthcoming) and presented in Chapter One has received considerable support from the analyses we have defended. Of particular import has been the consequence that adjunction to a barrier (more specifically, IP) creates a configuration from which further extraction is barred. This feature of the analysis has been used to capture the frozen character of SI as well as the differences in extraction possibilities from PTI in contrast to HNPS. We saw evidence in the analyses of both PTI and SI for a specific interpretation of the Strict Cycle Condition consistent with our view of Subjacency. Under this interpretation, the Strict Cycle Condition is satisfied for Move α applying on a given maximal projection no matter which segment of that projection Move α takes as its domain.

We have also observed that a phrase that has been moved by adjunction is itself a barrier in its derived position, and thus is an island to extraction even by further adjunction.[3] From this follow the remaining frozen properties of SI, HNPS, and PTI. The fact that adjuncts (that is, non-arguments) in general are islands to extraction suggests a configurational definition of the distinction between adjuncts and arguments, and more specifically of "L-marking" and "θ-government." In particular, we conjecture that a given phrase is θ-governed and therefore is L-marked if, and only if, it appears within the first maximal projection of a lexical head. We will not pursue here the very wide ranging consequences of this proposal. We note only its potential feasibility. We do note one consequence, that the frozen character of phrases in extraposed position follows from their appearance in adjunct position under our analysis of EX in Chapter Two.

We note finally that the analysis of Subjacency and the definitions of government and c-command elaborated in Chapter One have forced us to distinguish two notions of maximal projection, categorial and topological. A categorial maximal projection is the maximal value of a projection of some category, that is, X^{max}. A topological maximal projection is a node that counts as maximal in a syntactic configuration. In the configuration $[\alpha [\alpha . . .]]$, where α is X^{max}, both α's are categorial maximal projections, but only the higher α is a topological maximal projection.

The categorial notion is required for Subjacency to operate as we have assumed in the configurations of adjunction to IP with islandhood. The topological notion on the other hand is crucial to the consequences that derive from our formulations of c-command and government, particularly in regard to the ECP and lexical government.

2   Two alternatives

In this section we will consider two distinct alternative proposals for reducing the class of stylistic rules in the sense of Rochemont (1978) to independently motivated principles of UG, those of Newmeyer (1987) and Coopmans (1987). We will not discuss the proposals in Maruta (1985), though he too seeks to eliminate the category of stylistic rules, as we have already argued against relevant segments of the analyses of Stowell (1981) and Safir (1985), upon which Maruta's account is based.

2.1   Newmeyer (1987)

Newmeyer (1987) presents an analysis of PTI that is in many respects similar to our own. He argues that the postposed subject appears at S-structure adjoined to IP, and that the newly created IP node serves as an additional barrier in such configurations. His account of the extraction restrictions in PTI, however, hinges not on Subjacency, as does our account, but rather on the ECP. In particular, he assumes that the ECP can be satisfied in the relevant cases only under antecedent government from COMP, and that the adjoined IP configuration, in creating a barrier for elements dominated by the newly created IP, blocks the required antecedent government relation. Thus in (1), movement of I to C leaves a trace in I that may not be antecedent governed from C due to the intervening barrier (the higher IP).

(1)   a. *Did there walk into the room a man with long blond hair?
       b. $[_{CP}$ did$_i$ $[_{IP}[_{IP}$ there t_1 walk into the room] NP]].

Similarly in (2), if the trace of the *wh* phrase is properly governed only under antecedent government from COMP, then the intervening IP barrier in (2b) may once again be seen as the source of the ungrammaticality.

(2)   a. *I wonder which room there walked into a man with long blond hair?
       b. ... $[_{CP}$ which room$_i$ $[_{IP}[_{IP}$ there walked into $t_i]$ NP]].

Our principal objection to this analysis is that it attributes the extraction restrictions in PTI to the ECP. But if the restriction against extraction in PTI is due to the ECP, then the analysis in fact provides no account of the ungrammaticality of (2). The reason is that given that the antecedent government requirement for the trace of a non-subject argument may be satisfied in its immediate environment (by the θ-marking head) without reference to the most local COMP, the extra barrier created by adjunction to IP should prove irrelevant to satisfaction of the ECP for such a trace, in contrast to the trace of an adjunct which must be antecedent governed from the most local COMP position. That *which room* in (2) behaves as an argument for purposes of the ECP and not as an adjunct is shown by the contrast in acceptability of the examples below, where both *wh*-phrases are construed with the embedded sentence.

(3)   a. ??Which room did John ask why Mary walked into?
       b. *Why did John ask which room Mary walked into?
       c. ??What did John ask why Mary bought?

Which room in (a) patterns like *what* in (c) with respect to long extraction, and· not like *why* in (b). Thus in the analysis of Lasnik and Saito (1984) or Chomsky (1986b), in (3a, c) there is a violation only of Subjacency, in contrast to the added ECP violation in (3b). The ungrammaticality of (2) then cannot be attributed to the ECP, since as (3a) shows, the trace of the *wh* phrase does not require a local antecedent in COMP.[4] This objection is especially damaging given that Subjacency is readily satisfied in the cases Newmeyer considers of movement to COMP in PTI under the theoretical assumptions (those of Chomsky [1986b]) that he adopts. Newmeyer's ECP analysis then is evidently left without an account of (2).[5]

The argument just presented, however, is not complete. Newmeyer in fact may provide an account of (2) that attributes it neither to the ECP nor to Subjacency, but rather to the general inapplicability of PTI in embedded contexts, its "root" behavior in the sense of Emonds (1976). More specifically, Newmeyer proposes to capture the root behavior of processes like PTI through the requirement that in configurations of clausal complementation as in (4), V must govern C and C must govern I.

(4)
```
          VP
         /  \
       V      CP
             /  \
           C      IP
                 /  \
                     I
```

If PTI is derived by adjunction to IP, and the newly created IP serves as a barrier to government of I by C, then the required government chain in configurations such as (4) is broken, resulting in ungrammaticality. Newmeyer accommodates the proposal of Hooper and Thompson (1973) that root transformations may apply in embedded clauses if these clauses are asserted by allowing the IP of asserted clauses only to undergo extraposition by adjunction to the governing VP. In the resulting configuration, IP is no longer a complement to C and so is exempt from the government requirement on complementation. As Newmeyer shows, there is independent reason to think that only asserted complements may undergo movement in contexts of topicalization and parenthetical formation. In short, Newmeyer's proposal very elegantly captures in syntactic terms the root/non-root asymmetry in applications of PTI and other processes analyzed in terms of adjunction to IP, while still accommodating the objections of Hooper and Thompson (1973). We note that it is in fact consistent with our own analyses of root constructions previously analyzed as stylistic.

Returning now to (2), and assuming this account of the root behavior of certain constructions, note that Newmeyer might attempt to attribute the ungrammaticality of (2) to the root nature of PTI. Then in (2) either the embedded IP may not undergo extraposition (since *wonder* is perhaps not an assertive predicate), and the required government relation between C and I is blocked by the adjunction configuration, or extraposition of the embedded IP is allowed, and the *wh*-phrase in COMP fails to c-command its variable in the extraposed IP.[6] But then this account would falsely predict that (5) should be grammatical.

(5)   *Which room did you say that there walked into several people with canes?

In (5) *say* is indisputably an assertive predicate, so that the embedded application of PTI should be possible only under extraposition and adjunction to the matrix VP of the embedded IP. But in the resulting configuration, the *wh*-phrase in the matrix COMP does c-command its variable in the extraposed IP, and the ECP is satisfied for the trace of the *wh*-phrase quite apart from the *wh*-phrase itself. Even assuming Newmeyer's account of the root/non-root asymmetry, then, the ECP analysis provides no account of the ungrammaticality of (5), and an insufficient account of the ungrammaticality of (2). We conclude that an analysis that attributes the extraction restrictions in PTI to Subjacency, as ours does, is preferable to one in terms of the ECP.

2.2   Coopmans (1987)

Coopmans (1987) considers primarily the analysis of D/L, ultimately extending his account to PTI as well. The central feature of his account is his claim that verbs that participate in D/L (and PTI) must be intransitive, specifically either passive or unaccusative.[7] In his view, the postverbal subject is base generated as the thematic object of the intransitive verb (so accounting for the lack of objects in D/L), but due to the preposing of the argument PP may remain in its D-structure object position at S-structure.[8] The topicalized PP serves to license the expletive pro that appears in the thematically empty subject position, and Case marking of the postverbal subject is accomplished by lowering of INFL to V prior to S-structure. The restrictions on extraction in D/L Coopmans attributes to the Doubly Filled COMP Filter, under the assumption that the topicalized PP appears in COMP.

Our primary objection to this analysis is that the class of verbs participating in D/L and PTI are not exclusively unaccusative, although it is certainly true that many unaccusative verbs readily allow both D/L and PTI. Nevertheless, there are standardly unergative verbs that also participate in either construction, such as *walk* or *run*.

(6)   a. Into the room walked/ran John.
       b. There walked/ran into the room several young men with long hair.

Coopmans argues that a number of unergative verbs may in fact appear as unaccusatives in Dutch just in case they cooccur with locative adverbials. Nevertheless, his claims for these verbs in Dutch do not hold for their English counterparts, as seen by the contrast in grammaticality between the examples in (7) and the corresponding cases in (6b).

(7)   a. *There walked a man into the room.
        b. *There ran two joggers down the street.

Following Milsark (1974), we hold that unaccusative verbs in English typically tolerate the presence of Existential *there* with corresponding effects on word order (the unaccusative object immediately follows the verb), definiteness (the unaccusative object must be indefinite), and heaviness (the unaccusative object need not be heavy), as below.

(8)   a. There appeared an/*the angel before him.
        b. There arose a/*the question during the meeting.
(9)   a. There appeared before him the angel he had seen in his dreams.
        b. There arose during the meeting the one question everyone wanted to avoid.

Clearly verbs such as *walk* and *run* do not pattern with *appear* and *arise* in these respects even when accompanied by a locative adverbial.

   In addition, it is not the case that any unaccusative or passive verb freely gives rise to D/L. Consider the contrast between *appear* and *disappear* in examples (10) and (11), and the failure of D/L with the passive verbs in (12).

(10)   a. John appeared out of the mist.
       b. Out of the mist appeared John.
(11)   a. John disappeared into the mist.
       b. *Into the mist disappeared John.
(12)   a. *Out of the country was flown the president.
       b. *In the arm was shot Bill.

In our view the predominance of unaccusative and passive verbs in D/L does deserve an explanation, but does not itself characterize the restriction. In the account we offer in Chapter Three, the restriction to intransitive verbs is a consequence of the raising of V to I in conjunction with the principle that the trace of V may not assign Case (see Baker [1988]). We propose, following Rochemont (1978), that the further restriction to just a subclass of intransitive verbs may be attributed to the presentational requirement on V in these constructions.[9] The predominance of unaccusative verbs is a consequence of this presentational requirement. Since unaccusative verbs typically do not have agentive subjects, they are quite readily construed as presentational in the required sense. Unaccusative and passive verbs that may not readily have a presentational interpretation are correspondingly restricted from D/L, as with (11b) and (12).

Coopmans' analysis encounters other difficulties as well. It does not characterize the full range of data in connection with D/L that we presented in Chapter Three and used to motivate our analysis of D/L as derived in part through the topicalization of VP rather than PP. It also fails to capture the correspondence of heaviness of the postverbal subject with PTI in contrast to D/L both in the simple case and under extraction of the PP, as we discussed in sections 1 and 5 of Chapter Three. In addition, the proposal to capture the restrictions on extraction in D/L and PTI through appeal to the Doubly Filled COMP Filter and the corresponding analysis of Topicalization as movement to COMP fails to accommodate the full range of extraction restrictions analyzed in Chapter Three. Finally, the use of expletive pro in English gives rise to a series of problems concerning its very limited distribution (it may appear only in D/L and PTI) that remain for the most part unaddressed by Coopmans. Since Coopmans' paper, like Newmeyer's, is to some degree programmatic, these failures might conceivably be overcome in a more well-developed analysis of the sort Coopmans advances. Nevertheless, we think that any attempt to derive the major properties of D/L or PTI through appeal to an unaccusative analysis must of necessity either ignore some of the pertinent data as we have discussed above, or render ad hoc the characterization of the class of unaccusative verbs.

3   The Focus Effect

At the beginning of our study we raised two questions concerning the class of stylistic constructions of Rochemont (1978).

> (i) Why are these constructions syntactically restricted in the way that they are?
>
> (ii) Why do these constructions require that a specific phrase be focused, and why that phrase?

As we noted, Rochemont (1978) attempted to answer these questions by relegating the derivation of the constructions in question to the stylistic rule component of Chomsky and Lasnik (1977) and by reformulating the contribution of PF level information to semantic representations, requiring that such contributions be restricted to non-truth-conditional functions such as focus. We have seen that this answer is too strong on both counts. The so-called stylistic rules may in fact interact, though in a limited fashion, with pre-S-structure applications of Move a, and they may also affect aspects of the truth-conditional interpretation of sentences they apply in. For these reasons, our study has been devoted to finding a different set of answers to questions (i) and (ii).

Our strategy in responding to (i) has been to assume that these constructions are not in fact stylistic in the sense intended by Rochemont (1978) but are rather derived prior to S-structure by whatever mechanisms exist for derivation at that level, especially Move a. Then the failure and the ability of these specific cases to interact with other applications of Move a must be attributed to independent principles of grammar. For the most part, we have been able to reduce the syntactic restrictions in question to applications of Subjacency and the ECP, given the very detailed investigation of the constituent structure of these constructions that we have undertaken here.

Thus, our answer to (i) hinges on Universal Grammar. In particular, we claim that these constructions must show the restrictions they exhibit because of their syntactic form, the manner of their derivation, and the properties of English syntax as determined by UG. This account appears to us very reasonable, especially given the highly stylistic flavor of the constructions, their relative infrequence in some cases, and the necessary paucity of evidence concerning their properties and restrictions in the course of acquisition. That English speakers agree as extensively as they do in judgments of the relative acceptability of germane examples would otherwise be not only surprising but beyond explanation. Whether our specific account is correct or not, we take it that any potentially successful attempt to answer (i) must adopt the same general strategy that we have adopted here, to derive the syntactic restrictions in evidence in such cases from a principled view of grammatical theory seen as a function of UG.

Let us then consider how we might find an answer to question (ii) posed above. We suggest that (ii) should be answered in the same way that we have answered (i). That is, the obligatory focusing in these constructions should be attributed to their specific syntactic configurations in interaction with a principle of UG from which it follows that these constructions must exhibit the FE with respect to a specific phrase.

Such an approach is rendered all the more attractive when it is considered how knowledge relating to the focusing property of these constructions might be acquired. Knowledge of the FE amounts to the knowledge that a specific phrase in some construction must be a focus, in the sense that the sentence in which the phrase occurs is deemed acceptable in a given context of utterance only if the phrase in question is not c-construable.[10] A speaker with this knowledge therefore recognizes the contrast in acceptability of examples (2a, b) in the context of (1).

(1)   Where did John sit?
(2)   a. John sat at the head of the table.
        b. At the head of the table sat John.

More specifically, in part what must be acquired with the FE is the knowledge that (2b) is not a possibly appropriate response to the question in (1).

It is by now widely recognized that acquiring knowledge that a given sequence is unacceptable poses difficulties for any account of the acquisition of knowledge concerning language. In the case under consideration here, it does not appear plausible, even without solid empirical evidence, to claim that each learner of English is instructed by adult speakers in the proper discourse use of sentences like that in (2b). It is similarly implausible that the learner comes to have the required knowledge through the influence of direct or indirect negative evidence.[11] It is therefore reasonable to consider that some feature of the constructions in question signals the presence of the FE, and that this feature is identified for the learner as a function of UG. On this model, knowledge of the contrast in acceptability of (2a,b) in the context indicated is acquired with the feature, common to this and similar constructions, that identifies the FE. Adopting this perspective, let us then ask what this feature might be.

There are several hypotheses that we may dismiss immediately given the results of our syntactic investigation in the foregoing chapters. The Stylistic Rule Hypothesis (SRH) of Rochemont (1978) we have already noted encounters empirical difficulties in suggesting that the FE is associated with constructions derived in a stylistic (postcyclic) component of rules in sentence grammar. Moreover under the SRH, derivation in the stylistic rule component is only a sufficient and not a necessary property of a structural focus construction since in the analysis of Rochemont (1978), English *it* clefts are not derived by stylistic rule and yet they display the FE.

A second hypothesis is that the FE is obligatorily associated with all instances of rightward movement or dependency in English. However, to claim that the FE is uniquely associated with constructions derived by rightward movement of the focused phrase is not consistent with the available syntactic evidence, as we have seen. Of the constructions we have examined in detail here, only one (NP Shift) is derived by the rightward movement of a phrase. Moreover, although NP Shift and EX share the property that they involve a rightward dependency of sorts (i.e., a phrase in A-bar position is related to an A-position to its left), this feature is not shared by SI given our account of this construction in Chapter Three. Thus, the FE may not be predictably associated with rightward dependency.

A similar hypothesis is suggested by Whitney (1984). Whitney proposes to characterize all constructions involving movement to A-bar position as obligatory focusing constructions in terms of her A-bar Focus Principle (Whitney [1984, 191]).

A-bar Focus Principle
      If a results from adjunction to an A-bar position, then a is necessarily focused.

There are several problems with this account. First, in considering only constructions in which the focused phrase has undergone movement, the A-bar Focus Principle is too weak in that it incorrectly excludes EX and SI, given our analyses in the preceding chapters. Second, the A-bar Focus Principle is too strong in that it requires obligatory focusing in all leftward A-bar movement constructions. Whitney recognizes this difficulty and attempts to argue that all leftward movement to A-bar position results in focusing of the moved phrase. While this is a plausible analysis in the cases of *wh*-question movement and the *it*-cleft construction (cf. Rochemont [1986]), as well as with Negative Constituent Preposing (cf. Rochemont [1978]), it is not at all plausible in the case of topicalization.[12] The A-bar Focus Principle, then, is both too weak and too strong for our purposes.

Rochemont (1986) and Culicover and Wilkins (1984) suggest a further alternative, that the FE in such cases is associated with the movement or appearance of a phrase in a universally identified focus position in the sentence. These authors take that position to be a VP adjoined one. However, our analysis of relevant cases (SI and PTI in particular) shows clearly that this hypothesis cannot be upheld. In NP Shift the structural focus is not always adjoined to VP (compare HNPS and PTI) and in SI the focused phrase appears at S-structure in its D-structure position. Thus, while this alternative has the virtue of associating the FE with a unique structural configuration, the proposed configuration is not empirically adequate.

We think a more successful alternative is one that adapts the proposal of Rochemont (1986, chapter 5) to accommodate the similar focusing effect of the cleft construction. Rochemont suggests that a cleft focused phrase is one that appears at S-structure in a subcategorizable position but is not θ-marked in that position by the governing head. We propose below a suitable revision of this principle that subsumes the cleft cases analyzed in Rochemont (1986) and the constructions examined here under a single generalization, which we will refer to simply as the Focus Principle. By "structural focus" in (3), we mean a focused phrase that is identified as a focus by virtue of its appearing in a specific position in a given construction, with the attendant consequences for well-formedness of relevant question-answer sequences, as we have seen.

(3)   *The Focus Principle*[13]

α is a *structural focus* if

> (i) α = NP, CP, PP
> (ii) there is a β = X° such that β canonically governs α and α is neither Case-marked nor θ-marked by β
> (iii) β is not excluded by any γ, γ = X^{max}, that dominates α

Requirement (ii) of (3) is designed to accommodate the structural configurations we have been most directly concerned with in this study. "Canonical government" refers to the canonical government configuration of Kayne (1983), which for English is to the right.[14] Consider this requirement in light of the structural focus configurations below.

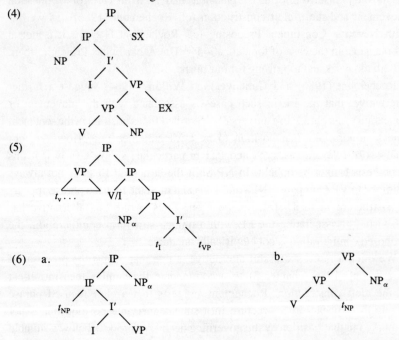

(4)
(5)
(6) a.   b.

Figure (4) gives the structural representations for EX defended in Chapter Two, figure (5) the representation for SI, and figures (6a, b) the configurations for PTI and HNPS, respectively. In each structure, $a = \text{NP}_a/\text{EX}/\text{SX}$ is canonically governed by a $X°$ (either I or V) that neither Case-marks nor θ-marks it.[15]

Given that I is not a lexical head, the stipulation in (iii) is designed to exclude the configuration in (7), where C canonically governs NP and neither Case- nor θ-marks, NP, yet NP is not a structural focus.

(7)

Note that I in (7) does not qualify as an appropriate $X°$ governing NP for the purposes of (3) because I does not canonically govern NP in (7). The canonical government requirement is evident also in (8), the structure corresponding to an example like (9), where NP is again governed by I but not canonically.

(8)

(9)   Into the room nude he walked.

The requirement of canonical government has several further consequences. It satisfactorily distinguishes topicalization, which we have assumed to be derived by left adjunction to IP, from PTI. Only the latter is identified as a focus construction, as required. Further, it prevents any element appearing in SPEC,CP from being necessarily identified as a structural focus under government by C.[16] Finally, it correctly distinguishes English, where canonical government is to the right, and German. In German, the focused phrase evidently appears to the left of the governing head. The simple observation that English structural foci appear at the apparent right periphery of the sentence is also accommodated.

The restriction of a to NP,CP,PP in (3i) is meant to characterize the fact that adjuncts appearing in X,VP or X,IP position are not necessarily focused in the manner of (4)–(6) with the corresponding effect on the well-formedness of question–answer sequences. This point is readily illustrated. Consider for instance the following.

(10)   a. Did anyone arrive nude?
         b. Yes. A friend of Mary's arrived nude.
(11)   a. Did anyone leave early?
         b. Yes, John left early.

That the question–answer sequences in (10)–(11) are fully well-formed shows that adjuncts are not structurally focused.

While the Focus Principle as stated in (3) is evidently empirically adequate to the task of identifying just the constructions in English that yield the FE, the stipulations it requires in (i) and (iii) in particular are *ad hoc* and thus unappealing.[17] Let us therefore reconsider these stipulations and ask whether they may be plausibly derived under another point of view. Consider first (i). As we have just seen, (i) is required to exclude adjuncts as structural foci. Now let us suppose that base-generated adjuncts are predicates, as for example in the analysis of Culicover and Wilkins (1984). Then (i) is restateable as a condition that a not be a predicate. This revised condition is significantly more natural than (3i) when considered in the light of the requirement in (3ii) that a not be in a Case- or θ-relation with the canonically governing head. In particular, it appears that any phrase in a canonically governed position that has no immediate relation to the governing head must be a structural focus. We assume that in the typical case (compare pseudoclefts) predicates either take the governing head as an argument or undergo merger with the projection of the head to seek an argument outside. (See Higginbotham [1985], Culicover [1988].) The set of categories stipulated in (3i) are just those categories that may fail to be interpreted as predicates when appearing in the position of an adjunct.

Consider next the stipulation (iii) of (3). As noted, this structural requirement excludes NP in (7) from being identified as a structural focus under canonical government by C. It might be possible to eliminate (iii) if we restricted the requirement of government to government by a lexical head. At first glance, this appears too strong, since while it excludes C as a possible governor for (3), it also excludes I. Canonical government by I is not in fact critical in identifying SI as a focusing construction (cf. [5]), given our analysis of this construction as requiring V raising to I. We have assumed that the amalgamated head has the features of V as well as I and thus is readily interpreted as lexical in the required sense. Thus, in (5) NP_a is canonically governed by a lexical head as required. (Note that for PAB we must assume *be* to be lexical in the required sense.) In contrast, in PTI in (6a) the structural focus is identified only under canonical government by I. So PTI would appear to provide a major obstacle to eliminating condition (3iii) in favor of a stronger statement of condition (ii).[18]

Suppose, on the other hand, that we were to assume that PTI does involve V raising to I, similar in this respect to SI. Then NP_a in (6a) would in fact be canonically governed by a lexical head (the amalgamated V/I) and so correctly identified as a structural focus. We could then conveniently eliminate condition (iii) from (3) without adverse consequences. An advantage of this analysis is that it provides an account of the predicate of appearance restriction in PTI and of the similarity of verb classes that may participate in PTI and SI. Moreover, this analysis suggests an account of the well-known observation that in both PTI and SI the participating verb must generally be intransitive.[19] Let us suppose that there is a parameter differentiating English and languages where there is unrestricted raising of V to I, such as Vata, German, etc., to the effect that only in the latter may the trace of a verb assign Case. In English we continue to assume that only the head itself may assign Case after movement and only when it governs and is adjacent to the NP to be Case-marked. Since in its derived position in I, V neither governs nor is adjacent to its object, the object may not be Case-marked. This establishes a strict correlation between V raising to I in SI and PTI and the possible presence of an object, as desired.

An apparent difficulty for this account arises with the assignment of nominative Case in configurations of SAI, as in (12).

(12)   Did John t_I leave?

By the account just suggested, t_I may not assign Case. But now note that *did* in (10) appears under our assumptions in the head position of CP, and from that position governs the subject NP *John* directly. It is therefore available to Case-mark *John* from its derived position. There is some evidence in support of this account of (12). Note that while leftward assignment of nominative Case in English by I does not apparently require adjacency, adjacency of I in its derived position and NP is required in SAI contexts like (12). Thus, compare the examples in (13).

(13)   a. John probably will leave.
  b. *Will probably John leave?
  c. Will John probably leave?

The ungrammaticality of (13b) is accommodated if we assume that the adjacency requirement on Case assignment in English holds in cases of canonical government only.

Let us assume then that the stipulation in (3iii) may be eliminated entirely, in favor of a stronger statement of condition (ii) requiring canonical government by a lexical head only. Then the Focus Principle may be reformulated as (14).[20]

(14)   *The Focus Principle*
  α is a *structural focus* if
  (i) there is a lexical head β that canonically governs α and α is neither Case-marked nor θ-marked by β
  (ii) α is not a predicate that is θ-related to β

The Focus Principle as stated in (14) properly characterizes the constructions we have investigated in this study, as summarized in (4)–(6), assuming now that PTI is derived in part through V raising to I.[21] Principle (14) also accommodates the cleft and pseudocleft constructions, under appropriate assumptions.[22] We have already seen that the Focus Principle does not apply to topicalization, Left Dislocation, and all constructions involving movement to COMP (e.g. relative clauses, embedded *wh*-questions, comparatives, etc.) The Right Node Raising construction of English is also excluded if we assume that the corresponding representation is a three-dimensional structure joined at the ''raised'' constituent (Goodall [1984]).

While our discussion of English constructions has not been fully exhaustive, it appears to be broad enough to render (14) a plausible working hypothesis. It remains to be seen how (14) will stand up under crosslinguistic testing, and whether it is subject to parametric variation in any respect.

4 The Heaviness Effect

As a final point let us consider whether it is possible to subject the Heaviness Effect (HE) identified in Chapter One: 4 to a structural analysis similar to that just proposed for the FE. Recall that the problem here was that the HE, while apparently related to the FE, does not follow from it. In particular, the HE is associated only with HNPS and PTI, and not for example with SI. We suggest that the HE is predictably associated with the structural configuration identified in (15).

(15) *The Heaviness Principle*
> If (referential) NP appears in A-bar position and is canonically governed by a lexical head, then NP must be heavy.

Since in order to satisfy (15), NP must also satisfy (14), the relation of the HE to the FE is appropriately characterized.

5 Conclusion

In the Introduction to this book we articulated two main goals. First, we sought to explain the well-known restrictions on so-called "stylistic" constructions in terms of independent principles of grammar such as the ECP and Subjacency, in conjunction with specific structural analyses of the stylistic constructions in question, involving applications of Move a. Second, we sought to account for the fact that there is a class of constructions in English (as well as in other languages) that are necessarily "stylistic". Our hypothesis at the outset was that what characterizes many if not all stylistic constructions is that they display "structural focus", that is, focus that is tied necessarily to properties of the configuration.

The results of this study are in some respects even stronger than those that we set out to achieve. Most importantly, we have seen that the general application of Move a in English, subject to ECP and Subjacency, inevitably yields constructions that have otherwise been seen as "stylistic" or peripheral. In a sense, these constructions are as central to English as are Passive or *wh* movement. To put it in another way, the existence of constructions such as Stylistic Inversion, Heavy NP Shift and Presentational *there* Insertion in a language such as English is a necessary consequence of the fact that English has syntactic *wh* movement, canonical government to the right and discrete modal anxiliaries in INFL.

What is special about these constructions, then, is not that they are "stylistic," i.e. that they form a distinct category of constructions outside of "Core Grammar" along the lines of Chomsky and Lasnik (1977) and Rochemont (1978). Rather, they are stylistic simply in virtue of the fact that as a consequence of their configuration, they require a particular focus interpretation that limits their distribution in discourse.

For future research we pose the hypothesis that the general perspective articulated here can be maintained in the further analysis of English and in the detailed analysis of other languages. If this perspective is a correct one, at least in its general outlines, one immediate and desirable consequence is a significant reduction in the expressive capacity of the theory of grammar.

To the extent that all syntactic constructions are derivable by applications of Move α subject to Subjacency and the ECP it is possible to rule out entirely the possibility of "stylistic" or "peripheral" constructions that are subject to different or more relaxed constraints. The range of possible grammatical hypotheses made available by linguistic theory is thereby narrowed, the explanatory power of the theory is enhanced, and we move closer towards the overarching objective of linguistic theory: to account for the ability of a language learner, faced with a complex range of linguistic data from a language, to accurately and rapidly acquire the grammatical knowledge that these linguistic data exemplify.[23]

Notes

Introduction
1 Since in the coming chapters we will be dwelling at length on the specific properties of each of the stylistic constructions in (1)–(4), for the purposes of the present discussion we will present examples freely from among them, leaving a detailed discussion for later chapters.
2 In fact, this effect of stylistic rules is not represented in (5), and motivates a revision of the grammatical model proposed in Chomsky and Lasnik (1977), as discussed in Rochemont (1978). Rochemont proposes that PF should be permitted to feed semantic interpretation independent of LF, but only with respect to discourse-related notions, perhaps restricted to focus. LF is assumed to provide all information relevant to the truth-conditional interpretation of sentences.
3 In fact, the arguments we present to this effect, and the account of focus that we presuppose and summarize in Chapter One, are drawn exclusively from Rochemont (1986), which builds on the account of focus and sentence stress presented in Culicover and Rochemont (1983).
4 See also Maruta (1985), Newmeyer (1987) and Coopmans (1987), who independently propose to derive the category of stylistic rules under principles of UG. We criticize these accounts in Chapter Five: 2.

1   Theoretical assumptions
1 In this regard, see Jackendoff's (1972) critique of EQUI. Jackendoff argued specifically that EQUI had to be a rule of interpretation, because the use of semantic conditions violated the view of EQUI as a rule of autonomous syntax. As further evidence to support the methodological principle of autonomy, Jackendoff showed that the traditional transformational account of EQUI could not work anyway.
2 Obviously this methodological restriction limits one's options severely in cases where there are surface order constraints on noun phrases in terms of features like [animate], [human] and so on. If the methodology is well-founded, these limitations should prove to be productive. For discussion see Hale et al. (1977).
3 This is in essence the Head Movement Constraint (HMC) of Travis (1984), adapted in Baker (1985). We propose an amendment to the HMC in Chapter Three, taking it to follow from the ECP, as proposed in Baker (1985), Chomsky (1986b).
4 In fact, the definition of L-marking in (3) is in need of a more careful formulation, as argued in Chomsky (1986b). For our purposes here, however, we can safely assume the formulation in (3).

159

5 We note here that if a maximal projection is L-marked then all its segments must be L-marked as well. The reason is that configurations of adjunction that are base generated are not islands to extraction, as with adjuncts to VP or small clause structures.

6 For an account of the Subjacency parameter as it applies to Italian and related cases adapting the model of Subjacency presented here, see Rochemont (1988).

7 Note that in contrast to the analysis of Chomsky (1986b), adjunction to a barrier will not improve the prospects for extraction, since movement from the adjoined position itself must also satisfy Subjacency, but can do so only if the position being moved to is contained within the next higher maximal projection. As noted, we follow Chomsky (1986b) in assuming that a maximal projection can move only to a SPEC position or by adjunction to X^{max}. If the SPEC position is free, then movement directly to it would not have violated Subjacency in the first place. On the other hand, movement to an adjoined position will continue to violate Subjacency, as illustrated in the diagram below.

(i) $[_{\gamma'} [_{\gamma} \ldots [_{\beta'} [_{\beta} \ldots t \ldots]]]]$

If β in (i) is a barrier for t, then movement from β to a position adjoined to γ ($= X^{max}$) (i.e., γ') is non-subjacent, given the presence of γ, whether movement proceeds through β' or not.

8 We must assume following Chomsky (1986b) that sentential complements to N are also generated as adjuncts, in order to characterize the oddity of (i).

(i)   *Who did you make the claim that Bill saw?

9 See Baltin (1981) and Rochemont (1978) for analyses of topicalization as adjunction to IP (S). Rochemont (1988) provides further argument that English topicalization is best derived by adjunction to IP, while rejecting the arguments of Baltin (1981) and Rochemont (1978).

10 Note that it must be assumed that *what* cannot move by adjoining first to the topicalized phrase, producing a S-structure equivalent of absorption (see May [1985]), and presumably satisfying Subjacency.
   Note also that Lasnik and Saito's analysis presumes that each segment of a maximal projection counts as maximal in the application of Subjacency, and also in the application of the ECP to be discussed below.

11 At least under the plausible assumption that there is no θ-relation between C and t in (11). We note that in fact, the very examples Lasnik and Saito (1984) use to justify a definition of the lexical government in terms of θ-government, involving intermediate traces in COMP, require a configurational definition if the ECP is to be seen as a conjunctive requirement, as we propose below.

12 The notion that traces must meet a requirement of lexical government independent of any requirement for antecedent government has been argued or assumed by numerous other authors, among them Jaeggli (1982), Stowell (1985), Aoun et al. (1987), Rizzi (1987), and Longobardi (1987).

13 This analysis would also be consistent with an account of the sort advanced by Aoun et al. (1987), where the ECP (taken to be a binding requirement) requires

antecedent government and the lexical government requirement is established at PF and holds independent of the ECP. We do not pursue such an analysis here, but we note that it would appear to be equally consistent with the full range of phenomena we analyze in the coming chapters.

14 This proposal may suggest a different account of the lack of *that-t* effects with adjuncts (cf. (i)) than the LF *that* deletion analysis of Lasnik and Saito (1984).

(i) a.   Why did John say [(that) Bill left *t*]?
    b.   Who did John say [(*that) *t* left]?

In particular, if the overt complementizer is relevant only to lexical government of the subject trace and does not in fact block antecedent government from the SPEC,CP position, then since the adjunct trace is lexically governed within VP, the presence or absence of an overt complementizer should be irrelevant to whether the adjunct trace satisfies the ECP. Rather the adjunct trace will fail to satisfy the ECP just in case the most local SPEC,CP position is filled with some phrase other than its antecedent, so that it will appear that the only thing relevant to the licensing of an adjunct trace for the ECP will be antecedent government. This account is appealing in that it extends also to the contrast in (ii).

(ii) a.   Why did John leave?
     b.   *Who did leave?

We will not, however, adopt this proposal, since we will consider evidence in Chapter 4 that when there is an overt complementizer in cases such as (ib), the subject trace is neither lexically nor antecedent governed. Thus, we must retain the *that* deletion analysis of Lasnik and Saito (1984).

15 This account must be extended to configurations of Exceptional Case Marking, as in the analysis of Chomsky (1986b), presumably under the mechanism of SPEC-head agreement. To avoid the assumption that coindexing with a lexical head gives rise to antecedent government, we might alternatively make appeal to a disjunctive definition of the ECP that requires either θ-government or lexical and antecedent government, essentially as in Stowell (1985).

16 There are two other focusing constructions in English that we will not discuss here, the *it* cleft and the pseudocleft constructions. For a discussion of the former, see Rochemont (1986, chapter 5). On the focusing requirement associated with VP Fronting in its various manifestations, see Chapter Three.

17 There is of course a rich and varied tradition concerning the identification and interpretation of focus to which we cannot begin to do justice here. The perspective developed in Rochemont (1986) and presupposed here is heavily influenced in particular by earlier work on this topic by Bolinger, Halliday, and Chomsky, among others. For more detailed discussion and references, the reader is referred to Culicover and Rochemont (1983) and Rochemont (1986).

18 Throughout our discussion in this book, our presentation of example sentences makes use of upper case letters to indicate locations of sentence accents. Where this usage overlaps with conventional usage, as with the first person singular nominative pronoun *I*, the surrounding discussion will serve to clarify the intended

interpretation. As a rule, we will not indicate the location of accents in context sentences, unless it is critically relevant.

19 It is of course true that new information in the response that is not requested will also be focused, as follows on the accounts in our earlier work on this topic.

20 We follow Chomsky (1971) in assuming that a string focused in this way must always be a syntactic constituent, although this assumption is not always made; see for instance Jackendoff (1972) and Selkirk (1984). It appears that if we adopt the analysis of Rochemont (1986, chapter 3), we can maintain the assumption that focus applies to syntactic constituents, even in the face of the criticisms advanced by Jackendoff and by Selkirk.

21 Unless of course we make further restrictive assumptions about the discourse context preceding the question (5). See Rochemont (1986) for discussion.

22 In a "typical" question/answer sequence, unlike (10), it is the truth value of the response that is focused by accenting the auxiliary element. For example, in response to (10A):

> No, he DIDN'T (talk to his brother).
> Yes, he DID (talk to his brother).

23 We say "must" because even where the constituent that is focused in the response is not "new" (as is likely to be the case in a response to a question like (i)), the information conveyed by the response is.

> (i)   Who talked to Mary – John, or Bill, or both?

24 It should be noted that both Chomsky (1971) and Jackendoff (1972) acknowledge that the two uses of the term presupposition may be distinct. This caveat has not been expressly indicated by others who have adapted the presupposition account of focus to other descriptions. In our view, the choice of terminology has simply been unfortunate.

25 We use the term *syntactically unanalyzed* to draw an informal distinction between semantically compositional and noncompositional compounds, where the former evidently may have accent assigned internal to the compound, whereas the latter may not. Thus, compare our examples with *bluebird* below, with the following example modelled on a parallel case in Ladd (1980).

> (i) A: Did the faculty discuss that issue yet?
>   B: No, they are going to talk about it at the faculty MEETING later TODAY.

Out of context, the compound *faculty meeting* is pronounced with prominence on the first member, *faculty*, but context may influence this assignment of prominence internal to the compound, as in (i).

26 It may be that failure to assign a focus-related accent appropriately in the stylistic constructions to be discussed here in fact parallels contrastive stress assignment in being restricted to contexts of repair. See Rochemont (1986) for discussion.

27 The English pseudocleft construction, illustrated in (i), is typically assumed to parallel the cleft construction with regard to these properties.

> (i)   What John bought for his wife was a fur coat.

Thus, (i) also is not a possible response to (25), though it is to (24). We will not extend our discussion to include the pseudocleft construction in the present study.

28 It is of course true that structural foci must be accented. In the framework of Rochemont (1986) this requirement follows as a consequence of well-formedness conditions on the LF representations of structural focus constructions, together with assumptions regarding the LF representation of accent-related focus assignments.

29 It is argued in Rochemont (1986) that HNPS constructions and *it* clefts are not fully functionally identical, even though they both serve to focus a given phrase. In particular, these constructions seem to identify different focus interpretations for the phrases in question – a Presentational interpretation in the case of HNPS and a Contrastive one in the case of *it* clefts. Rochemont coins the terms *constructional focus* and *cleft focus*, respectively, to distinguish the two cases. We will ignore this distinction in the discussion to follow and accordingly coin the term *structural focus* to refer to both types of cases.

30 The Focus Effect with Extraposition from NP seems not as strong as in the other cases. For example, though we have marked it as odd, (39b) is not as odd as the (b) examples of (40)–(45). We have no account of this, but will continue to assume that Extraposition from NP too identifies a structural focus.

31 The FE and the HE are confused also in the discussion of Rochemont (1986, 120ff.).

32 Even for subjects, the DE cannot be tied to the presence of an overt expletive element in the vacated subject position. For instance, Portuguese is a null subject language with postverbal subjects characterized by the HE (cf. Safir [1985] for discussion).

33 Subject possibly to parametric variation, as for example in Italian where postposed subjects seem not to exhibit the HE, or in French *wh* triggered Stylistic Inversion. Of course, this issue depends critically on the resolution of a prior one, concerning the proper grammatical analysis of the Italian and French constructions.

2   Extraposition from NP

1 Earlier and somewhat different versions of the analysis in section 1 of this chapter have appeared as Rochemont and Culicover (1988) and Culicover and Rochemont (to appear).

2 These contrasts have been treated in various ways by many authors, including Ross (1967), Andrews (1975), Rochemont (1978), Baltin (1981, 1983, 1987a, b), Guéron (1980), Culicover (1980), Taraldsen (1981), Huang (1982), Guéron and May (1984), Chomsky (1986b).

3 See especially Ross (1967), Baltin (1981, 1983, 1987b). It might be thought that a stipulation distinguishing leftward and right movement is in fact independently motivated by the Presentational *there* (PTI) construction (cf. (i)), also assumed to involve rightward movement.

(i)   There walked into the room a man no one knew.

However, we argue in Chapter Four that in PTI the postverbal subject is adjoined to IP. Thus, a single unbounded application of Move a in PTI is excluded in the same fashion as non-cyclic unbounded leftward movement. Moreover, it would be mistaken to attribute the strict boundedness of rightward movement of heavy NPs to the Generalized Subjacency Condition of Baltin (1981) for example, even assuming a movement analysis for EX. As the sentences in (ii) show, NP Shift of heavy NPs in general (of which we treat PTI as a specific case) is more restricted than EX.

(ii) a.   Mary talked with someone yesterday who she hadn't seen in years.
     b.   *Mary talked with yesterday someone she hadn't seen in years.

In Chapter Four: 3, we provide an independently motivated account of cases like (iib), making reference to a general condition on rightward movement. Our account, which is related to the Uniformity Condition of Chomsky (1986a), extends beyond such cases to those for which Generalized Subjacency is irrelevant. It is therefore less *ad hoc* than Generalized Subjacency.

It is a noteworthy consequence of the analysis we offer in Chapter Four that EX may not be derived by rightward movement since it would be in obvious violation of the principle we propose. To the extent that our account of examples such as (iib) is motivated, then, we have a further argument against a movement account of EX.

4 Although it must be noted that Guéron and May (1984) appeal to successive cyclic applications of movement through COMP in the derivation of numerous instances of EX, so rendering an account of the contrast between (3a, b) even more difficult on a movement account of EX. Baltin (1987a, 20) also invokes a presumably successive cyclic analysis of movement in EX in order to allow degree complements to take scope outside the clause that most immediately contains their antecedents at S-structure.

We observe that the failure of Subjacency to block successive cyclic movement might be remedied, but only by appeal to a stipulation regarding (uniformity of) direction in applications of Move a. This stipulation might be thought to be independently required to block successive cyclic unbounded movement in PTI constructions, as below.

(i) a.   ??John explained that there had appeared to him a vision of the future to everyone who would listen.
    b.   *John explained that there had appeared to him to everyone who would listen a vision of the future.
    c.   *John explained had appeared to him to everyone who would listen a vision of the future.

We provide a different account of the ungrammaticality of (ib, c) in Chapter Four.

5 Analyses of the sort advanced by Gazdar (1981), Huck (1985), Sag (1987), and Kroch and Joshi (1987), to the extent they require the postulation of a "gap" within NP, are subject to the arguments against movement accounts that we present in C&R.

6 We ignore here the possibility that β is an A-bar binder of a trace elsewhere in the structure.

7 If β is a predicate or an operator, then the PFI will be satisfied only if β satisfies the well-formedness conditions specific to its type. We return in section 4 to one of the conditions that must be satisfied for predicates. See also Williams (1980), Rothstein (1983) and Culicover and Wilkins (1984), among others.

8 In fact, the analysis of C&R does not specifically exclude the possibility for rightward application of Move α to a phrase base-generated in non-extraposed position. In fact, extraposition in this fashion from a position within the subject NP must violate Subjacency and the ECP, so it is excluded. However, extraposition by movement of a phrase contained within an object, if it proceeds by adjunction to VP, satisfies both Subjacency and the ECP and is consistent with all the facts considered. The availability of such a derivation in these cases alone might be appealed to in an account of the less severe restrictions on OX in contrast to SX (for instance restrictions on verb classes, transitivity, etc.). (But see note 3.)

9 We have also assumed that adjunction by a maximal projection is possible only to a maximal projection, so barring adjunction to I' in these cases. See Chapter One and Chomsky (1986b).

10 Baltin (1987b) argues that the extraposed phrase must be Chomsky adjoined to VP, and not simply adjoined outside V' for instance. We do not reproduce this argument here, but we take it to be valid. The arguments in C&R against Baltin's analysis of EX remain consistent with this conclusion.

11 As in Chapter One, upper case signals the required *sole* locations of sentence accents in these examples and wherever else employed. Thus, in our judgment, (7a) for example is not as good if pronounced as in (ia), and even worse if pronounced as in (ib).

(i) a. A MAN came in with blond HAIR, and a WOMAN did TOO.
    b. A man came IN with blond hair, and a WOMAN did TOO.

We cannot overemphasize the importance of assigning accents in the reading of examples only as indicated.

12 Our definition of government is adapted in part from Chomsky (1986b), although it makes no reference to the notion "barrier". That it should is indicated by the examples below.

(i) a. I found it in a magazine yesterday that was on the coffee table.
    b. John talked to many people at the party that he already knew.

In the S-structures for (i) the NP antecedent of the extraposed phrase is contained within a maximal projection (PP) that excludes the extraposed phrase. The PP in this case, however, is not a barrier, being L-marked. In parallel cases where the PP is not L-marked, it in fact serves as a barrier to government for purposes of the CP, as would be expected under Chomsky's approach.

(ii) a. *In which magazine did you see it which was on the table?
     b. *I noticed the mistake in a picture by accident of Ronald Reagan.

Example (iia) is drawn from Baltin (1978, 82), and illustrates that PP in COMP is not L-marked in the required sense. In (iib) the PP is an adjunct and not an argument to the verb, evidently blocking the government relation between the extraposed complement and its antecedent.

We note in addition that Chomsky's assumption that VP is not L-marked, contrary to our assumption in Chapter One following Lasnik and Saito (forthcoming), is supported by these observations and the claim that OX may not adjoin higher than VP. That is, unless VP is a barrier, OX may govern its antecedent from the adjoined to VP position.

These observations conceal a more general difficulty for our approach. Our assumptions in Chapter One give rise to definitions for government, Subjacency and antecedent government such that only the latter two make reference to barrier-hood in their statements. But the examples in (i) and (ii) suggest a different view, if the CP is formulated to require government and is responsible for the contrast between (i) and (ii).

13 C&R provide no account of cases including violations of the CP (or Subjacency in a movement analysis of EX), as in (i). (see Guéron [1978].)

(i) a.   How much of a proof exists of this theorem?
     b.   Have all of the commentaries appeared on Mary's work?
     c.   The construction of a bridge was proposed which would span the Delaware River.
     d.   Several pounds of apples were bought that turned out to be rotten.

We note that in all of the examples of (i) extraposition of the higher PP within NP leads necessarily to ungrammaticality.

(ii) a.   *How much exists of a proof of that theorem?
     b.   *Have all appeared of the commentaries on Mary's work?
     c.   *The construction was proposed of a bridge which would span the Delaware River.
     d.   *Several pounds were bought of apples that turned out to be rotten.

If the correlation between (i) and (ii) is sufficiently strong, it suggests that the lower head noun of the subject NP is in such cases acting as the head of the full NP subject, so that the CP is in fact satisfied.

14 Rochemont (1986, notes 125, 126) discusses some variation in acceptability for a range of examples of the interaction of SX and VP Topicalization. The position we adopt here is that these cases are to be generally excluded.

15 Williams (1974, 123) observes that only CP may appear extraposed from a *wh*-phrase. He provides example (i).

(i)   *Who does he know with any sense?

While we do find (i) odd, we find (ii) considerably less so.

(ii)   Who do you know with blond hair?

Note that the non-extraposed counterpart of (i) in (iii) is also distinctly odd, as is the *wh*-in-situ with a PP modifier in (iv).

(iii)   *Who with blond hair do you know?

(iv)   *Who talked to who with blonde hair at the party?

We note also that the restriction against PP with *wh* does not hold in the same fashion for determiner *wh* phrases such as *which* and *how* as it does for nominal *wh*-phrases such as *who*.

(v) a.   Which woman with blonde hair did you talk to?

     b.   ?Which woman did you talk to with blonde hair?

(vi) a.   How many women with blonde hair do you know?

     b.   How many women do you know with blonde hair?

16 As C&R observes, this result makes a variety of predictions concerning the range of coreference readings possible in EX sentences with *wh*-phrase antecedents. We do not reproduce that discussion here, but we do note that the reconstruction effect for PP in *wh*-movement configurations is preserved under extraposition. Thus, (i) and (ii) are equally ungrammatical under a reading of coreference.

(i)   How many books about John did he read?

(ii)   How many books did he read about John?

17 This predicts that unlike SX and OX an extraposed phrase with a *wh* antecedent in COMP may not delete with VP under ellipsis. The prediction is apparently verified in the examples below.

(i) a.   *Who did John say would come to the party that everyone knew, and who did Mary say would?

     b.   *How many adults came into the room with red hair, and how many children did?

     c.   *Which of your friends didn't come to the party that you wanted to, and which of your friends did?

     d.   *How many women came to the party that you've never met before, and how many men did?

     e.   *Who did you invite to the party that I haven't met before, and who did Bill.

The critical cases are (i a–d), since (i e) may be independently excluded by the restriction against *wh* movement out of a deleted VP. It should also be expected, however, that an extraposed phrase with a *wh* antecedent in COMP may fail to delete with VP under ellipsis, but relevant examples such as those below do not appear to us to be any more acceptable than (i).

(ii) a.   *Who did John say would come to the party that everyone knew, and who did Mary say would that everyone disliked?

     b.   *How many adults came into the room with red hair, and how many children did with blond hair?

c.   *Which of your friends didn't come to the party that you wanted to, and which of your friends did that you dislike?

Given that ellipsis of VP in a *wh* question fails to interact with EX at all, examples (i) may not provide a valid test of constituent structure for the case in question.

18 With echo and quiz format questions it may be the LF position of the *wh*-phrase that conditions the height of attachment of the extraposed complement, as seen by the grammaticality of (i) on either of these readings.

(i)   Bill told her$_i$ that Sam was dating which student that the teacher$_i$ liked?

If echo and quiz format questions involve LF raising of the *wh*-in-situ, as in the analysis of Hendrick and Rochemont (1982), then the CP is presumably satisfied in these cases only at LF, on a par with result clauses as demonstrated by Guéron and May (1984).

May (1985, 61) claims that echo *wh* do exhibit weak crossover effects (WCO), suggesting that they undergo LF movement. This claim is undermined by the apparent lack of a WCO effect in (ii) in contrast to (iii).

(ii)   The woman he loved betrayed WHO?
(iii)   Who did the woman he loved betray?

19 We will see reason below to revise this conclusion for cases of result clause and comparative extraposition (RX and CX, respectively). Evidently, the CP must be satisfied at different levels dependent on the quantificational character of the antecedent. If the required antecedent is a non-quantified expression, the CP is satisfied at S-structure, and if the antecedent is a quantified expression, the CP is satisfied at LF.

20 The CP shows an additional restriction which we have not accommodated here on the range of A-bar phrases that may serve as antecedent for an extraposed phrase. Thus, in contrast to *wh* phrases in COMP, the antecedent may not appear in topic or in cleft focus position.

(i) a.   *That man, Bill didn't invite to his party who drinks heavily.
    b.   *It was that man that came to the party who drinks heavily.

The ungrammaticality of these cases may perhaps be related to the failure of an extraposed PP to undergo topicalization, as in (ii).

(ii)   *By Chomsky, a book appeared *t*.

Note that the CP is otherwise satisfied in both (i a) and (ii), assuming topicalization to proceed by adjunction to IP.

21 Note incidentally that the CED continues to provide an account of the lack of a noncontrol reading in (6b) if such result clauses are adjoined to VP as adjuncts, and not within VP as arguments as with controlled *too* result clauses (cf. Chomsky [1986b], Baltin [1987a]).

22 See also Chomsky (1981, 81ff.), Rouveret (1978). Akmajian (1975, 128) observes that EX is sometimes not strictly bounded, as in (i).

(i)   A number of stories soon appeared about Watergate.

He suggests that the structure of NPs with quantifier-like elements such as *a number of* may not be "two-tiered." In this case, presumably the head of the subject NP in (i) is *stories* and not *number*, and *a number of* is perhaps a QP specifier on the head.

23 This assumption has been common in many analyses of RX, especially in light of examples such as (11a). See for example Liberman (1974), Williams (1974).

Guéron and May (1984) argue that a movement analysis is favored in that it establishes the selectional relation between the QP antecedent of the result clause and the complementizer within the RX at D-structure. We assume that the selectional relation is instead satisfied at LF. In this view, D-structure represents only a partial satisfaction of selectional requirements, as seems appropriate. Consider for instance the selectional relation between a verb selecting an interrogative sentential complement and the *wh* phrase in SPEC,CP position. In some languages this relation is not satisfied until LF, and in no language is it evidently satisfied prior to S-structure.

24 Rouveret (1978), while adopting a movement analysis for result clauses in French, argues convincingly that the site of attachment of the result clause is conditioned by the scope of its QP antecedent at LF. (See also Williams [1974]). As Rouveret (p. 172) observes, his analysis is consistent also with an account of RX not involving movement. His concern is to represent the extent to which the RX/antecedent relation is bounded.

Chomsky (1981, 81ff.) explicitly invokes a construal and not a movement analysis for RX.

25 In fact, we will see directly below that LF movement of *so* does show certain bounding effects not considered by Guéron and May.

26 Liberman (1974, 88) observes that *so* may only take wide scope when it is not contained within the domain of a nominal head or a nonbridge verb. Thus, neither of the examples in (i) allows the wide scope interpretation.

(i) a.   Mary made the claim that John was so weird that we didn't invite him to dinner.
  b.   Mary announced that John was so weird that we didn't invite him to dinner.

Andrews (1975, 167) adds the observation that *so* may not take wide scope outside a sentential subject. While the narrow scope only reading of (i a) and the sentential subject effects might be made to follow from the ECP under current formulations (cf. Lasnik and Saito [1984], Chomsky [1986b]), that in (i b) may not. (Though see Stowell [1985].)

Rouveret (1978, 168ff.), in considering related examples in French RX, concludes that the boundedness restrictions on RX do not follow from Subjacency but rather from LF restrictions on the operation of QR. An ECP approach is potentially consistent with this conclusion, as we show below.

27 As expected, failure of the RX to be included with the VP under ellipsis is possible in (34a) only.

(i) a.   *John invited so many people to the party that Mary laughed, and Bill did that she cried.

   b.   So many men came to the party that Mary was thrilled, and so many women did that she cried.

28 These examples with ROX and RSX mirror the superficially parallel examples considered earlier with OX and SX. Nevertheless, the account of the paradigm we have offered for RX differs from that we offered for EX. We might alternatively characterize the contrast between (35) and (36) by assuming that the CP is in fact a twofold requirement for both binding and government, as in Rochemont and Culicover (1988), and claim that the binding requirement of the CP holds for RX at S-structure, as for EX. We do not adopt this solution here for the reasons that we must still assume that the government requirement of the CP holds at LF for RX and at S-structure for EX, thus undermining the notion that the CP is a uniform requirement. Note also that taking the CP to be a dual requirement of both government and binding also yields a redundancy since both relations require c-command, as pointed out to us by Geoffrey Pullum.

29 While this line of reasoning correctly accommodates our earlier example (11a), it presupposes that one of the NPs must always c-command the other. This assumption is not sufficient to exclude a multiple antededent reading for the extraposed complement in example (i) below.

(i)   John talked to a man about a woman on Saturday who he had just met.

Note that not only does (i) not allow a multiple antecedent reading, it also apparently allows only a single reading, where the antecedent of the extraposed phrase is *a woman* and not *a man*. Following Gazdar (1981), we take this property of (i) to be a function of the processing strategy that attaches incoming material as low as it can on the parse tree, as proposed in Frazier and Fodor (1978). From this it follows that (i) will independently fail to allow a multiple antecedent reading.

30 We must assume that a node does not dominate itself. Note that the lack of a government relation between both QPs and their respective RX phrases blocks the LF representation for (32) in which the instances of RX appear adjoined to IP rather than CP.

31 Andrews (1975, 165) claims otherwise on the basis of example (i) below.

(i)   Bill's teachers said he was smarter than anyone else.

To our ears, (i) does not sound especially good. Consider also:

(ii) a.   *Bill's mother doesn't realize that Bill is more intelligent than anyone else does.

   b.   ?*John thinks that more people came to the party than Bill does.

   c.   *?Susan said that more people came to the party than Bill did.

32 Thus, (41c) does not have the reading in (i).

(i)   More men than we invited met more women than we invited at the party.

Andrews (1975, 164) notes that multiple antecedents for a single CX is possible in conjoined structures, as in (ii).

(ii)   More men were singing and more women were dancing than I had ever seen on a stage at once.

33 This is also the analysis of CX advanced by Andrews (1975). The paradigm analysis of the comparative construction offered in Bresnan (1973) assumes otherwise, but is consistent with this view.
34 This would be the case if the *more* were adjoined to IP/VP or to the NP containing it. In any case, the properties of CX illustrated in (47) follow from the antecedent/ complement relation that holds between the CX and the NP.
35 Our judgment of the grammaticality of the examples below, drawn from Chomsky (1981, 82) differs from Chomsky's.

(i) a.   Pictures that more critics admired were for sale than I expected.
    b.   Pictures that were admired by more critics were for sale than I expected.

To our ears, these sentences are ungrammatical, in contrast to the other examples considered by Chomsky in this context, where the scope of *more* remains clause bounded. To the extent that (i) may be grammatical, we predict that the relevant intepretations are on the higher N *pictures*, assuming an LF raising analysis for *more* on a par with our account of similar examples with *so*.

Chomsky (1981, 83) argues that there is yet a further type of CX, as in (ii).

(ii)   John likes more people than Bill.

His claim is that *than*-NP CX pattern with sentence level CX in regard to construal properties. Again, we are inclined to agree overall, though we disagree with the judgment of grammaticality on the relevant interpretation for the example below.

(iii)   No one saw pictures that were admired by more excellent critics at the exhibit than John.

In our judgment, (iii) cannot be interpreted with wide scope for *more*, though it does allow a narrow scope interpretation.
36 We note here an unresolved problem for this analysis. If it is the IP that serves as the antecedent for the extraposed comparative in sentence level CX, then in such cases the comparative phrase may presumably only be adjoined to IP or higher. We therefore expect that sentence level CX, in contrast to the examples with CX considered in the text, will fail to pattern with VP under ellipsis or dislocation, regardless of the argument status of the NP containing the *more*. This prediction, however, is incorrect, as illustrated below for ellipsis.

(i) a.   John invited more people to the party than I expected, and Bill did too.

b.   More men came to the party than I expected, and more women did too.

37 Stucky (1987) disputes this claim for specific cases, also providing some counter-examples to the analysis to be presented below. Nevertheless, it is readily demonstrated that her claim (p. 402) that "non-heads that do not ever precede their heads can follow their respective heads in any number and in any order" is too strong, as seen for instance in the behavior of extraposed result clauses, which she fails to consider.

While some of the data we consider in this section may be disputed, we will present the relevant generalizations as firm and seek to provide a systematic account here, leaving the discussion of more recalcitrant cases for later research.

38 Though some authors have made appeal to the sort of nesting requirement we will defend here. See Williams (1974), Andrews (1975).

39 We emphasize that given the complexity of the examples required to illustrate the distributional generalizations, the judgments indicated are relative and not absolute.

40 Guéron and May (1984, 27) claim that multiple EX in a single sentence is impossible, on the basis of the example in (i).

(i)   Many books have been published by many authors recently who I know which I've enjoyed reading.

Their claim is that (i) is ungrammatical. We think it just clumsy. Thus, we think that (ii) is better, and that (i) and (ii) contrast with (iii), which has the wrong order of SX and OX.

(ii)   Many books have been published by many authors recently who I know personally that I've really enjoyed reading.

(iii)   *Many books have been published by many authors recently that I've really enjoyed reading who I know personally.

41 Note that, as might be expected with CX and EX, when pragmatically plausible, the extraposed complement is preferably construed with the lower NP. Thus, compare (6a) and (i).

(i)   Many women invited more men to the party than we talked to who were from Chicago.

In (i) it is difficult to get the SX reading on the extraposed complement.

42 Example (8) is taken from Guéron and May (1984, 3). The observation that RX must be final is made also in Williams (1974).

43 Examples similar to (15) (cf. (i)) are presented in Guéron and May (1984, 29) as a problem for their analysis of sentence level CX.

(i) a.   So many people ate more hush puppies at the fair than we expected that we ran out of them early.

    b.   *So many people ate more hush puppies at the fair that we ran out of them early than we expected.

Even for sentence level CX, our account correctly predicts the relative order restriction exhibited in (i), as will be seen below.

Incidentally, notice that example (14a) is improved with a sentence level CX (cf. (ii)). We have no explanation for the oddity of this example as it stands. We note only the contrast in degree of acceptability between (14a) and (14b).

(ii) a.   ?More people came to so many parties last year than we expected that we stopped having them.

    b.   *More people came to so many parties last year that we stopped having them than we expected.

44 Williams (1974, 127) observes a similar nesting requirement for clauses that are dependent on items with scope. He was concerned in particular with RX and EX constructions with QP antecedents and with RX and *must . . . in order to . . .* cases. The analysis we present extends beyond these to the interaction of relations that are not scope related.

45 There are some relative order restrictions our analysis does not presently handle which perhaps it should. For instance, Williams (1974, 124) notes that there are relative order restrictions on the interaction of EX and *because* clauses appearing within and without the scope of negation. He provides the following examples.

(i) a.   *Not everybody went to Bill's who was at Sam's because Sam's is smaller.

    b.   *Not everybody went to Bill's because Sam's is smaller who was at Sam's.

(ii) a.   Not everybody went to Bill's who was at Sam's, because Sam's is smaller.

    b.   *Not everybody went to Bill's, because Sam's is smaller, who was at Sam's.

In (i) the *because* clause is interpreted within the scope of negation, and in (ii) without. The ungrammatical sentences in (i) and (ii) should be due, we think, to the interaction of constituent structure for EX and *because* clauses and possibly also to the interpretive nesting requirement. A similar analysis should also accommodate the observation, also made by Williams (1974), that when the *because* clause appears within the scope of negation, an extraposed result clause may follow it, in contrast to (ib). His example is (iii).

(iii)   So many people didn't come to our show because they found our ad offensive that we have decided to remove it.

46 Contrary to the claim of Guéron and May (1984), it seems to us that a given sentence may contain two instances of RX, one RSX and the other ROX, but the antecedent – result clause relations must be nested.

(i) a.   So many people ate so many beans that they were sick that we had to call the doctor.

    b.   *So many people ate so many beans that we had to call the doctor that they were sick.

Note that (ib) is possibly good, but only on a pragmatically odd reading that is not available for (ia).

47 The example in (i), showing the interaction between HNPS and SX, would seem to provide an argument that EX patterns with configurations that involve rightward movement.

(i) a. Several people were trying to sing last night some awful song from the sixties who simply couldn't sing at all.

   b. *Several people were trying to sing last night who simply couldn't sing at all some awful song from the sixties.

In (i), the nested ordering of phrases, assuming the presence of traces for both HNPS and EX, is grammatical in (a) and the non-nested ordering in (b) is ungrammatical. Note that even properly nested examples do not always sound good. Thus, compare (ia) and (ii).

(ii)   ??Many people brought to the party more food than they were expected to who I had never met before.

Moreover, when we consider the interaction of HNPS and OX precisely the opposite array of judgments arises.

(iii) a. John told a man yesterday that he met at the party some very outrageous stories about Mary.

   b. *John told a man yesterday some very outrageous stories about Mary that he met at the party.

Finally, we observe that OX and PTI interact in such a way as to apparently require nesting, as in (iv).

(iv) a. There walked into the room this morning that John was painting someone who claimed to know him.

   b. *There walked into the room this morning someone who claimed to know him that John was painting.

Since we argue in Chapter Four that PTI is derived by adjunction to IP and we have already argued that OX may adjoin no higher than VP, the facts in (iv) are irrelevant to the issue of nesting of rightward dependencies of various types.

48 In fact, it may be that (24) is mistaken in allowing the SP to adjoin to either IP or VP, given the ungrammaticality of (i).

(i)   *She$_i$ ate the meat wearing Mary$_i$'s new dress.

If so, the obligatory attachment of SP to VP may be due to a requirement that unselected predication must merge with the main predication of the sentence, in the fashion described in Culicover (1988).

49 For some reason, some cases in which SP precedes OX or CX are not entirely unacceptable, especially where the predicate is relatively "light."

(i) a. ?John ate some beans yesterday nude that should have been cooked.

   b. John came to more parties nude than we invited him to.

Not all speakers agree with these judgments, however. For simplicity we restrict our analysis to the examples in the text.

50 Some of these examples are subject to other, irrelevant interpretations. The reader is cautioned to assign only the relevant interpretation in judging acceptability.

51 Joseph (1977) notes an interesting potential subject/object asymmetry in extraposition from such NPs as *the claim*.

   (i) a.   The claim was made by Columbus that the earth was round. [Joseph's (1a)]

      b.   ??I believe the claim with all my heart that she is innocent. [Joseph's (2b)]

However, if we focus on absolute minimal pairs, the robustness of this asymmetry is open to question.

   (ii) a.   The claim was made by Columbus that the earth was round.

      b.   Columbus made the claim several years ago that the earth was round.

   (iii) a.   The suggestion was advanced by John that we should phone out for pizza.

      b.   John advanced the suggestion at dinner time that we should phone out for pizza.

We speculate that the unacceptable examples noted by Joseph fall under the Name Constraint, however it is to be properly formulated, and are not indicative of a true subject/object asymmetry.

52 In developing this analysis, we elaborate upon a suggestion originally made by Guéron (1978).

53 The failure of partitive phrases to appear in extraposed position, as in (i), must be due on this account to the nature of the semantic relation holding between the head noun and its partitive complement.

   (i) a.   *Many came to the party of the people that John dislikes.

      b.   *A pound was sold of apples.

54 For some reason, it is impossible for an appositive relative clause to appear in extraposed position.

   (i) a.   John, who I've known for many years, just came into the room.

      b.   *John just came into the room, who I've known for many years.

   (ii) a.   Mary invited John, who she's known for many years, to the party.

      b.   *Mary invited John to the party, who she's known for many years.

We presume that whatever rules out the ungrammatical sentences in (i) and (ii) also rules out an appositive interpretation for extraposed clauses that violate the Name Constraint. See for example (1b) in the text. See also Ziv and Cole (1974).

55 In this discussion we treat only cases of extraposed relatives. Extraposed PPs pattern in the same way, in particular in allowing just the antecedent or just the extraposed phrase to be focused.

(i) a.   Is there anyone here with blond hair?/Is there anyone with blond hair here?

b.   YEAH, a SOLDIER just came in with blond hair.

(ii) a.   Did you meet any soldiers last night?

b.   YEAH, I met a soldier last night with blond HAIR.

56 This observation also contradicts the analysis of Guéron and May (1984), who claim that the antecedent of an extraposed phrase must be a quantified expression. We have already argued that this stipulation is too strong, but example (9) shows that even the weaker claim that the antecedent must be focused (and so an LF operator) is also too strong.

57 There is no parallel requirement on OX, despite the very similar Focus Effect in operation.

58 We have already seen in 4.2 that the focusing requirement is not necessarily restricted to the subject. This may not be a damaging criticism of the statement in the text because even when the subject is unfocused, it is still related to the focused constituent, the extraposed phrase.

3   Stylistic inversion

1 For ease of presentation, we will not in future discussion provide contexts of this sort for every such example as (6). Nevertheless, the reader is cautioned that reliable judgments for much of the data we consider here are highly sensitive to context manipulation in the fashion just illustrated for (6). In particular, contexts must be constructed to satisfy the exigencies of the FE.

2 However, it is noted in Gundel (1974) and Rochemont (1978) that this typical phrasing of topic constructions is absent when the topicalized phrase is itself the focus of the sentence. Thus, in the examples below, (iii) is a well-formed response to (i) only with a pause following the topicalized phrase, and to (ii) only without such a pause.

(i)   What do you think about John?

(ii)   Is there anybody you don't like?

(iii)   John I don't like.

3 As R. Kayne (p.c.) points out, the examples of (i) sound considerably better than the corresponding cases in (9).

(i) a.   ?To John, a book on linguistics, I would never give.

b.   ?A book on linguistics, to John, I would never give.

Consider also such cases as (ii).

(ii) a.   On Wednesday, with John, I'm going to the opera.

b.   In front of the house, in a new car, Mary claims she saw Bill.

Evidently, crosslinguistic variation in the possibility for multiple topics is not reducible to a simple parameter distinguishing languages that do and those that do not allow multiple topics. In English, PP plus NP or PP sequences are more easily topicalized in some cases (compare (9b, c) with (i)). Nevertheless, examples

(9a, d) have, to our knowledge, no grammatical structural equivalents, showing conclusively that even if English does restrictively allow multiple topics, it cannot be that the examples of (6) are derived through multiple topicalization.

4 Examples (10) have a possible derivation under a different intonation as in (i), derived from the corresponding sentences in (ii) as instances of D/L.

   (i) a.   *Nude into the room walked John.
       b.   *Smiling in front of her stood Bill.
   (ii) a.   *John walked nude into the room.
        b.   *Bill stood smiling in front of her.

We note that the (b) examples above are not as bad as those in (a), because they allow for another reading in which the PP complement *in front of her* is a complement to *smiling* rather then *stood*.

For reasons that we do not understand, examples such as (9b) sound slightly better when there is no comma intonation after the second topic. It is possible that this fact is related to the fact noted in footnote 2 that there are in fact two types of topicalization constructions in English, those that bear comma intonation and those that do not.

5 In this we go against the assumptions of Akmajian, Steele, and Wasow (1979), though as will become clear below, for VP Ellipsis, our assumptions will yield equivalent results.

6 As noted in Culicover (1971), focused auxiliaries may also focus time, realis/ irrealis, or modality. For example, focus on *will* may contrast with *did*, with *won't*, with *would*, or with *may*. Note that focus on I as the head of IP is very much restricted in just the manner indicated, so that only features inherently associated with I may be interpreted within the domain of the focus. See (19) for example.

7 However, we will argue in Chapter Four that the postposed subject in a Presentational *there* construction is in fact adjoined to IP. This will not affect our discussion here.

8 It will be noted that (24b) is improved if the predicate is made heavier, as in (i).

   (i)   ?There walked into the room a man no one knew nude from the waist up.

We contend, though, that (i) is grammatical only with a different structure than that relevant to the discussion in the text, in particular where the entire sequence following *room* is a single phrase. On this interpretation, (i) is roughly equivalent to (ii).

   (ii)   ?A man no one knew nude from the waist up walked into the room.

Note that the simple predicate in (24b) cannot be interpreted as part of the postposed subject on a par with (i) because the source sentence, unlike (ii), is fully ungrammatical.

   (iii)   *A man no one knew nude walked into the room.

9 Sentence (27b) is marginally grammatical, we claim, on another derivation, in which *John* has undergone Heavy NP Shift and the PP has been topicalized. On this derivation, (27b) parallels (i).

   (i)   ?There walked into the room NUDE, JOHN.

We discuss these derivations of sentences such as (i) and (27b) in detail in section 5.

10 Emonds (1976) presents an inversion analysis of roughly the type we have given in (38ii) for Directional Inversion constructions only. We argue against this particular realization of the inversion analysis in section 6.

11 Note that it is not possible to analyze the material following the copula in (41b) as a small clause (cf. Safir [1983]), given the ungrammaticality of (i). (Compare (ii).)

   (i)   *An old iron statue rusting was standing at the edge of the park.
   (ii)   An old iron statue was standing at the edge of the park rusting.

12 Though note that inversion in VP Topicalization constructions apart from PAB and D/L is blocked for some reason, indicating that *be* assimilates in some manner to the class of D/L verbs, whose properties we elaborate in more detail in section 4.

   (i) a.   *They said someone would walk into the room nude, and walk into the room nude did John.
      b.   *They said someone she liked would sit beside her, and sit beside here will Mary.

Compare (i) with (ii).

   (ii) a.   They said someone would walk into the room nude, and into the room nude walked John.
      b.   They said someone she liked would sit beside her, and sitting beside her will be Mary.

13 Notice that collapsing PAB with SI ignores the restrictions on the copula in PAB.

   (i) a.   Being chased around the park is Mary.
      b.   *Chased around the park is being Mary.

Nevertheless, the oddity of (iib) is likely due to an independent restriction on the behavior of *be* in VP constituent operations. See Akmajian and Wasow (1975) and Akmajian, Steele, and Wasow (1979) for discussion and examples.

14 See for instance Jackendoff (1971) and Stillings (1975). Goodall (1984) provides a very interesting account of Gapping constructions in terms of parallel structures and a grammatical process of linking. To explicitly adapt this account to our analysis of D/L in interaction with Gapping constructions would take us well beyond the scope of this discussion. However, we see no principled objection to such an adaptation, provided the linking process is taken to apply at, or after, S-structure, as Goodall himself seems to assume.

15 Wexler and Culicover (1980) note examples like (i) (compare (ii)), where this claim is apparently falsified.

(i)   John gave a book to Mary, and Bill a magazine to Fred.
(ii)   *John gave Mary a book, and Bill Fred a magazine.

See also Ross (1967), Kuno (1976) for additional apparent counterexamples.

Nevertheless, we are aware of no counterexamples to the claim that only a single constituent may precede a gapped sequence. Accordingly, our arguments for a VP Topicalization analysis of D/L on the basis of Gapping stand without qualification.

16 As already noted, a sentence such as (i) also involves VP Topicalization without the verb.

(i)   Into the room nude Susan walked.

Given this, the oddity of (iia), with the relevant S-structure analysis (iib), is expected only if we assume that some overt constituent must follow the gapped sequence. Consider (iii).

(ii) a.   *Into the room nude Susan walked, and out of the room smiling Jack.
    b.   [$_{VP}$ out of the room smiling] Jack [$_V$ ø] t_{VP}
(iii)   *In the room Mary sat and on the patio John.

17 Some speakers find (6a, b) better than we have indicated. We presume this difference is tied to a further difference among speakers regarding the acceptability of Gapping constructions. For some speakers the gapped verb may evidently have multiple constitutents following it.

18 VP Ellipsis, which we have used as a diagnostic for containment in VP, gives unexpected results in these cases.

(i) a.   *Her son sat beside her in the ambulance but her husband did in the waiting room.
    b.   *Mary walked down the stairs into the kitchen and Bill did into the living room.

It is conceivable that the oddity of these examples is related to that of the example in (ii).

(ii)   *Mary put the book in the fire, after Bill did on her table. (= Bill put the book on her table.)

Culicover and Wilkins (1984) use cases such as (ii) to argue that all of the complements to *put* occur within V^1. Perhaps a similar view should be taken of the multiple complements to V in examples such as (i). If so, then our analysis would require a distinction between VP and V′, contrary to our earlier claim. We might further assume following Akmajian, Steele, and Wasow (1979) that VP Topicalization is actually V^n Preposing.

19 Some speakers disagree with the judgments we have labeled in (22b). For these speakers, the judgments are rather:

(i)   , and into the room walked JOHN nude/*NUDE.

20 Further, the difference in grammaticality between (29) and similar cases in nonrestrictive relative clauses, as in (i), may be due, we hypothesize, to a special feature of the analysis of nonrestrictive relatives, namely that these are derived not by movement of a *wh* phrase to CP, as in restrictive relatives and questions (cf. (iii) and (30)), but rather by topicalization (that is, adjunction to IP) of a phrase containing a *wh* element.

(i) a.   Mary will pass by a room, into which will walk John.
   b.   Mary passed a bench, sitting on which was an old man.
(ii)   *Sitting on which bench was an old man?
(iii) a.   *The room into which will walk John is that one.
   b.   *The bench sitting on which was an old man was that one.

We will not pursue this line of investigation further here.

21 Alternatively, we might assume that the VP is adjoined to CP rather than in SPEC,CP, consistent with our conclusion in the preceding section. This derivation meets with the same criticism we offer below against (4) on the basis of (1b).

22 In fact, (5b) does not completely reflect the derivation Chomsky proposes. It is missing a trace in the adjoined to VP position, but since it is irrelevant to the present discussion, and not required on the analysis we have adopted, we have not included it.

23 Note that we must distinguish the trace of VP from pro$_{VP}$ in this regard. In particular, t_I may serve to satisfy the government requirement for pro$_{VP}$ where it may not for t_{VP}. Thus, compare (6b) and (i).

(i)   I know that John will eat his dinner, but will Bill t_I pro$_{VP}$?

Ultimately, the analysis of empty VPs of various types and their respective relations to I is a complex topic with many consequences which we will not develop in any detail here. The reader is referred to Zagona (1982) and Lobeck (1986) for discussion and analysis.

24 One might seek to find a solution to the difficulty posed by (7) for a structural analysis of D/L that parallels (5b) by making appeal to the proposal of Chomsky (1977) that posits an S^2 node, distinct from S^1, containing a topic position that may be embedded under S^1. We will not pursue such a solution since it would be otherwise inconsistent with our restrictive assumptions concerning X-bar theory.

25 The problem of lexical government might be overcome for t_V by a higher verb, given our assumptions in Chapter One about government and lexical government. Alternatively, we might follow Baker (1988) in requiring the trace of a head to satisfy the ECP through antecedent government only. Nevertheless, the real problem here is antecedent government for t_V, which can only be satisfied by V in I, except that V does not c-command t_V in (9).

26 Of course, the derivation of (10a) should also violate Subjacency. But the oddity of (10a) is considerably more striking than similar Subjacency violations (cf. (i)).

(i) a.   ?*This book, I've always wondered who wrote.

b.   ?*To Mary, John asked which letter Bill had sent.

27 By the same token, there can be no topicalization of the subject in SI.

(i)   *John, [$_{VP}$ into the room] t walked t_{VP}.

Despite our analysis of Subjacency in cases of multiple adjunction to IP, the trace of the subject will fail, among other things, to be antecedent governed.

28 We establish the point that D/L is strictly bounded in section 5 below. We return in that section to examples very similar to the second examples of (17), though grammatical.

29 We note one consequence of this result under our theoretical assumptions. Since we take VP to be L-marked, it must be that L-marking of a maximal projection does not extend to the head. (See also Baker [1988].) It should follow that no heads are L-marked, and therefore that movement of a head must always be as an adjunct.

30 Belletti and Rizzi (1986) argue on the basis of extraction from postverbal subjects in Italian that a, the adjoined node in a configuration of Chomsky adjunction such as (22), is a barrier to extraction, again on a par with the CED.

31 Example (i), involving extraposition, is excluded on independent grounds, given our analysis in Chapter Two, by the CP.

(i)   *Into the room nude walked John that Mary was working in.

32 Examples such as (i) may be considered as instances of D/L, but they are far more restricted in their distribution than typical cases (cf. (ii)).

(i) a.   Here comes the bus.
     b.   There lay John.
     c.   There goes the ball.
(ii) a.   Up to the house/*Here drove John.
     b.   Into the room/*There walked John.
     c.   Off the shelf/*There rolled the ball.

We assume that the tight lexical restrictions on constructions such as (i) follow on the Lexical Parameterization Hypothesis of Wexler and Manzini (1987), following Borer (1984).

33 Culicover (1980) observes a contrast between the examples in (i).

(i) a.   Into the room marched several soldiers.
     b.   *In the room marched several soldiers.

These cases imply that the directional reading is preferred for verbs that cooccur with both directional and locative phrases. As the examples in (ii) illustrate, the locative reading is in fact available when forced.

(ii) a.   Up and down in the hallway marched the students.
     b.   Inside the hall marched the students.

34 This contrast might be tied to the unaccusative nature of *arrive/appear* and so

tied to the restriction against objects in D/L. This approach would seem to be justified when we consider other examples of unaccusative verbs in English.

(i)   *During the meeting occurred a riot.

It is further justified by the behavior of passives in D/L, though judgments here tend to be somewhat more variable.

(ii) a.   *Through the window could be seen John.
    b.   *On the table was put the book.
    c.   *In the back was shot John.
    d.   *Next to the body was found a bullet.

But compare (iii), which seems significantly better.

(iii)   Seen in the park last Tuesday reading a newspaper was the mayor.

35 As Rochemont (1978) notes, (12) cannot give rise to an instance of D/L.

(i) a.   *Beside him stood up his mother.
    b.   *Up beside him stood his mother.

36 Akmajian, Steele, and Wasow (1979), Emonds (1976), and Culicover (1976). The analysis is originally due to Klima.

37 Kyle Johnson points out to us that further data bearing on our proposal here should stem from the behavior of *not* in D/L. In particular, if V moves to I and then adjoins to IP, *not* might be expected to either move with VP or stay behind. In fact, it can do neither.

(i) a.   *Into the room walked John not.
    b.   *Into the room walked not John.

Further, the only marginally acceptable example corresponding to (i) is (ii).

(ii)   ??Into the room didn't walk John.

We might exclude the examples of (i) by simply blocking movement of V to I in case there is an intervening *not*. Then (ii) might be derived by the process of restructuring suggested in the text for the derivation of sentences such as (iii).

(iii) a.   Into the room will walk John.
    b.   ??Into the room won't walk John.

The oddity of (ii) and (iii b) is due we think to an independent feature of numerous structural focus constructions, that negation is excluded (cf. Rochemont [1978] for discussion).

38 It might appear that V can undergo raising to I even without topicalization of the VP, as below.

(i)   John walked into the room and Mary ran.

We think it likely, however, that the relevant interpretation of the second sentence is inferred rather than grammatically indicated.

39 That government might in fact be directional either in some cases or more generally is considered by, among others, Kayne (1983).

40 Wexler and Culicover (1980) argue on the basis of Gapping constructions that *slowly walked* in examples such as (22) is a constituent. Consider (i).

(i)   John completely finished the ice cream and Mary the pizza.

We have been operating under a different assumption here, however. In particular, we take it that the adverb-V sequence is only a constituent as a function of restructuring, and this in the restricted manner we have discussed. These restrictions preclude treating the adverb-V sequence as a unit in examples such as (i). See Goodall (1984) who argues that Gapping constructions may be used to test constituenthood, but of the nongapped rather than the gapped material. See also our discussion in section 2 and earlier in this section.

41 Sentence (23a) is grammatical on another, though irrelevant, reading, in which the complete pre-subject sequence is a topicalized PP, on a par with (i).

(i)   Down the stairs that lead into the ballroom, the Queen walked slowly.

42 The ungrammaticality of example (23b) provides a further argument against an analysis of D/L constructions that considers these cases to be derived in part by a rule of subject postposing, since on this account there will be no account for the contrast in grammaticality between (23b) and sentence (i).

(i)   Into the ballroom there walked slowly a procession of visiting dignitaries.

43 Following the line of analysis initiated in Rochemont (1978), we might propose that the lexical restrictiveness of D/L, and the restriction to directional/locative complements in particular, is due to the Presentational Focus requirement on the construction. This view would seem to be supported by the contrast in acceptability of the sentences below, where (b) sounds considerably worse than (a) or (c), presumably because of the greater difficulty in retrieving a Presentational Focus interpretation for the postverbal subject.

(i) a.   Down the stairs came John.
   b.   Down the stairs fell John.
   c.   Out of the box fell John.

   However, this approach cannot be correct, since as already noted, PAB constructions also force a presentational interpretation on the postverbal subject, but the lexical restriction is of a different sort (i.e., auxiliary *be* only). In particular, example (ii) is odd, but fine as an instance of PAB. Cf. (iii).

(ii)   *In the garden was playing Mary.
(iii)   Playing in the garden was Mary.

44 In fact, the ungrammatical examples in (8) are due to the Subjacency condition adopted in Chapter One, for the purposes of which the topicalized phrase is an adjunct, hence a barrier.

45 See the discussion and analysis in section 3, from which the ungrammaticality of (9) follows as well.

46 In fact, in Chapter Four we will argue against this assumption, and propose that the postverbal subject is instead adjoined to IP, except for these cases.

47 There is a problem ultimately with this assumption, and this is that *wh* movement in cases that are otherwise entirely parallel is ruled out by Subjacency, as we discuss in more detail in Chapter Four.

(i) a.   *In front of whom did there sit knitting a woman she didn't know?
    b.   *Into whose office did there run screaming a group of frantic girls?
    c.   *I wonder in front of whom there sat knitting a woman she didn't know.

The contrast between (i) and (10) is as expected given our assumption that topicalization is derived by adjunction to IP and our interpretation of the Strict Cycle Condition, as outlined in section 3. Note also that we predict a contrast between (10) and examples in which the topicalized phrase has escaped from its clause by movement through SPEC,CP, as in (ii).

(ii)   *In front of her Mary didn't believe there could be sitting knitting a woman she didn't know.

48 It is also predicted on this view that there will be a difference in acceptability between examples (i) and (ii).

(i)   ?Into the room nude will slowly walk the Queen.
(ii)   *Into the room nude will walk slowly the Queen.

These judgments are, we think, very subtle, especially given the improved acceptability of (ii) with sufficient pause before and emphasis on the postverbal subject. Nevertheless, the judgments indicated support our claim that some apparent instances of D/L are in fact derived by Presentational *there* insertion with proper government of empty subject parasitic on the preposed PP.

49 Notably, both Stowell (1981) and Safir (1985) claim that PAB is more restricted than D/L, a perspective which we think is not motivated by the facts. See section 4 of this chapter.

50 As we will see, this point holds irrespective of whether the ECP is seen as a conjunctive or a disjunctive requirement.

51 See for instance Safir's (12), page 305: "For which pair, Px and y, where Px is *into the room*, y walked Px."

52 Notice also that the difference of agreement in presentational Stylistic Inversion is dependent on the presence of *il*. Compare the corresponding examples in (17)/ (18) and (19).

4   NP Shift

1 The parallel between heavy NP shift and stylistic *there* was first suggested by Jespersen (1949, VII: 113ff.). He writes "sometimes the reason for the *there*-construction seems simply to be the length of the subject which has made it difficult to place it at the beginning of the sentences."

2 Culicover and Wilkins (1984) observe that a complex VP may have at least two points of attachment for an NP shifted from object position. When there are two or more adjuncts in the VP, the NP may adjoin to the right of any one.

(i) a.   Mary gave a book about earthquakes to John in the garden last night for his birthday.

   b.   Mary gave to John a book about earthquakes in the garden last night for his birthday.

   c.   Mary gave to John in the garden a book about earthquakes last night for his birthday.

   d.   Mary gave to John in the garden last night a book about earthquakes for his birthday.

   e.   Mary gave to John in the garden last night for his birthday a book about earthquakes.

These potential alternations play no role in the discussion to follow, and we will not mention them further.

3 As elsewhere, we occasionally speak of ellipsis as "omission" or "deletion" of a VP, without intending to suggest that there is a transformational rule that deletes the VP.

4 Not all relevant examples are as bad as might be expected. Thus, compare (i).

(i)   ?John predicted there would walk into the room while he was waiting someone he had not seen in a long time, and there did.

5 This observation meets with apparent counterexamples in the form of the little understood operation of sluicing, as in (i).

(i)   I know that Bill talked to someone, but I don't remember who.

6 Note that the reconstruction effect assumed to be operative in clefts is of a different sort than that assumed for topicalization, as shown by examples such as (i). (See Higgins [1973].)

(i) a.   What John did to Mary was arrive late.
   b.   *John arrived late to Mary.

Examples corresponding to (10b) are considerably improved if modeled on (ia) and if they do not involve any operation of HNPS.

(ii)   What John did with the books he found was give them to Mary.

As a separate point, note that even this manipulation will not improve (10b) itself, since the NP in this case is a quantified expression.

(iii)   ?What John did with every book he could find was buy it for Mary.

The pronoun in (iii) must be interpreted as a bound variable, but does not satisfy the binding requirements for pronouns as bound variables.

7 See the discussion of VP trace and the ECP in section 3 of Chapter Three.

8 This leaves unexplained a range of cases with topicalization of VP in PTI where the result sounds much worse to us than (14).

(i)　　　*Present at the coronation, there were all the King's allies.
(ii)　　　*Sitting in front of her, there were her closest friends.

Note that examples (i) and (ii) are fully grammatical without *there*, as instances of SI.

(iii)　　　Present at the coronation were all the King's allies.
(iv)　　　Sitting in front of her were her closest friends.

In our analysis, however, the derivations of (i)/(ii) and (iii)/(iv) differ radically. In both cases there has been topicalization of the VP, but only in the former has the subject undergone movement. Thus the ungrammaticality of (i)/(ii) remains a mystery despite the existence of (iii)/(iv).

9 Certain other cases that are relatively acceptable are not instances of movement of a subject. For instance, in the following it can be argued that the final NP originates in the VP, and thus does not have to move out of VP in order to appear in VP-final position.

(i) a.　　　?There were expected to occur several unusual events, but there didn't.
　　b.　　　John says that there would be found in the group a man capable of doing the job, and there was.

We note also that acceptability sometimes depends on the particular verb, so that *occur* for instance is much better than *enter*.

(ii)　　　There should have occurred a riot, but there didn't.

We speculate, following Milsark (1974), that *occur* allows an unaccusative construction, in which the NP is in an underlying direct object position, and is not moved from subject by NP Shift. Further examples along the same lines support this analysis. In (iii), for example, the NP in question may precede an adjunct to VP. Such a sequence is ruled out for Move a from subject position, as shown in (iv).

(iii)　　　You may think that there will eventually occur a great revolution in the Soviet Union.
(iv)　　　*You may think that there walked a veritable army of revelers into the room.

10 For a refinement and development of this account, see Davis (1984).
11 Culicover and Wilkins (1984) argue against the existence of NP-t on different grounds, and from a set of different assumptions than those that we have adopted here.
12 See Safir (1985, 158). A "θ-set" is a composite θ-position (Safir 1985, 75) such that a given θ-role (specifically the external θ-role) may be assigned to one of two positions: either SPEC,IP position or the adjoined to VP position. Only one

of the two positions in a θ-set may contain an argument or there will be a violation of the θ-Criterion.

Safir observes in a footnote (n. 17, p. 338) that his analysis encounters a difficulty for which he has no solution, in the form of the example in (i) below.

(i)   *How many men did there seem to like fish?

Note that on the account we will give, insertion of *there* is not possible in the relevant structure for (i), since the empty category in subject position is lexically governed if there is no inversion (cf. (ii)), and fails to be antecedent governed if there is.

(ii)   How many men seem to like fish?

13 Cf. Koopman and Sportiche (1986), who cite Chomsky, class lectures.
14 Note that examples such as (i) must on our account be derived first by NP movement of the embedded subject to matrix subject position, with subsequent NP Shift of the derived subject.

(i) a.   There seems to have walked into the room a man with long blond hair.
    b.   There were believed to have walked into the room several people wearing gold headbands.

This analysis is supported by the observation that VP Ellipsis appears not to be able to include the sentence final subject in such cases in its target.

(ii)   *Yesterday there seemed to have walked into the room a man with long blond hair, and today there (does/seems to have) too.

15 Unfortunately, not all such cases are as relatively easy to judge as the examples in (7), or as promising for our prediction. Compare the examples in (i).

(i) a.   I saw ?(?there) walk into the room a man with long blond hair.
    b.   I made *(?there) walk into the room a man with long blond hair.
    c.   I want ?(*there) to leave early anyone who is not having a good time.
    d.   I believe ??(?there) to have walked into the room a man with long blond hair.
    e.   I expect *(?*there) to fall on Bill a massive wall hanging from Peru.

Note also that examples such as (ii) are only seemingly relevant, since they may be derived by shifting the NP from the VP internal position rather than from the subject position.

(ii) a. I believe *(there) to be waiting for me in my office someone I haven't seen in years.
     b. I expect *(there) to arise during the meeting a host of problems and unanswered questions.

16 A Case-based account is also possible, we think, for pleonastic and for weather *it*.
17 Williams (1984) argues against Safir's (1985) proposal that E-*there* occupies the

position of a variable at LF as a result of the application of QR to the quantified NP following the copula in an existential construction. This dispute is not relevant to our present concerns, since the required differentiation of E-*there* and P-*there* is stateable at S-structure, independently of the respective LF configurations. To adopt Safir's proposal, however, either the ECP would be required to apply at S-structure as well as at LF to guarantee the presence of P-*there*, or the requirement for lexical government is not in fact a part of the ECP but a separate PF requirement, as in the analysis of Aoun et al. (1987).

18 While it is difficult to verify the claim that the trace left by NP Shift is a variable in the case of PTI, it has been shown that in NP Shift more generally the trace behaves as a variable licensing the presence of a parasitic gap (cf. Chomsky [1982]).

(i)   John filed without reading every report that Mary placed on his desk.

If movement of an object *that*-complement to VP final position is a special case of heavy NP shift, then we would expect to find that such a constituent also licenses a parasitic gap. With this in mind, consider the following examples.

(ii) a.   Mary heard all of the stories you told without mentioning it to Susan.
    b.   *Mary heard all of the stories you told without mentioning [e] to Susan.
    c.   Mary heard *t* without mentioning [e] to Susan all of the stories you told.
    d.   Mary heard you had committed several crimes without mentioning it to Susan.
    e.   *Mary heard that you had committed several crimes without mentioning [e] to Susan.
    f.   Mary heard *t* without mentioning [e] to Susan that you had committed several crimes.

(iii) a.   Fred believed all of the stories you told without admitting it to anyone.
     b.   *Fred believed all of the stories you told without admitting [e] to anyone.
     c.   Fred believed *t* without admitting [e] to anyone all of the stories you told.
     d.   Fred believed that you had committed several crimes without admitting it to anyone.
     e.   *Fred believed that you had committed several crimes without admitting [e] to anyone.
     f.   Fred believed *t* without admitting [e] to anyone that you had committed several crimes.

The examples show that VP-final CP functions just like a heavy NP in regard to the licensing of parasitic gaps.

However, there are significant differences between VP-final CP and shifted heavy NP.

(I)   It is possible to extract out of CP, but not out of shifted heavy NP. As we have seen, the latter are adjuncts, and as such are extraction islands for Move *a* in the syntax.

(II)   VP-final CP does not block extraction from an adjacent PP, while shifted NP does. Compare (iv) with the examples in the text.

(iv) a.   Who was it obvious to *t* that Mary would be a candidate?
    b.   Who did you mention to *t* that Mary would be a candidate?

The fact that it is possible to extract from VP-final CP suggests that VP-final CP may also be generated in final position, and are not necessarily moved there by heavy NP shift. Corroborating this view is the fact that unlike shifted NPs, VP-final CP does not display the constructional focus properties associated with heavy NP shift.

Along related lines, we find that *it* extraposition does not have the special focus properties of heavy NP shift and stylistic *there* insertion. Extraction from extraposed clauses is not blocked, and extraposed clauses do not block extraction from an adjacent PP, as in (iva). Following Stowell (1981), we postulate that there is a base generation analysis of *it* extraposition in which the *that* complement is directly assigned the subject θ-role. We allow also for the possibility of Move α applying in the derivation of *it* extraposition.

19 We note the following potential problem with the analysis. Suppose that topicalization is attachment to IP, as we have assumed (see Chapter One). What is to stop topicalization of the subject? It must be stopped because if it occurs, the subject trace will not be lexically governed. In this case we would predict the grammaticality of

(i)   *John, there left.

which has the structure [C [NP [*t* [I VP]]]]. So either attachment to IP is impossible for the subject, or topicalization of the subject must be independently ruled out.

Suppose that attachment of the subject to IP is ruled out by a general constraint against string "vacuous movement." (See Wexler and Culicover [1980].) Then this problem does not arise.

20 The notion *c-subjacent* developed here is unrelated to that appealed to in Rouveret and Vergnaud (1980).

21 The account just offered might seem equivalent to one in which antecedent government can only be satisfied by an X°, as proposed by Lasnik and Saito (forthcoming), following Stowell (1981) and Rizzi (1986). However, while it is true that in the critical cases discussed here both the subject and object traces are taking antecedents that are heads, restricting the antecedent in this fashion would lead to abandoning any account of the distribution of P-*there* in terms of the ECP. This is so because what must be expressed is that P-*there* can salvage the potential ECP violation that arises in (i) but not in (ii) – see (iii), as we have observed in the discussion above.

(i)   There walked into the room a man with long blond hair.
(ii)   *Who did you say that left?
(iii)   *Who did you say that there left?

22 We observed in Chapter One that the LF *that* deletion analysis of Lasnik and

Saito (1984), proposed to overcome the lack of *that-t* effects with adjunct extraction, could be abandoned in favor of our new account of the *that-t* effect for subjects. Under the current proposal, however, the LF *that* deletion analysis must be reinstated.

23 This analysis also accommodates the failure of inversion in *wh* movement of a subject in matrix clauses (cf. Koopman [1983a]).

   (i)   *Who did leave?

In the S-structure of (i), *did* appears in the C head position of CP, so blocking COMP Indexing and thus both lexical and antecedent government of the subject trace.

24 This same analysis would be forced for French (the *que/qui* alternation) and other languages where the complementizer position must be lexically filled, I continues not to be a lexical governor for the subject (compare Chinese), and there is no free inversion of the subject to VP final position, as in Italian.

25 Essentially the same account may be given of the overt trace of V in the Vata predicate cleft construction, assuming that t_V, which in all other respects behaves like an adjunct, also requires both lexical and antecedent government. See Koopman (1984) and Koopman and Sportiche (1986) for discussion and examples.

26 Or of the sentence in (i).

   (i)   *Who do you wonder what there bought?

27 Koopman and Sportiche argue that the distribution of R is not predictable in terms of the ECP, and that there is need for a further constraint, their Condition on Long Extraction. Our account of the ECP removes the need for this constraint.

28 Our account might be realized in a different fashion, following Aoun et al. (1987). In particular, we might suppose the ECP to require only antecedent government, perhaps as an instance of a more generalized binding theory (see Aoun [1985, 1986]). We might then impose a lexical government for trace at PF, as argued in Aoun et al. (1987). Then the presence of English P-*there* and Vata R would be a PF conditioned phenomenon, with insertion of the overt trace only after S-structure. While we think this account has much to recommend it, we have not pursued its various consequences, and we will not adopt it in our analysis here. We note only that it is a plausible alternative.

29 See also Newmeyer (1987) who expresses a similar point of view and analysis, though with different theoretical assumptions, outlined in Chapter Five

30 We note that this effect is rather weak, and we emphasize that the judgments given are comparative rather than absolute. Thus, the significance of (8) lies in the contrast with the corresponding examples in (5).

31 As we note in Chapter Three: 6 and later in this section, the possibility for topicalization in the presence of P-*there* is ruled out when the sentence in question can only be derived as an instance of SI.

   (i)   Out of the room screaming (*there) ran twelve jurors and a sheriff.

32 Though it must be noted that in the case of multiple topicalization in English,

the situation is somewhat more complex, as we observe in Chapter Three. For instance, not all cases where the categorial restriction is satisfied are good.

(i) a.   *Nude, into the garden, John followed Mary.
    b.   *Into the garden, nude, John followed Mary.
(ii)   *To John, a letter, Mary sent.

33 Compare also the following minimal pairs that are similarly accommodated.

(i) a.   It was Bill that John sold Mary a picture of.
    b.   *It was Bill that John sold to Mary a picture of.
(ii) a. Who did John sell Mary a picture of?
     b. *Who did John sell to Mary a picture of?

34 We note that not all cases of extraction from PP are as bad as those given here.

(i) a.   ?We slept in when we were in Connecticut a marvelous bed that had belonged to George Washington.
    b.   ?We looked at last night a wonderful film about New York that had been made during the Depression.

It is conceivable that the examples in (i) are derived by a restructuring of the P under V, so that HNPS of the object is not from a position within PP. This proposal is supported by the observation that parallel cases where a restructuring account is unavailable are significantly worse than the examples above.

(ii) a. *We slept under when we were in Connecticut a marvelous bed that had belonged to George Washington.
     b. *We talked during last night a wonderful film about New York that had been made during the Depression.

35 For a discussion of the latter see Chapter Two.
36 Chomsky's statement of the Uniformity Condition is given in (i).

(i)   If α is an inherent Case-marker, then α Case-marks NP if and only if α θ-marks the chain headed by NP.

Since Case-marking and θ-marking proceed under government only, (i) requires that a head that inherently Case-marks and governs the head of a chain must also govern the tail of that chain.

37 Note that condition (16) automatically excludes a movement analysis of Extraposition from NP, consistent with our account of this construction in Chapter Two.
38 Note that these examples all include an adjunct to VP preceding the shifted NP. Parallel cases without an adjunct (cf. [7a, c] of section 2) are much improved. Consistent with (16), these can only be derived by adjunction of the shifted NP to the small clause itself.
      Note also the contrast between (i) and (22b).

(i)   John saw leaving the room last night a man with long blond hair.

This follows on our account if the structure of a gerund is not that of a small clause but rather of a sentential NP without a N head whose subject is governed by V in (i).

39 This is the analysis assumed in most prior work. See for example Stowell (1981), Culicover and Wilkins (1984), Safir (1985), Rochemont (1986), among others.

5   English focus constructions

1 As we have noted throughout, the alternative proposed by Aoun et al. (1987), that the requirement for lexical government is not part of the ECP but belongs instead to the PF component, is apparently consistent with relevant features of our analysis, though we have not investigated this matter in detail.

2 Chomsky (1982, 165) attributes the essentials of this definition to Reinhart (1976).

3 The failure of extraction from cleft and pseudocleft focus positions may very well be attributed to the non-L-marking of these positions by specificational *be*.

(i) a.   *Who was it a picture of *t* that Bill saw?
    b.   *What was what Bill saw a picture of *t*?

In contrast, predicational *be* apparently does L-mark its complement.

(ii)   Who is that a picture of?

4 Similarly it cannot be claimed that there is a dual ECP violation in the S-structure for sentence (i).

(i)   *Which room did there walk into several young men with long hair?

5 Note that the ungrammaticality of (2) cannot be attributed to failure to satisfy the ECP because P may not act as a proper governor since this would incorrectly also exclude (3a).

6 That *wonder* may in fact be an assertive predicate is indicated by the possibility of PTI in contexts where there has been no movement to COMP, as in (i).

(i)   I began to wonder whether there might be sitting behind me someone with a grudge and an axe to grind.

7 Baker (1988) makes a similar proposal for the analysis of Locative Inversion in particular. This proposal is subject to many of the same criticisms we make against Coopmans' analysis.

8 One argument Coopmans offers in favor of this structural analysis, drawing on the discussion in Maruta (1985), concerns the failure of the postverbal subject in D/L to serve as controller for a sentence final infinitival adjunct (see Postal [1977]).

(i)   Bill stood beside her to take advantage of her.
(ii) .   *Beside her stood Bill to take advantage of her.

But Coopmans and Maruta fail to observe that (ii) is considerably improved when the infinitival adjunct appears with the PP sentence initially, as in (iii).

(iii)   Beside her to take advantage of her stood Bill.

We conclude that whatever the proper account of (ii) is, it can make no appeal to the claim that the postverbal subject is a S-structure direct object, given the contrast between (ii) and (iii).

9 Though see note 43 of Chapter Three. This objection might be overcome by appeal to a requirement that V in I must be presentational in character.

10 See Chapter One: 4. This specific formulation presupposes the account of Rochemont (1986), Chapter 4, which may be too strong.

11 The possibility that the required negative evidence might be indirect is perhaps not so readily dismissed. It might for instance be claimed that the consistent and necessary association of accent with the postverbal subject in cases like (2b) in every token of this construction in the learner's primary data base may be used by the learner to indirectly determine that there must be a structural focus in this position. We note two problems with such a hypothesis. First, the focus/accent relation is not isomorphic, as we have argued elsewhere (see Culicover and Rochemont [1983], Rochemont [1986]). And second, the account we will ultimately advance would appear to hold crosslinguistically irrespective of the role of accent. (See Rochemont [1986] for discussion.)

12 Whitney (1984) proposes that topicalization creates a Contrastive Focus of the topicalized phrase in the manner argued by Rochemont (1986) for the cleft construction. But this proposal can only be maintained if it can be shown that clefting and topicalization have parallel discourse effects specifically in the determination of well-formedness for question-answer sequences. That they do not is shown in the examples below.

(i)   Did anybody vote for John?
(ii) a.   It was John that several people voted for.
     b.   John, several people voted for.

While (iib) may serve as a response to (i), (iia) may not, without further contextual manipulation.

13 Note that we state this principle in terms of ''if'' and not the stronger and more desirable ''iff.'' At this point, it is not clear to us whether all instances of structural focus can be made to accommodate this formulation of the Focus Principle, or a suitable revision (see for example [14] below). The question of whether necessary conditions for structural focus can be found is one for future research.

14 See Kayne (1983, 225):
W and Z (Z a maximal projection, and W and Z dominated by some Y) are in a *canonical government configuration* iff

a.   V governs NP to its right in the grammar of the language in question and W precedes Z or
b.   V governs NP to its left in the grammar of the language in question and Z precedes W.

15 Note the required assumption that Case and θ-roles are assigned to positions. Thus, NP in (6a) for instance is not in fact Case-marked by I. Rather t_{NP} is. If NP_a in (6) requires Case, it receives it in virtue of being in a chain with t_{NP}.

16 Culicover and Rochemont (1983) and Rochemont (1978, 1986) argue that the *wh*-phrase of a direct *wh*-question is necessarily a focus, but they employ a mechanism distinct from that developed here to identify it as one. Hendrick and Rochemont (1982) argue that the *wh*-phrase of an indirect question is not a structural focus.

17 We have not explicitly considered how focusing is derived in the VP Fronting construction here, as the precise generalization eludes us. We have also excluded from consideration the focusing aspects of English elliptical constructions, a topic we reserve for future research.

   Whitney (1984) provides a fairly convincing argument that the Parenthetical Formation construction identifies the post-parenthetical phrase as a structural focus. If this construction is indeed derived by rightward movement of the sentence final phrase, as argued by Emonds (1976), then the resulting configuration would be subsumed under the Focus Principle as stated in (3), if it were generalized beyond the restriction in (i) and some account of the non-obligatory focusing of predicates were given. (See [14].)

18 SX in (4) positioned in X,IP would appear to provide a further obstacle, but in fact may not. Recall from our discussion in Chapter 2 that we found no empirical reason to prevent SX from appearing in either VP or IP adjoined position. We did not therefore restrict the locus of attachment for SX. It might perhaps be reasonable in light of this discussion to restrict SX to VP adjoined position, so eliminating any problem posed by the positioning of SX in (4) for revising the stipulation in (3 iii).

19 This requirement is less stringent in PTI than in SI.

   (i) a.   ?There followed her into the room a horde of screaming children.
       b.   *Into the room there followed her a horde of screaming children.

   Note though that sentences like (i a) are marginally possible only with pronominal (cliticized) objects, suggesting a restructuring of sorts that is unavailable for SI. (See Chapter Three: 4.)

   (ii)   *There followed Mary into the room a horde of screaming children.
   (iii)   *There walked the dog around the park an old well-dressed lady.

20 A remaining difficulty with (14) concerns the status of *wh*-phrases in embedded COMP positions governed by the higher lexical head. We could exclude these phrases from qualifying as instances of α in (14) by requiring that α not appear in the SPEC position of a phrase that serves as complement to β.

21 The problem remains that V raising in PTI is not forced by any mechanism. We might claim, in the absence of any preferable alternative, that the NP right adjoined to VP is uninterpreted if it is not identified as a structural focus, and so violates the Principle of Full Interpretation of Chomsky (1986a). That it may be uninterpreted is plausible given that it is neither an argument, nor a predicate, nor a quantified expression, and it is an R-expression appearing in A-bar position but not as a topic.

22 On clefts, see Rochemont (1986, chapter 5). We leave the detailed analysis of pseudoclefts to subsequent work.

23 Chomsky (1965, chapter 1) first articulated the intimate relationship between linguistic theory and the problem of explaining how it is that human beings can acquire language. For discussion of the specific relationship between grammatical theory and language acquisition see Wexler and Culicover (1980), Culicover and Wilkins (1984), Borer and Wexler (1987) and Wexler and Manzini (1987), Davis (1987).

References

Akmajian, A. (1975). "More Evidence for an NP Cycle," *Linguistic Inquiry* 6, 115–129.

Akamjian, A., S. Steele, and T. Wasow (1979). "The Category AUX in Universal Grammar," *Linguistic Inquiry* 10, 1–64.

Akmajian, A. and T. Wasow (1975). "The Constituent Structure of VP and AUX and the Position of the Verb BE," *Linguistic Analysis* 1, 205–245.

Andrews, A. (1975). *Studies in the Syntax of Relative and Comparative Clauses*, Garland Press, New York, 1985.

Aoun, J. (1985). *A Grammar of Anaphora*, MIT Press, Cambridge.

(1986). *Generalized Binding*, Foris Press, Dordrecht.

Aoun, J., N. Hornstein, D. Lightfoot, and A. Weinberg (1987). "Two Types of Locality," *Linguistic Inquiry* 18, 537–577.

Aoun, J., N. Hornstein, and D. Sportiche (1981). "On Some Aspects of Wide Scope Quantification," *Journal of Linguistic Research* 1, 69–96.

Atkinson J. (1973). *The Two Forms of Subject Inversion in Modern French*, Mouton, The Hague.

Baker, M. (1985). "Incorporation: A Theory of Grammatical Function Changing," Ph.D. dissertation, MIT.

(1988). *Incorporation: A Theory of Grammatical Function Changing*, University of Chicago Press, Chicago.

Baltin, M. (1978). "Toward a Theory of Movement Rules," Ph.D. dissertation, MIT.

(1981), "Strict Bounding," in C. L. Baker and J. McCarthy, eds., *The Logical Problem of Language Acquisition*, MIT Press, Cambridge.

(1983). "Extraposition: Bounding vs. Government-Binding," *Linguistic Inquiry* 14, 155–162.

(1984). "Extraposition Rules and Discontinuous Constituents," *Linguistic Inquiry* 15, 157–163.

(1987a). "Degree Complements," in G. Huck and A. Ojeda, eds.

(1987b). "Do Antecedent-Contained Deletions Exist?," *Linguistic Inquiry* 18, 579–595.

Barss, A. (1986). "Chains and Anaphoric Dependence: On Reconstruction and Its Implications," Ph.D. dissertation, MIT.

Belletti, A. (1988). "The Case of Unaccusatives," *Linguistic Inquiry* 19, 1–34.

Belletti, A. and L. Rizzi (1986). "Psych-Verbs and θ-Theory," *Lexicon Project Working Papers* 13, MIT, Cambridge.

Bolinger, D. (1961). "Contrastive Accent and Contrastive Stress," *Language* 37, 83–96.

Borer, H. (1984). *Parametric Syntax*, Foris Press, Dordrecht.

Borer, H. and K. Wexler (1987). "The Maturation of Syntax," in T. Roeper and E. Williams, eds., *Parameter Setting*, Reidel, Dordrecht.

Bresnan, J. (1973). "Syntax of the Comparative Clause," *Linguistic Inquiry* 4, 275–345.

(1976). "Nonarguments for Raising," *Linguistic Inquiry* 7, 485–501.

(1977). "Variables in the Theory of Transformations," in P. Culicover, T. Wasow, and A. Akmajian, eds.

Chomsky, N. (1965). *Aspects of the Theory of Syntax*, MIT Press, Cambridge.

(1971). "Deep Structure, Surface Structure and Semantic Interpretation," in D. Steinberg and L. Jacobovits, eds., *Semantics*, Cambridge University Press, London.

(1973). "Conditions on Transformations," in S. Anderson and P. Kiparsky, eds., *A Festschrift for Morris Halle*, Holt, Reinhart and Winston, New York.

(1975). "Questions of Form and Interpretation," *Linguistic Analysis* 1, 75–109.

(1977). "On Wh Movement," in P. Culicover, T. Wasow, and A. Akmajian, eds.

(1981). *Lectures on Government and Binding*, Foris Press, Dordrecht.

(1982). *Some Concepts and Consequences of the Theory of Government and Binding*, MIT Press, Cambridge.

(1986a). *Knowledge of Language*, Praeger, New York.

(1986b). *Barriers*, MIT Press, Cambridge.

Chomsky, N. and H. Lasnik (1977). "Filters and Control," *Linguistic Inquiry* 8, 425–504.

Coopmans, P. (1987). "Where Stylistic and Syntactic Processes Meet: Inversion in English," unpublished ms., University of Utrecht.

Coopmans, P. and I. Roovers (1986). "Reconsidering Some Syntactic Properties of PP-Extraposition," Utrecht Formal Parameters Yearbook II, 21–35.

Culicover, P. (1971). "Syntactic and Semantic Investigations," Ph.D. dissertation, MIT.

(1976). *Syntax*, Academic Press, New York.

(1980). "Adverbials and Stylistic Inversion," *Social Science Working Papers* 77, University of California, Irvine.

(1981). "Negative Curiosities," Indiana University Linguistics Club, Bloomington, Indiana.

(1988). "Autonomy, Predication and Thematic Relations," in W. Wilkins, ed., *Thematic Relations*, Academic Press, New York.

Culicover, P. and M. Rochemont (1983). "Stress and Focus in English," *Language* 59, 123–165.

(to appear). "Extraposition and the Complement Principle", *Linguistic Inquiry* 21.

Culicover, P., T. Wasow, and A. Akmajian, eds. (1977). *Formal Syntax*, Academic Press, New York.

Culicover, P. and K. Wexler (1977). "Some Syntactic Implications of a Theory of Language Learnability," in Culicover, P., T. Wasow, and A. Akmajian, eds.

Culicover, P. and W. Wilkins (1984). *Locality in Linguistic Theory*, Academic Press, New York.

Davis, L. (1984). "Arguments and Expletives," unpublished Ph.D. dissertation, University of Connecticut.

Davis, H. (1987). "The Acquisition of the English Auxiliary System and its Relation to Linguistic Theory," unpublished Ph.D. dissertation, Univ. of British Columbia.

Dowty, D., R. Wall, and S. Peters (1981). *Introduction to Montague Semantics*, Reidel, Dordrecht.

Emonds, J. (1976). *A Transformational Approach to English Syntax*, Academic Press, New York.

Fodor, J. (1978). "Parsing Strategies and Constraints on Transformations," *Linguistic Inquiry* 9, 427–473.

Frazier, L. and J. Fodor. "The Sausage Machine: A New Two-Stage Parsing Model," *Cognition* 6, 291–325.

Gazdar, G. (1981). "Unbounded Dependencies and Coordinate Structure," *Linguistic Inquiry* 12, 155–184.

Gazdar, G., E. Klein, G. Pullum, and I. Sag (1985). *Generalized Phrase Structure Grammar*, Harvard University Press, Cambridge.

Goodall, G. (1984). "Parallel Structures in Syntax," Ph.D. dissertation, University of California at San Diego.

Guéron, J. (1978). "The Grammar of PP Extraposition," unpublished ms., Université de Paris VIII.

   (1980). "On the Syntax and Semantics of PP-Extraposition," *Linguistic Inquiry* 11, 637–678.

Guéron, J. and R. May (1984). "Extraposition and Logical Form," *Linguistic Inquiry* 15, 1–31.

Gundel, J. (1974). "The Role of Topic and Comment in Linguistic Theory," Ph.D. dissertation, University of Texas at Austin, reproduced by Indiana University Linguistics Club, 1977.

Haegeman, L. and H. van Riemsdijk (1986). "Verb Projection Raising, Scope, and the Typology of Rules Affecting Verbs," *Linguistic Inquiry* 17, 417–66.

Hale, K., L. Jeanne, and P. Platero (1977). "Three Cases of Overgeneration," in P. Culicover, T. Wasow, and A. Akmajian, eds.

Halliday, M. (1967). "Notes on Transitivity and Theme in English (Part II)," *Journal of Linguistics* 3, 199–244.

Hendrick, R. and M. Rochemont (1982). "Complementation, Multiple wh and Echo Questions," published in *Toronto Working Papers in Linguistics* 11, 1988.

Higginbotham, J. (1985). "On Semantics," *Linguistic Inquiry* 16, 547–594.

Higginbotham, J. and R. May (1981). "Questions, Quantifiers and Crossing," *The Linguistic Review* 1, 41–80.

Higgins, R. (1973). "The Pseudocleft Construction in English," Ph.D. dissertation, MIT.

Hooper, J. and S. Thompson (1973). "On the Applicability of Root Transformations," *Linguistic Inquiry* 4, 465–498.

Horvath, J. (1981). "Aspects of Hungarian Syntax and the Theory of Grammar," Ph.D. dissertation, UCLA.

—— (1985). *FOCUS in the Theory of Grammar and the Syntax of Hungarian*, Foris, Dordrecht.

Huang, J. (1982). "Logical Relations in Chinese and the Theory of Grammar," Ph.D. dissertation, MIT.

Huck, G. (1985). "Discontinuity and Word Order in Categorial Grammar," Ph.D. dissertation, University of Chicago, distributed by IULC.

Huck, G. and A. Ojeda, eds. (1987). *Syntax and Semantics*, Volume 20: *Discontinuous Constituency*, Academic Press, New York.

Jackendoff, R. (1971). "Gapping and Related Rules," *Linguistic Inquiry* 2, 21–35.

—— (1972). *Semantic Interpretation in Generative Grammar*, MIT Press, Cambridge.

—— (1983). *Semantics and Cognition*, MIT Press, Cambridge.

Jaeggli, O. (1982). *Topics in Romance Syntax*, Foris, Dordrecht.

Jespersen, O. (1949). *A Modern English Grammar*, George, Allen, and Unwin, London.

Joseph, B. (1977). "On the Cyclicity of Extraposition-from-*the-claim*," *Linguistic Inquiry* 8, 169–173.

Kayne, R. (1979). "Rightward NP Movement in French and English," *Linguistic Inquiry* 10, 710–719.

—— (1980). "Extensions of Binding and Case-Marking," *Linguistic Inquiry* 11, 75–96.

—— (1983). "Connectedness," *Linguistic Inquiry* 14, 223–249.

Kayne, R. and J.-Y. Pollock (1978). "Stylistic Inversion, Successive Cyclicity, and Move NP in French," *Linguistic Inquiry* 9, 595–621.

Koopman, H. (1983a). "ECP Effects in Main Clauses," *Linguistic Inquiry* 14, 346–350.

—— (1983b). *The Syntax of Verbs*, Foris, Dordrecht.

Koopman, H. and D. Sportiche (1986). "A Note on Long Extraction in Vata and the ECP," *Natural Language and Linguistic Theory* 4, 357–374.

Kroch, A. and A. Joshi (1987). "Analyzing Extraposition in a Tree Adjoining Grammar," in G. Huck and A. Ojeda, eds.

Kuno, S. (1975). "Conditions for Verb-Phrase Deletion," *Foundations of Language* 13, 161–175.

—— (1976). "Gapping: A Functional Analysis," *Linguistic Inquiry* 7, 300–318.

Ladd, R. (1980). *The Structure of Intonational Meaning*, Indiana University Press, Bloomington.

Lasnik, H. and M. Saito (1984). "On the Nature of Proper Government," *Linguistic Inquiry* 15, 235–289.

—— (forthcoming). *Move α*, MIT Press, Cambridge.

Liberman, M. (1974). "On Conditioning the Rule of Subj-AUX Inversion," in E. Kaisse and J. Hankamer, eds., *Papers from the Fifth Annual Meeting of the North Eastern Linguistics Society*, Harvard University, Cambridge.

Lobeck, A. (1986). "Syntactic Constraints on VP Ellipsis," Ph.D. dissertation, University of Washington.

Longobardi, G. (1987). "Extraction from NP and the Proper Notion of Head Government," unpublished ms., Scuole Normale Superiore, Pisa.

Manzini, R. (1983). "Restructuring and Reanalysis," unpublished Ph.D. dissertation, MIT.

Maruta, T. (1985). "Is Stylistic Inversion 'Stylistic'?" *Cahiers Linguistique d'Ottawa*, no. 14, University of Ottawa.

Massam, D. (1985). "Case Theory and the Projection Principle," Ph.D. dissertation, MIT.

May, R. (1985). *Logical Form*, MIT Press, Cambridge.

Milsark, G. (1974). "Existential Sentences in English," Ph.D. dissertation, MIT.

   (1977). "Toward an Explanation of Certain Peculiarities of the Existential Construction in English," *Linguistic Analysis* 3, 1–29.

Montague, R. (1973). "The Proper Treatment of Quantification in Ordinary English," in J. Hintikka, J. Moravcsik, and P. Suppes, eds., *Approaches to Natural Language*, Reidel, Dordrecht.

Newmeyer, F. (1980). *Linguistic Theory in America*, Academic Press, New York.

   (1987). "Presentational There-Insertion and the Notions 'Root Transformation' and 'Stylistic Rule,' " Papers from the Twenty-Third Regional Meeting of the Chicago Linguistics Society.

Perlmutter, D. and J. Ross (1970). "Relative Clauses With Split Antecedents", *Linguistic Inquiry* 1, 350.

Pesetsky, D. (1982). "Paths and Categories," Ph.D. dissertation, MIT.

Pierrehumbert, J. (1980). "The Phonology and Phonetics of English Intonation," Ph.D. dissertation, MIT.

Postal, P. (1977). "About a 'non-argument' for Raising," *Linguistic Inquiry* 8, 141–154.

Reinhart, T. (1976). "The Syntactic Domain of Anaphora," Ph.D. dissertation, MIT.

   (1980). "The Position of Extraposed Clauses," *Linguistic Inquiry* 11, 621–624.

Rizzi, L. (1982). *Issues in Italian Syntax*, Foris, Dordrecht.

   (1986). "On Chain Formation," in H. Borer, ed., *Syntax and Semantics* 19: *The Syntax of Pronominal Clitics*, Academic Press, New York.

   (1987). "Relativized Minimality," unpublished ms., University of Geneva and LSA Summer Institute, Stanford.

Rochemont, M. (1978). *A Theory of Stylistic Rules in English*, Garland Press, New York, 1985.

   (1979). "Remarks on the Stylistic Component in Generative Grammar," in E. Engdahl and M. Stein, eds., Papers Presented to Emmon Bach by his Students, University of Massachusetts, Amherst.

   (1982). "On the Empirical Motivation of the Raising Principle," *Linguistic Inquiry* 13, 150–154.

   (1986). *Focus in Generative Grammar*, J. Benjamins, Amsterdam.

   (1988). "Topic Islands and the Subjacency Parameter," unpublished ms., University of British Columbia to appear in *Canadian Journal of Linguistics*.

Rochemont, M. and P. Culicover (1988). "A Non-Movement Analysis of Extraposition from NP," ERIC Clearing House for Linguistics, Washington, DC.

Ross, J. (1967). "Constraints on Variables in Syntax," Ph.D. dissertation, MIT.

Rothstein, S. (1983). "The Syntactic Forms of Predication," Ph.D. dissertation, MIT.

Rouveret, A. (1978). "Result Clauses and Conditions on Rules," in S. J. Keyser, ed., *Recent Transformational Studies in European Languages*, MIT Press, Cambridge.

Rouveret, A. and J.-R. Vergnaud (1980). "Specifying Reference to the Subject: French Causatives and Conditions on Representation," *Linguistic Inquiry* 11, 97–202.

Safir, K. (1983). "On Small Clauses as Constituents," *Linguistic Inquiry* 14, 730–735.

___ (1985). *Syntactic Chains*, Cambridge University Press, London.

Sag, I. (1976). *Deletion and Logical Form*, Garland Press, New York, 1979.

___ (1987). "Grammatical Hierarchy and Linear Precedence," in G. Huck and A. Ojeda, eds.

Schmerling, S. (1976). *Aspects of English Sentence Stress*, University of Texas Press, Austin.

Selkirk, E. (1984). *Phonology and Syntax: The Relation Between Sound and Structure*, MIT Press, Cambridge.

Sperber, D. and D. Wilson (1986). *Relevance*, Harvard University Press, Cambridge.

Stillings, J. (1975). "The Formulation of Gapping in English as Evidence for Variable Types in Syntactic Transformations," *Linguistic Analysis* 1, 247–274.

Stowell, T. (1981). "Origins of Phrase Structure," Ph.D. dissertation, MIT.

___ (1985). "Null Antecedents and Proper Government," in *Proceedings of NELS* 16, Univ. of Mass., Amherst.

Stucky, S. (1987). "Configurational Variation in English: A Survey of Extraposition and Related Matters," in G. Huck and A. Ojeda, eds.

Taraldsen, T. (1981). "The Theoretical Interpretation of a Class of Marked Extractions," in A. Belletti, L. Brandi, and L. Rizzi, eds., *Theory of Markedness in Generative Grammar*, Scuola Normale Superiore, Pisa.

Torrego, E. (1984). "On Inversion in Spanish and Some of its Effects," *Linguistic Inquiry* 15, 75–102.

Travis, L. (1984). "Parameters and Effects of Word Order Variation," Ph.D. dissertation, MIT.

Wexler, K. and P. Culicover (1980). *Formal Principles of Language Acquisition*, MIT Press, Cambridge.

Wexler, K. and R. Manzini (1987). "Parameters and Learnability in Binding Theory," in T. Roeper and E. Williams, eds., *Parameter Setting*, Reidel, Dordrecht.

Whitney, R. (1984). "The Syntax and Interpretation of A-bar Adjunctions," Ph.D. dissertation, University of Washington.

Williams, E. (1974). "Rule Ordering in Syntax," Ph.D. dissertation, MIT.

___ (1980). "Predication," *Linguistic Inquiry* 11, 203–238.

___ (1984). "There-Insertion," *Linguistic Inquiry* 15, 131–153.

Zagona, K. (1982). "Government and Proper Government of Verbal Projections." Ph.D. dissertation, University of Washington, Seattle.

Ziv, Y. and P. Cole (1974). "Relative extraposition and the scope of definite descriptions in Hebrew and English," in M. W. La Galy, R. A. Fox, and A. Bruck, eds., *Papers from the Tenth Regional Meeting of the Chicago Linguistic Society*, Chicago, Ill.

Zubizarreta, M. L. (1985). "Morphophonology and Morphosyntax: Romance Causatives," *Linguistic Inquiry* 16, 247–89.

Index of names

Akmajian, A. 100, 168 n.22, 177 n.5, 178 n.13, 179 n.18, 182 n.36
Andrews, A. 36, 38, 163 n.2, 169 n.26, 170 n.31, n.32, 171 n.33, 172 n.38
Aoun, J. 160 n.12, n.13, 188 n.17, 190 n.28, 192 n.1
Atkinson, J. 112, 114, 115

Baker, M. 87, 91, 95, 147, 159 n.3, 180 n.25, 181 n.29, 192 n.7
Baltin, M. 34, 36, 39, 40, 135, 160 n.9, 163 n.2, n.3, 164 n.4, 165 n.10, 166 n.12, 168 n.21
Barss, A. 89
Belletti, A. 28, 181 n.30
Bolinger, D. 22–4, 161 n.17
Borer, H. 181 n.32, 195 n.23
Bresnan, J. 29, 101, 107, 171 n.33

Chomsky, N. 1, 2, 5, 6, 7, 8, 10, 11, 12–13, 14, 16, 19, 21, 27, 33, 34, 40, 41, 42, 44, 50, 51, 73, 77, 87, 91, 93, 100, 101, 102, 111, 121, 124, 133, 135, 138, 141, 142, 144, 145, 148, 157, 159 n.2, n.3, n.4, 160 n.7, n.8, 161 n.15, n.17, 162 n.20, n.24, 163 n.2, 164 n.3, 165 n.9, n.12, 168 n.21, n.22, 169 n.24, n.26, 171 n.35, 180 n.22, n.24, 187 n.13, 188 n.18, 191 n.36, 192 n.2, 194 n.21, 195 n.23
Cole, P. 175 n.54
Coopmans, P. 7, 66, 143, 146–8, 159 n.4, 192 n.7, n.8
Culicover, P. 2, 3, 5, 17, 20, 32, 34, 35, 36, 68, 73, 80, 81, 82, 100, 118, 133, 151, 154, 159 n.3, 161 n.17, 163 n.1, 164 n.5, 165 n.7, 166 n.13, 167 n.16, 170 n.28, 174 n.48, 177 n.6, 179 n.15, 179 n.18, 181 n.33, 182 n.36, 183 n.40, 185 n.2, 186 n.11, 189 n.19, 192 n.39, 194 n.16, 195 n.23

Davis, L. 186 n.10
Dowty, D. 6

Emonds, J. 69, 77, 96, 108–9, 120, 145, 178 n.10, 182 n.36, 194 n.17

Fodor, J. 55, 170 n.29
Frazier, L. 170 n.29

Gazdar, G. 6, 38, 164 n.5, 170 n.29
Goodall, G. 156, 178 n.14, 183 n.40
Guéron, J. 2, 25, 27, 33, 35, 36, 37, 38, 39, 41, 42, 43, 44, 45, 48, 49–50, 51, 52, 60–1, 64, 65, 66, 67, 163 n.2, 164 n.4, 166 n.13, 168 n.18, 169 n.23, n.25, 172 n.40, n.42, 173 n.46, 175 n.52, 176 n.56
Gundel, J. 176 n.2

Hale, K. 5, 159 n.2
Halliday, M. 19, 161 n.17
Hendrick, R. 168 n.18, 194 n.16
Higginbotham, J. 111, 154
Higgins, R. 185 n.6
Hooper, J. 145
Hornstein, N. 160 n.12, n.13, 188 n.17, 190 n.28, 192 n.1
Horvath, J. 2
Huang, J. 8, 9, 14, 15, 16, 44, 163 n.2
Huck, G. 164 n.5

Jackendoff, R. 5, 21, 159 n.1, 162 n.20, n.24, 178 n.14
Jaeggli, O. 160 n.12
Jeanne, L. 5, 159 n.2
Jespersen, O. 184 n.1
Johnson, K. 182 n.37
Joseph, B. 175 n.51
Joshi, A. 164 n.5

Kayne, R. 12, 111–15, 116, 152, 176 n.3, 183 n.39, 193 n.14
Klein, E. 6
Klima, E. 182 n.36
Koopman, H. 88, 91, 93, 95, 129–31, 141, 187 n.13, 190 n.23, 190 n.25, n.27

Index of subjects